Dennis Look

JOY
OF
BACKPACKING

People's Guide to the Wilderness

Jalmar Press, Inc.
Sacramento

Collaborator:
Arthur S. Harris, Jr.

Library of Congress Catalog Card Number: 76-9649
International Standard Book Number (ISBN): 0-915190-06-0
Jalmar Press, Inc. Sacramento, California
© by Dennis Look
First Printing 1976
Printed in the United States of America

Illustrations by Suzanne D'Arcy and Dennis Look
Cover by: Thaddeus Lewandowski

Textual Acknowledgements
Reprinted from
Albert Saijo, THE BACKPACKER, 101 Productions, San Francisco
Reprinted from HIKING THE APPALACHIAN TRAIL © by Rodale Press, Inc.
Permission granted by Rodale Press, Inc., Emmaus, PA 18049

Distributed by Price/Stern/Sloan Publishers to Retail Book Trade
410 North La Cienaga
Los Angeles, CA

Distributed by Jalmar Press to Educational and Religious Institutions
391 Munroe Street
Sacramento, California 95825

Contents

1 **WILDERNESS LIVING**   1
   Loving it or laying it low.

2 **BOOTS**   9
   Walking, stalking, hiking.

3 **PACKS**   25
   The pack on your rack is the home on your back.

4 **SLEEPING BAGS**   39
   Wilderness bedrooms.

5 **CLOTHING**   57
   Glad rags, wilderness style.

6 **SITE SELECTION AND SHELTERS**   68
   The best in helter shelter and how to choose it.

7 **FOOD AND STOVES**   89
   The art of the stomach and how to serve it.

8 **TRAVELING**   115
   On the trail. Perils and pleasure.

9 **WINTER CAMPING**   136
   A look at the snug life . . . below zero.

10 **GRAB-BAG**   158
   A medley of backpacking tips.

ACKNOWLEDGMENT

I wish to thank my parents, Mildred and Tony Look, for raising me in an environment of love and respect for the wilderness. Without these precious gifts this book would not have been possible. The summers spent in the mountains as a youth have left a lasting impression on me as an adult. The result is that I have a tremendous feeling of love for the wilderness.

I would also like to thank my close hiking companions, Wayne, Ron, Ray and Bob for all their input into this book. And to Pat, a lady who loves to walk and camp no matter what the season is. Her love and affection make my life worthwhile.

I would also like to thank everyone at JALMAR PRESS for all their support, especially Publisher Alvyn M. Freed who saw a full length book lurking in the pages of my outline-form teaching manual. And to JALMAR editor-in-chief, John Dickinson Adams, who first joined with good friend, Helen Friend, in editing the book, and later to speed up the publishing process, personally handled the production and interior design of the book.

Art Harris of Arlington, Vermont deserves high praise for his stimulating contributions to the book. His sound knowledge of structuring the basic book and his familiarity with Eastern and European wilderness regions enabled me to craft a book that has relevance to both national and international backpacking.

And lastly to the wilderness of America, may we love it and not lay it low. For in the wilderness lies the preservation and renewal of people, and to these two entities, this book is dedicated.

Dennis Look
Sacramento, California
July 1976

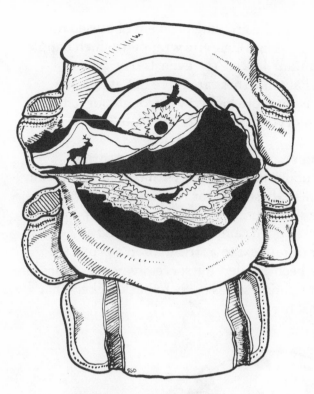

Wilderness Living

Loving it or laying it low.

Chapter One

Few books have become as outdated as those written several years ago on backpacking. Over the years writers have viewed forests as everlasting. Hikers were advised to cook over open fires at campsites, to build themselves bough beds by stripping nearby trees. Chapters were devoted to wood-based wilderness camps, axe handling, and finding dry wood. It seemed that no hike was complete without a roaring campfire and green saplings holding marshmallows toasting over an open flame.

Invariably these books on camping advocated going into the woods with an axe or belt hatchet. Hikers were sometimes advised to bury their empty tin cans. (We know today how easily animals can dig up cans and scatter them around.) All these books had one thing in common: a view that wilderness was inexhaustible. It never occurred to any writers of the so-called "woodsman school" that as more and more campfires were built, wood surrounding a favorite campsite or shelter would become scarce. They never anticipated that the vicinity of lean-tos or trail shelters would eventually resemble denuded, defoliated areas of Viet Nam as hikers foraged in ever-expanding circles around these structures seeking wood. Running out of fallen timber, hikers put their axes to use taking down anything that looked burnable.

It has become impossible to ignore the growing problem of buried tin cans dug up by animals, broken glass and cigarette wrappers which dapple the grounds and polluted mountain lakes. Yet even today when environmentalists are warning that wilderness areas are not everlasting, they are attacked by those who want more highways through our national parks, more trails and lean-tos — even fast-food restaurants and trailer campsites.

Fortunately the old "woodsman" school seems to be disappearing, although a backpacking book published recently says that a small saw can be a very handy piece of equipment, best used for "cutting such things as skillet extension handles, dingle sticks (used for hanging cooking pans), tent stakes, walking staffs." Today open campfires are regarded as wasteful. All too many fine campsites next to a stream or in a protected cove of a mountain lake have been spoiled by successive generations of wood seekers. A heightened consciousness has come to backpackers that flows with nature and not against her.

Along with this ecological awareness have come advances in equipment and food — lightweight trail items, long-contour pack frames to carry the weight higher than in a rucksack, and all sorts of freeze-dried and dehydrated foods. New fabrics have contributed to a revolution in raingear, tents, jackets, outer parkas. The old hobnailed hiking boot, common after World War II, has gone the way of the belt hatchet, replaced now by footwear with rubber-cleated soles which grip well on rock or muddy trail. Thus even a sensible book on backpacking (or packbacking, if you wish) written two decades ago may be obsolete today. That may be hard to believe, but backpacking books are not like geometry texts — things keep changing in this field pretty fast. I doubt if there ever will be a nostalgic return to the roaring campfire and the pine-bough bed, although today's obsession with exactly the right equipment fortunately seems to have peaked. Many backpackers are getting back to basics once again, discovering that an empty one pound coffee can makes a stove, that an old shower curtain can be a poncho or a tarp, that a throwaway frozen pie plate is a perfect, lightweight trail item.

I wish I could say that along with new equipment and an awareness of the preciousness of forests, recent backpacking books were also free of male chauvinism, but they are not. A book published only last year says on the second page" . . . backpacking represents an attempt by *man* to reintegrate *himself* with *his* environment. *Man* wants to see, smell and touch nature again. Modern life removed *man* from *his* natural environment and exposes *him* . . . " The italics are mine, but the prose is someone else's. Most backpacking books are written (and illustrated) as though the wilderness belonged only to the male of the species. They are sprinkled with claims that while a **man** may easily carry one-third the weight of his body on his back, a member of the **"fairer sex"** will be doing well to carry one-fourth of her body weight. Sometimes among all the prose about man and his environment, there may be a gratuitous paragraph welcoming women to the woods — as though our forests belonged somehow to men. In uncharitable moments, I sometimes think the writers of these books ought to be sentenced to accompany an all-woman expedition to Himalayan peaks just to see whether males are more competent than these females at 26,000 feet above sea level!

Fortunately the proportion of women on wilderness trails is increasing. The Boy Scouts may have been organized first, but the Girl Scouts were not far behind, and from what I have seen lately, male domination of the woods is disappearing along with the campfire. It is sad to have to admit that the stripped forests and campsites which look like bomb craters were largely the work of males.

If any defense can be summoned for the overexploitation of our forests, the best that can be said is that it was done in honest ignorance: our natural resources were regarded as infinite. Also wilderness trails were not well-travelled even twenty years ago. An enormous number of people have recently discovered what I call "the wilderness experience" and once remote trails are often heavily travelled today.

Wilderness travel — or backpacking — is now a Movement in itself. People are aware that since backpacking is a self-propelled, non-mechanical means of travel, the wilderness can be experienced with a small impact upon nature — if all those trail axes and small saws are left behind. The natural setting can be left relatively undisturbed and often can be observed in its natural state — except for occasional trail markings and candy wrappers.

While I don't want to belabor a point and catalog all the reasons backpacking is coming into its own, let me quickly tick off some of the reasons why mountaineering equipment stores are doing a brisk business and increasing numbers of people are venturing into the woods:

Getting Away From It All: With the growth of cities and urban sprawl, there is a counterbalancing urge to get away from it all — from high-rise condominiums of cement and glass, and those fast-food operations which chew up the trees by dispensing French fries, hamburgers, and thick shakes in layers of forest destroying paper. Many describe backpacking as removing one from the artificiality of the urban experience — the tempo of everyday existence, the ruts one can so easily fall into, the time clock syndrome. In the woods one can forget time and measure days by dawns and dusks as Indians did. I confess I sometimes wear my wristwatch into the woods, but sometimes I don't look at it for days. If I want to eat at mid-day, I stop and relax and eat when it **feels** like mid-day, not when my watch says it's twelve noon.

As work in America, whether in an office or factory, has become depersonalized, one can sometimes find an identity in the woods. Most of the major decisions of my life have been made away from the city of Sacramento where I earn a living. Up in the high Sierra, with Sacramento — indeed with San Francisco and Los Angeles **down there** somewhere — off in the distance, my head seems to clear. As the expression goes, I really get my head together away from it all. I seem to gain a perspective, perhaps even a harmony with the land, that allows me to think clearly. And I am not alone in this, for hiking companions of mine seem to be more open, more "together" up on the ridges.

In truth, the mountain air may be as polluted as in the San Francisco Bay Area to the west because that city is well-ventilated and the pollution it produces is often air-borne eastward, passing over the state capital and running smack into the high mountains, but that scientific fact doesn't take away from the ethereal spirituality of it all. Stress seems to drain away in the mountains or forests once you get away from the highways with their cumbersome campers.

Seeking Out One's Roots: Lately there has been a tremendous interest in history, a sort of remembrance of times past. Until recently, it seems to me we were always looking forward. A few years ago the best selling book was **Future Shock**, but as I write this, a nostalgic novel of the early years of this century called **Ragtime** tops the best-seller lists. Now many backpackers are seeking roots, going into the woods because this is what America was once when it was all Indian land. Far enough away from the highway not to hear a Winnebago grinding up a steep incline, you can imagine yourself a pioneer of two centuries ago alone in the woods with the earth and the sky above. If an occasional jet leaves its white contrail in the sky en route to an international airport, it only serves to accentuate the contrast — the pristine wilderness on the ground much as it was when Lewis and Clark ventured west; overhead the world of today with imported champagne being served to movie-watching 747 passengers.

The Inexpensiveness of It All. True, a pair of good hiking boots may cost up to $75 (hardly comparable to $175 ski boots) and a good rucksack or contour packframe will not be cheap, but beyond these items, neither necessary, what great expenses are there? No lift tickets, fiberglass skis priced over $200 needing replacements at season's end because they've lost their flex. Compared with downhill skiing — and even cross-country skiing where some places charge for use of trails — wilderness back-packing is truly inexpensive. As one writer on backpacking has already asked, "In what other sport could a family of four spend a weekend at less than $20?"

The Simplicity of It All. Tennis, golf, and downhill skiing all require a considerable learning. Indeed, it is reported that more people **drop out** of skiing than **take it up** yearly, perhaps because of the frustration at learning to negotiate a mountainside on skis.

"Pros" abound in these sports, teaching (for healthy fees) how to drive for the green, how to return a blistering service, how to ski moguls aggressively. But whoever heard of a backpacking pro anxious to exchange experience for lots of cash? True there are mountaineering camps and courses (I teach several myself) but a backpacker can take off into the woods with no fancy personal instruction — just good common sense — and feel perfectly adequate the first day out. After all, most of us learned to walk somewhere along about age one or two, and have been at it ever since.

The Relative Safety of Backpacking. Alpine journals regularly report mountain accidents — hikers who get lost, fall off a rain-soaked cliff, or die of exposure above timber line, but let's face it — backpacking done sensibly is hardly a high risk sport. There are dangers in backpacking, but they are relatively rare and can be reduced almost to zero with proper attention to equipment, proper use of that equipment, and common sense regarding weather, health, campsites, and so on. That is why I shall devote so much space in this book to equipment and its use, as well as listing safeguards, even simple things like what to do when a lightning storm comes while you are in the woods.

I know I have an enormous feeling of well-being when, properly but not necessarily expensively equipped, I am in the wilderness. The solitude there, actually hearing oneself think without interruption, brings on a tranquility which is a superb tonic. But I would be less than honest if I didn't confess the wilderness is becoming more crowded, so much so that people today must be admonished to "Take nothing but pictures, leave nothing but footprints."

I shall try to avoid lecturing although it will not always be easy when I am seized with a vision of careless backpackers tossing empty Spam® cans into the brush and chopping living trees with axes. What I want to do most of all is make *your* wilderness experience as comfortable and enjoyable as possible, even if that means a detailed look at equipment, how to select what is right and best for your budget, and how to use it.

I know a man who bought an expensive virgin goose down sleeping bag made for a very low temperature and darned near froze in it because he did not know anything about under-the-bag or ground insulation. Nobody, it seems, had told him that all that expensive down would compress under his body weight and pick up coldness from the ground.

If I seem sometimes to over-simplify or belabor a point, just skip along to the next part that interests you. You see, this book is aimed at a wide range of people including beginning backpackers who've never done more than stroll through Central Park or Golden Gate Park and are venturing into the wilderness, packs on backs, for the first time.

One final note: those out-dated backpacking books did have an appreciation of budget. They suggested how one could improvise an oven out of metal roof flashing or how one could make a suitable bedroll out of blankets and big safety pins. Their authors had a marvelous make-do philosophy. This makes a refreshing change from some other trends in backpacking.

As technology increasingly touched our lives, it began to permeate backpacking. Canvas (as a tent or knapsack fabric) was **out**, ripstop nylon was **in**. The rucksack became **out** and a magnesium alloy packframe was

in. Other items became **out** — wool jackets (too heavy), rubberized ponchos (ditto), blanket rolls (so far **out** they were ridiculous). The **ideal** backpacker, some books implied, was one equipped with Fabiano boots, Scandinavian Ragg socks, a Kelty pack, a Gerry down jacket, Gokey grouse cap, a Svea 123 stove (because it was the stove Colin Fletcher seemed to favor), and maybe even custom hiking shorts from England. In short, books began to concentrate on equipment. There were seemingly endless, humorless discussions about the minute differences between two sleeping pads. In short, technology was taking over backpacking which was in danger of becoming as much of an elitist sport as skiing.

But not **quite.** Sensible voices began to speak up, at first in letter columns of backpacking magazines. "Are we prisoners of technology? Are we becoming equipment freaks?" What was really so bad about wearing sneakers, or using a salted-peanut-butter can to boil water in, or using an old shower curtain as a ground cloth? Did one have to buy $75 boots, or was there something at Sears, Penneys, or Wards that would do just as well?

This revolt against elitism has come at a good time, coinciding not only with America's 200th birthday, but with a renewed interest in a simpler, more natural way of doing things — whether it's growing vegetables or making ice cream without chemicals. The new thrust in backpacking today is: improvise and enjoy.

I have demonstrated this philosophy throughout this book. When I seem to have become a prisoner of the backpacking technology myself, such as in debating the relative merits of goose down versus duck down it is because this is currently a widely and loudly heard argument in packing circles. You may as well get some awareness of these areas to protect you against any hard sells.

Too often we assume that comfort and enjoyment go together, that if only one is comfortable on a backpacking trip the experience will be enjoyable. Amazingly I have seen thoroughly soaked hikers slogging through wet brush and enjoying it — perhaps because in everyday life we seldom allow ourselves to get wet. We have lost touch with rain. To be momentarily buffeted by chilling winds or find oneself out of breath by sweaty exertion on a steep pitch of trail may be worth discomfort. Such moments may be the most memorable of all.

If comfort and joy went together, the first-class world traveler whose bags are cared for by a succession of porters and bellhops would automatically have more joy than the $10-a-day knapsacked tourist. Pleasure comes at unexpected moments and sometimes out of adversity.

What I always remember is the sheer joy of backpacking — that wonderful feeling when you awake early in the morning in the woods (having gone to sleep at dusk) and feel the sharp cold as soon as you are out of the sleeping bag. Water is soon boiling for morning chocolate and cereal; another day on the trail approaches. Perhaps there will be blueberries on the sunny ledges up above; maybe a deer will bound through the woods today, its white-tipped tail flashing through the green and brown forest. Who knows what is in store? The anticipation itself is highly stimulating, for backpacking is about as authentic a return to old times as one can experience in this fast world, and it can be full of simple joy.

Boots

Walking, stalking, hiking.

Chapter Two

The following section is greatly detailed on the selection and construction of boots. It is optional reading. If you do not want to know the A to Z's of "bootdom" there is always expertise and advice available at a good mountaineering or backpacking store. - DL

In most sports attention is paid to proper footwear. But in backpacking there can be no question: the single, most important piece of equipment is footwear. The main concern here is the support of the foot. With all the extra weight and stress hiking entails, you need a foot covering that will protect the balls of the feet from damage.

SNEAKERS

It is possible to stand on many a mountain summit and see happy hikers come up the last pitch to the summit in sneakers, Hush Puppies,® even sandals. Sometimes entire summer camps, with camp counselors at either end of a snake-like column of advancing hikers, will reach a summit all outfitted in low-cut sneakers. Even experienced backpackers like writer Bob Rethmel recommend carrying sneakers to wade and cross streams. A whole group of climbers, boots lashed to packs to prevent them from getting wet, can cross a stream with one pair of sneakers being tossed back and forth.

But, generally, sneakers are for other uses — sandlot baseball, basketball, tennis, canoeing — and are not meant for serious backpacking. They do not give the foot or ankle much support; they get wet very easily (of course they also dry easily!); they can be slippery, especially if the tread is smooth or worn; and they can be mighty cold if one runs into a little frost or snow. An ordinary street shoe, even if it has a cleated or rippled sole, is not much better, for it is low, neither giving the foot or ankle needed support nor affording protection from pebbles and sticks that easily find their way inside.

WAFFLE-STOMPERS

Of course, low, laced shoes are not exactly an "in" item. You have advertising agency account executives who otherwise lead a pretty soft life coming to work in $50 Frye boots. They would not be caught dead in a pair of laced wing tips! Others, including college students who used to walk around the campus in a pair of Bass loafers, are going for a higher shoe — the so-called "waffle stomper." It provides more support than a low shoe, can take a lot of knocking around, is adaptable to rain and slush and some snow, provides pretty good traction with its rubber or simulated-rubber cleated soles. I know students who just about live in their "waffle stompers"— so-called because the impression left in mud or snow is not unlike the grid of a waffle iron.

As great as this shoe is — and it is really far more practical than a loafer — it is not for **serious** backpacking. Don't get me wrong — it is light years ahead of the low, laced shoe and the sneaker, but it simply is not sturdy or supportive enough (or even waterproof enough) to stand up under moderate to strenuous backpacking where a load is carried.

I am sure you realize that such shoes are fine for ordinary walking and even a little amateur touch football, but once you are carrying 25-40 pounds on your back, the importance of footwear will be evident. Have you ever looked at a weightlifter's shoes? And the weightlifter is not walking around very much. Obviously, plenty of support in the foot is needed if one is going to lift a weight, or, in the backpacker's situation, carry a pack on the back.

VARIOUS BOOTS

What is the best boot? There is no simple answer. What is great for rock climbing (flexible for narrow footholds, not too heavy) might not be so good on a squishy trail which slices through bogs and meadows where a strong, reasonably waterproof shoe would be required. A heavily-padded boot might be fine for winter mountaineering, but far too hot a boot (in fact, a "sweat box") on blistering summer days or in the desert.

There are heavy boots (which weigh five pounds) and lightweight boots that come in around two pounds. There are boots with the "rough" side of the leather out, and boots with the "rough" side inward — and endless debate about which is better. Some hikers have more than one pair of boots, just as a skier may have downhill skis and slalom skis which differ from each other in length and width. A hiker might wear a well-insulated, relatively heavy boot in winter conditions and switch to a much lighter-weight, non-insulated boot for summer hiking. I cannot recommend any single boot. The best way to buy boots is in person, although sometimes you can order and be well-fitted by mail.

Let's consider various boots in detail. What about welts, soles, leather tanning, lacing and even boot laces? A good background in fundamentals of boot construction can help you to make your choice based on terrain, load to be carried, weather, and so on. For example, if you lived in Vermont and wanted boots to backpack along the Long Trail, which extends the length of the state from Massachusetts border to Canada, one consideration would be the trail itself. There, the trail is almost entirely in the woods, often in low, wet areas; it seldom slants up a rocky face or slices across exposed surfaces above timber line. In this situation, I think waterproofing is most important. I would not want a boot which leaked around the welt, nor a boot in which swampy water could seep in around the tongue. On the other hand, if considerable hiking was to be done above timber line, often in fields of loose stone but where rainwater would tend to drain well, running off among the rocks rather than accumulating in soggy puddles. I would place a high premium on a boot that would take the chafing of rocks and give strong ankle support. Selecting boots is a highly subjective thing. The best I can do is outline some of the characteristics of boot construction and hope that the buyer will use reasoned judgement to select the proper boot.

BUYING BOOTS

Boston's EMS (Eastern Mountain Sports) devotes a good-sized section to ordering boots by mail. They tell the buyer exactly how to make a foot outline with two pair of socks and so on. EMS says there's a 75% chance of getting properly fitted the first time via mail if their advice is followed.

In general, the salespeople in a mountaineering or backpacking store are more savvy than those at a run-of-the-mill Army and Navy or Surplus store. In the backpacking store you can try on all sorts of boots and get a good fit. Do not be **overly** concerned with the size number stamped or marked on the boot. Some of the boots, built on European lasts, are made to European sizes. A size 44, for example, is not exactly translatable to our sizes. Besides if a size 10 boot feels right even if you think your size is 9½, trust your feet rather than the printed size.

When trying on boots, take two pair of socks with you. Some hikers prefer a cotton, silk, or synthetic fiber inner sock next to the foot, and a wool outer sock. Be sure there is ample toe space — a finger (or at the most two fingers) inserted behind the heel sideways with the boots unlaced and the toes pushed forward should give you a good feel of size. Sometimes a store will let you stand at a 45° downward-sloping angle to give you the feel of toe pressure against the front of a boot, since coming downhill off a mountain puts tremendous strain on the toe of a boot. The boot should be snug between the instep and heel. There shouldn't be more than ¼" inch heel lift. When your heel is lifting less than ¼" it is called "lift." When your heel lifts more than ¼", it is called a "slip." If you can find some stairs, it should be easier to check out the heel lift. If there seems to be too much heel slip, not only check the size of the boot (i.e., its length), but the width. Some people have narrow feet and need a narrower boot.

STIFFNESS OF SOLE

How stiff should a boot be? For rock-climbing, a relatively flexible boot is required. Generally, though, I think a fairly stiff boot, although harder to break in, is better; it tends to give much-needed support. However, if you get too much stiffness, you may get too much weight; then you're in the position of lifting an additional 2½ pounds each time you take a step (if the boots weigh in at five pounds a pair). Stiffness is partly determined by the midsole, made of leather or rubber, which is sandwiched between the innersole (where the foot rests) and the outer sole with its cleats or lugs. The more layers of midsole, the stiffer the boot. Most medium weight hiking boots range from one layer of midsole to 2½ layers of midsole, but in any event, the boots should be stiff enough to protect the feet from rough trails, but not so stiff as to prevent the foot from flexing. There is a delicate balance involved here. One's body weight and size of shoe determine how fast the midsole can be broken in. Too stiff a midsole can lead to blisters on the heel because the sole was not flexible enough. Boots should weigh in somewhere between 4 to 6 pounds per pair, but there are extremes on either end — especially on the low end. A Himalayan expedition concluded that one pound of boot is equal to carrying five pounds in the pack, so an excessively heavy boot is going to feel even heavier as it is lifted and lifted and lifted.

You will want to lace up the boots yourself and see if you can wiggle your toes slightly. Naturally, these new boots may feel stiff. I cannot honestly say that new boots should be absolutely comfortable when tried on in the store. One must surmise how they will feel after they are broken in. While they should be snug, they should not be too tight; there must be some allowance for a slight swelling of the feet. (Did you know that feet are often slightly larger at night than in the morning — that is, presuming one sleeps rather than works at night?) Leather does soften up and become more pliable. Ironically that is the reason leather is seldom used today in ski boots where an absolute stiffness gives the skier instant control of skis. In skiing, plastic has replaced leather, and a pair of plastic ski boots will feel on the foot after a whole winter of skiing exactly as they did the first day in the ski shop, but hiking boots are different. Leather is still the preferred material for boots, and it will adapt itself to the foot to some extent. If the boot, however, is too big, no amount of stuffing or strategically placed padding will make it right. Perhaps that is why you often see in mountain climbing journals ads like this: "Great Pair of Fabiano Mountain Boots, size 9½ N, for sale. Used twice."

SEX LABELING IN BOOTS

A word about boots for men and women. Wear what fits regardless of the sex label. Most Japanese who come to the United States find themselves buying "ladies ski boots" and I suppose they might find the somewhat narrower and shorter sizes of mountain boots similarly suitable. Boys often find a "ladies" style fits well. Men, swallowing their masculine pride, have been known to be content with a pair marked L — for ladies.

Perhaps all this will change. Not many years ago women wore blue jeans with a zipper on the side, while men went around with front zippered flies. Now jeans are pretty much (but not entirely) unisex. It must be noted, though, that while we may champion unisex clothing — particularly in backpacking — most of the accommodating has been by women to traditional men's clothing.

So far, at least, American men are not about to adopt much of anything from women's clothing, not even a kerchief when it might be practical. Men's boot, ladies' boot — what does it matter so long as it fits well and is sturdy? Traditionally, women's styles have narrower lasts, while men's and boy's are a little wider. It's entirely possible for a particular man to have narrower feet than a particular woman or vice versa. So, as a purchaser of new boots, why not ignore the sex labeling in boots and buy the boot that fits best?

HAIR INSIDE OR OUTSIDE?

Perhaps no more controversial subject has appeared in backpacking literature lately than this: should the hiker's boots have the hair outside or inside? In his marvelously illustrated book on backpacking, Harvey Manning reminds us all: "The cow wears its skin with the hair outside, the flesh inside." True enough — and the cow wears it that way **all the time** with no choice, but hikers do have a choice. They may select boots with the hair side outside, generally called **smooth leather** or **smooth-finish leather**. For years this was the only way European bootmakers fabricated their boots and thus the smooth-leather adherent became very well entrenched. The so-called "European hiking boot" was unquestioned as the best, but in recent years the animal's way of wearing its skin has been reversed in boots; the hair side has been turned inward and the so-called **rough** side is out. These so-called **rough-outs** are now very popular and cannot be dismissed as inferior; in fact, most American hiking boots are now "rough-outs."

The **"rough-outs"** seem to be more durable, but perhaps a little less water repellent than the **smooth-finish** boots. The theory today seems to be that while the smooth-finish leather is a good water repellent material, the relatively thin skin is exposed for slicing or gouging by rocks or stumps in normal trail use. With **rough-outs**, the thickness protects against superficial scuffing and abrasions, and the animal "skin" is inside, well protected from the hazards of rock, roots, and other normal trail terrain. Even my over-simplified statements about the relative merits of each may be debatable. In fact, one respected mountaineer maintains that the **smooth-leathers** are less water repellent than the **rough-outs** (sometimes called **reversed, reverse-tan leather, or rough-tanned**). Perhaps, there is no definitive answer, any more than one can say which construction makes the best ski. Perhaps, what matters more is the quality of the leather, the way it has been treated, and the care with which the boot was made.

TANNING

Obviously the animal skin would deteriorate without some sort of preparation, so it is put through many operations which are spoken of as **curing the leather.** If you have ever been to the city of Fez in Morocco, you probably have ventured (with or without guide) into the old medina and seen leather processing going on in open air just as it did thousands of years ago. The smell — all right, the **stench** — is something you must experience. In more up-to-date places like Lynn, Massachusetts, once the self-proclaimed leather-tanning capitol of the world, factories process animal hide into leather. With **chrome** or **dry tanning**, various chromium salts are employed, and the leather has a hard finish. This is common in many so-called street shoes. Sometimes another method is used: material derived from plants and trees and called **bark tannis** is used. This process called **vegetable tanning** (or **oil tanning**) gives a more moist, more supple appearance — some call it the oily look. As in the matter of which side of the animal hide should be outside the boot, the debate over which of these two tanning methods is superior continues unabated. What is really significant, however, is to determine which method was used in the boots you have selected because proper maintenance of one type of tanned

14

leather differs from the other. Ask the salesperson which method was used in tanning the leather, for it will determine how you treat the boots in the years following.

You might also want to know whether you have **full-grain** leather which is used in most mountaineering boots, **corrected-grain** (which has many grades) sometimes used in medium-weight boots, or **suede** which is leather which is sliced from inside the hide. Full-grain leather, favored by purists, will show imperfections just as natural wood shows grain and knotholes. A pair of boots from the same box may not match exactly in terms of color — but who cares, as long as the leather is durable? With corrected-grain, some of the inherent defects of the leather have been swept aside by a treatment which gives a uniformity in texture and color to the leather. Of course we are all familiar with suede, used in the so-called "Hush Puppy"®or "desert boot." While this shoe or boot is lightweight and good in warm climates, it is much less durable and generally cannot be waterproofed.

BOOT CONSTRUCTION

Many people automatically assume that a "padded boot" is best, partly because the term implies no blisters and also because these boots may be the most expensive in the store. In padded boots, between two layers of leather, there is a layer of polyurethane foam. Make no mistake, there **are** advantages: the foam tends to absorb moisture from the foot besides giving protection against sores, blisters, and abrasions of the foot. Moreover, such boots can often be broken in a lot easier because the foam tends to mold to the foot. Generally, these padded boots are the most comfortable — but not **always.** For one thing, the weight of all that padding makes them heavier, and a **little** heavier in the store may prove to be a **lot** heavier out on the trail where the feet may be lifted up and put down again more than 1,000 times an hour. Also, these boots, as I mentioned before, can be very warm in summer weather and be a source of great discomfort. If I were interested in four-season hiking and knew I would be doing some winter mountaineering, these boots would be attractive because they are much warmer in the winter. Who likes cold feet? I might endure an occasional "hot foot" just for the extra warmth in winter.

Normally a lined boot is perfectly adequate and gives reasonable protection to the foot. The largest percentage of hiking boots on display in any mountaineering store today will be lined boots (two layers of leather with smooth leather inside, rough-out on the outside) and they should be durable enough for most situations. Unlined boots, such as many "waffle-stompers," are much lighter in weight and more inexpensive.

There are other factors to consider:

*Shank, backbone of the boot, which can extend one-half to full length of the boot (insole), promotes flexing support. **Nylon shank** does not conduct hot or cold temperatures. It expands and contracts at the same rate as leather. **Steel shank** conducts hot or cold temperatures and may corrode.

*Hinged Instep — provides further flexing of the top portion of the boot.

*Scree collar, located on the top of the boot with a leather and rubber cover, may provide protection against entrance of pebbles and the like. (Some hikers prefer a breathable gaiter.)

*Heel counter — provides stiffening to heel for protection, and minimizes "side flex" of the boot.

*Toe counter. Stiffening of toe area of boot to provide greater protection. Most new hiking boots have some sort of hard toe.

TONGUE CLOSURES

For the buyer who is no shoe expert, it may be difficult to spot some of the features we have discussed so far, but, fortunately, the tongue closures are easy to spot and very handy to know about:

***Single tongue closure.** You will find this on an ordinary pair of street shoes where the tongue is stitched at the bottom. This sort of closure, common to sneakers and even waffle-stompers, provides a minimum of water protection and tends to slip from side to side at the top of the boot.

***Double tongue closure.** Here we have the single tongue, often padded, with an outer tongue stitched in from the sides of the boot, but with enough extra leather to make the shoe easy to get on and off. With this closure, there is water protection.

***Split tongue with single tongue.** Seems complicated, but it simply means we have two halves sewn to the sides of the boot and overlapping the single tongue when laced. (Tongues, by the way, not only provide protection from water, but protect the foot against laces.)

***Single tongue gusset with overlapping split tongue.** This provides maximum protection against the elements (rain, water, snow) and is found in the most expensive boots.

Here are two other terms which might appear in a discussion of hiking boots: **rocker last** — the sole is curved upward at the toe to promote flexing in the midsole. The boot should be more comfortable for walking. **Back stay:** stiffened portion of the back of a boot where the single piece of leather to make the boot is joined. Helps protect the Achilles tendon area.

16

WELTS

Let's take a brief look at welts. Technically, a welt is a "type of seam in which one edge is cut close to the stitching line and covered by the other edge which is stitched over it." Basically, we are talking about the little ridge area where the sole is attached to the boot proper. Of course, if there is a bonded sole, as in many waffle-stompers, no outside welt exists. There may not be much protection, but after all, this sort of shoe is made for everyday wear. Remember, though, that with the bonded sole it is almost impossible to put on a new sole. It can be done, but shoe-repair shop bonding always seems less satisfactory than factory bonding.

A good pair of hiking shoes will have some sort of welt, and it will be possible, of course, to resole the boot making it (if the uppers last) good for a lifetime of backpacking.

Here are some common types of welts:

Norwegian welt: This is the most common welt with many variations, ranging from single to triple stitching in the welt area. Advantages:

*Outersole can be replaced.

*This welt allows for further laminations of midsole, thus developing a stiffer boot. These laminations, or layers, can be made of rubber or leather. But if there are too many layers the boot may be too stiff.

*This welt will be found on medium weight to heavy weight (up to 7 lbs. per pair) technical climbing boots.

When a Norwegian welt is used on a medium weight with two or more laminations, a **storm welt** is desirable. A storm welt is a strip of leather that runs around on top of the welt area. Because the Norwegian welt allows the use of larger thread diameters to be used in sewing, larger needles must be used to penetrate more layers of laminations. A complement to this type of welt is the storm welt. It acts as a further backing of the stitching, plus, as the name implies, helps keep out moisture. The little ledge around the boot (welt area) is a great collector of moisture. Boiled linseed oil may be used to help prevent this moisture from penetrating the inner portion of the boot.

Goodyear Welt: A Goodyear welt is preferred by some manufacturers in medium weight hiking boots. It generally has the same qualities as the Norwegian, but where a single exterior stitch is required, a Goodyear welt is desirable. Where two or three exterior stitches are used, the Norwegian welt is more practical. A storm welt may be used in either welt system.

McKay [or Littleway] Welt: Now we have a mid-sole sandwiched between the inner and outer sole, but the most important difference is that the stitching of the welt is found **inside** the boot. Again, as with the Norwegian welt, the sole can be replaced. The foot has good protection from rocks and hard hiking trails. This type of welt offers no outside ledge to collect rain, but the stitches inside must be fine enough so that the bottom of the foot is not worn by stitching. Sometimes a Dr. Scholl's insoles will help.

SOLES

As I said earlier, the nailed or hobnailed boot, so common on American hiking trails, has practically disappeared. Instead, virtually all hiking boots have rubber or simulated-rubber soles with built-in cleats or lugs. Perhaps the most familiar name is Vibram ® sole. This outersole was originally made in Italy, but has since been licensed to be produced in at least two other countries: Switzerland and the U.S.A. The material is neoprene, and there are a number of different soles with special uses. Usually the specific name is either stamped into the sole or on the manufacturer's "logo" as follows:

*Roccia (Italian for rock): Since this outer-sole was developed for rock climbing, it is softer (less carbon and more neoprene) and has an excellent grip on rock. For extensive hiking, however, it wears out quicker, partly because its lug depth is not so great. This sole is usually found on lighter-weight boots.

*Montagna (Italian for mountain): This sole has a higher percentage of carbon which makes it hold up under ordinary hiking conditions with rock abrasions and general terrain hazards. It has a relatively deep lug depth and often will last twice as long as a Roccia sole under similar conditions.

*Montagna or Roccia Bloc: The unit is a one-piece sole and heel unit. The color of the labeling means nothing. The same sole may have the logo area in black or yellow. Glue is used to attach the outer sole to the midsole. Some manufacture use either staples, nails, or screws to secure the heel and toe areas (which are more vulnerable to delamination).

Note that many backpacking catalogs list a lightweight boot with a Roccia sole both in their rock-climbing sections and in their trailboot sections. While the boot may be perfect for rock climbing, it may also be ideal for ordinary trail hiking — something perhaps less than strenuous backpacking. Naturally, choice of the sole is dictated by the sort of hiking one expects to do.

All Vibram ® soles can be replaced. A new Vibram ® sole can be added for, perhaps, $17-$22. Try to get a genuine Vibram ® sole, with its special beveled holes in the lugs which act as suction cups around wet rocks. Some competing soles are comparable to the Vibram,® especially those made in France. You will want to watch out for any separation or delaminations between the midsole and the Vibram ® sole. If this delamination (it may never occur) is not caught in its early stages, water can rot out the leather in the midsole.

Since the Vibram ® sole has a lot of carbon in it, it can cause black streaks on floors, especially linoleum floors. Also, since the lugs are designed to be self-cleaning, wearing of these boots inside a house will result in little pockets of trail dirt being emptied here and there. Vibram ® soles are the greatest invention, say some, since canned beer. It might be more appropriate in **this** book to say that they are the greatest invention since the frame pack, which has revolutionized backpacking.

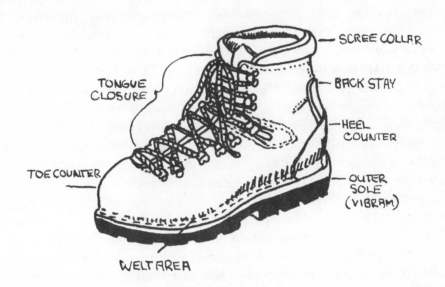

THINGS TO REMEMBER WHEN SELECTING BOOTS

Height: There is a great difference of opinion here. Too high a boot tends to restrict movement, but in heavy snake country, a high boot is sometimes preferable. I would say 5½ inches from welt to top gives minimum ankle support.

Feel of Boot: Unlike a plastic ski boot which will never compromise its stiffness, a leather boot will "give" with normal wear. Therefore, it will feel differently out on the trail than in the store. However, there should never be any sideways flex, even in the store. Such flex will only grow worse under normal wear; blisters will be inevitable or perhaps a twisted ankle. The sole should be stiff enough to protect feet from the sort of trails you will be hiking on, but not so stiff that it prevents the foot from flexing somewhat. The boot should breathe — and that is one other advantage of leather over plastic or neoprene.

Lacing: Originally all boots had grommeted eyelets like those found in laced street shoes. They are strong and can be replaced if they give away. (Even if one gives away, the hole in the leather will still be there for lacing). Many climbers prefer these grommeted eyelets all the way to the top of the boot even though it takes more time to lace and unlace the boot. Faster lacing is accomplished by using a combination of grommeted eyelets at the bottom of the shoe, then hooks toward the top. Since the lower laces do not have to be undone to pull the boot on or off, they can remain in the secure grommets, and the top can be laced and pulled tight in jig time using the hooks. You will also find swivel eyelets (little rings attached to the boot) and that fastest of all inventions — speed lacing, where little tunnel-shaped metal lace-carriers control the lacing all the way up the boot, so a good, hefty tug at the two top laces will pull everything tight. The speedy methods are handy, but sometimes all the hooks and rings and tunnel-like channels break off or get snagged on underbrush. For all its old-fashioned looks and the little extra time it takes, the grommeted eyelets are still hard to beat, although most hiking and climbing boots have one combination or another. Today nylon laces are very popular — one in particular is the Cordura flat lace. A rounded lace tends to let the knot slip, where a flat lace will hold. Cotton laces (flat or round) wear out quickly. In stress areas of lacing, leather still has some advantages, although mice are said to like to chew on leather laces.

You can do a lot of experimenting with lacing in order to make your feet most comfortable in the boots. Sometimes you may want to have two sets of laces so the bottom laces can be looser than the top laces. Going downhill, however, it might be better to lace your boots tightly through the bottom eyelets, (not too tight, it tends to cut off blood circulation), with a looser lacing on top. Each person develops his or her own style of lacing. For many hikers, going downhill, especially when the grade is steep, is much more difficult than climbing uphill as there is great pressure on the front of the boot — good reason not to have the toes touch the end of the boot when fitting a new pair of boots. Vasque (a division of Red Wing Shoe Company that makes mountaineering boots) catalogs have an excellent explanation and diagram on boot lacing.

In general, you will have to decide whether you are most happy with an extremely light boot (the waffle-stomper) which would be adequate for Sunday hikes without a pack. The trailboot (McKay welt, a little heavier weight boot than a lightweight) can be used with a pack on moderate trail walking and is considered an all-purpose backpacking boot. The scrambling boot or medium weight backpacking and climbing boot falls into the category of more ankle support for heavier pack weight, with cross-country (bushwacking) and moderate trail hiking. You will need a heavy weight boot for climbing and four-season backpacking. Of course there always exists slight differences from manufacturer to manufacturer. One last suggestion when selecting boots — if you intend to winter camp during your backpacking career, choose a boot that is slightly heavier in its **category**. You will usually end up with a full-grain leather, or a higher grade of corrected-grain leather. These leather thickness allow the boot to stay waterproofed much longer.

BREAKING IN THE BOOT

Leather is forgiving; it will soften with use. While a boot may develop a little more lateral give-and-take, it will not become any longer, but the mellowing process can be hastened so the boot can almost feel broken in when on the first pitch of trail. There are two approaches to this breaking in process, and I have used them both with success.

If you do not have a big wilderness excursion scheduled right away, just wear the boots around as much as possible — mowing the lawn, washing the car; if you are city-bound, you might just walk among the cement canyons of your city — anything to put a little mileage on these boots. (Some people prefer to walk around the house — with Vibram ® black-carbon soles ?? — on the theory that if the boots really don't fit, they can be returned if they show no wear.)

If the boot is a fairly heavy boot and somewhat stiff, it may need more than mere walking mileage to break it in properly. This method will sound a little squishy, but take my word for it — it works. Simply pour hot tap water into the boot right up to the top. Dump the water out right away. Now put on your nice socks (two pairs probably — we shall get to that soon) and wear around until the boots are completely dry. It is a funny moist feeling — but it does work. This way of breaking in the boots cannot harm them. Also you will be duplicating hours of your feet sweating inside the boots. This inside moisture helps mold the inner part of the boot to the shape of your foot. Avoid using any chemicals or chemical softeners on the boots and try this strange, yet natural, method to break them in.

MAINTAINING THE BOOTS

There is a theory (totally unproved, but, nonetheless, passed around by folks who run lodges which cater to skiers in the winter and backpackers in the summer) that backpackers are far more **considerate** than skiers. It may or may not be true, but I think when it comes to caring for their boots, the skiers win hands down. Note how they take them off, put them in ski-boot presses, then put them into a duffle bag or even a specially designed bag which zips up to the shape of the boot. Go early to a place like China Peak or Big Bromley and watch the skiers arrive, all carefully carrying their ski boots which they will put on inside the ski lodge.

Too many backpackers, sad to relate, neglect their boots. After a hike they stash the muddy boots somewhere without realizing that mud tends to dry the leather and make it more brittle. Or they commit that cardinal sin of backpacking — drying wet boots under severe heat. You have probably seen people place soggy boots close to a fire, or close to a radiator or car heater in the belief that a good, strong blast of heat will dry the boots out rapidly. Excessive heat — test the heat by seeing if your hands can take the same heat — will tend to stretch the leather and dry it up. (After all, although the leather has been tanned, it is still animal skin.) Even worse is putting a pair of boots in an oven and turning up the temperature to a cake-baking range of 475 degrees.

These mistreatments will cause problems. Unexpectedly the boot may fall apart in some strategic area; or the boot will change size; or the boot will lose its waterproof qualities.

If the boots get wet, they can be dried, but s-l-o-w-l-y in a temperature range that your exposed toes could take for a similar period of time. Some people put newspapers inside the boot on the theory that the newspaper will absorb moisture and hasten the drying process. All mud and trail debris should be brushed away from the boot before it is stored. A good stiff brush will help. Many hikers automatically dust off the boots with a car whiskbroom just as they return from the trail to the parked car. Better yet, use saddle soap and a little water to clean the dirt out of the pores of the leather. Then wipe with a dry towel and brush.

Thirty years ago that's all there was to it. One simply put the boots away, but in today's world, the chemist has taken over and there are a hundred preparations for maintaining the interior, the welt, the exterior, the tops — whatever. Some are more useful than others, but the important thing is to use the right preparation on the particular leather you have. Many people spray the interior of the boot with a preparation like Lysol spray — although I'm not very keen on aerosol sprays. Perhaps some antiseptic powders would work as well. This precaution will hopefully prevent any mold from developing, although during the rainy season in some areas, nothing will prevent mold.

I know one climber who puts his hiking boots in an Allsop Shoe Press (Allsop Automatic Co., Bellingham, Washington). It is a sort of boot press made for ski boots, but is adaptable to most hiking boots with a reasonable welt. Here are some more tips for boot maintenance:

*Saddle soap is still a good material for cleaning the leather.
*Silicones can be used for chrome tanned leathers, and Sno-Seal® is a waxy, silicone treatment for the same type of tanned leather.
*For oil-tanned leathers, Snow Shoe® is a fine boot grease. Neats foot

oil and mink oil may also be used on oil tanned leathers. Leath-R-Seal®may also be used, but read the label carefully to be certain you are using it on the properly tanned leather. Chrome-tanned leathers are treated differently from oil-tanned leathers. The general rule is that silicones may be used with chrome-tanned leathers, while oils and greases appropriately go with oil-tanned leathers. If I had a new pair of chrome-tanned leather boots, I would treat with some silicone preparation fairly soon after purchase.

*Many people smother the boots in preparations thinking they will make the leather more waterproof. But the leather must breathe and **water repellent** surfaces do have a saturation point which **waterproof** surfaces do not. If one makes a boot **completely** waterproof, sweat can easily build up inside the boot, creating more of a chance of blisters and cold feet. Some backpackers waterproof the lower portion of the boot where it is really needed and then try to make the upper part of the boot water repellent, thus having the best of both worlds! The upper portion of the boot can breathe and the lower portion, which gets more moisture, can afford to be waterproof.

*If your boot has a welt — that little ridge where the sole has been stitched to the upper — you can use Leath-R-Seal®or boiled linseed oil. These liquids will penetrate around the stitches and needle holes. Dacron thread, especially useful in putting on a storm welt, will not swell and cover needle holes, so such liquid aids to the welt are important for water-proofing.

*In general, less waterproofing is needed in the summertime, but this generalization may not apply if you are hiking in the Olympic rain forest in Washington in July, where it seems to be wet all the time.

*To apply Sno-Seal®(good on the lower portion of a boot and best used on chrome-tanned leathers), the Sno-Seal®mixture may be heated, although the "new, improved" Sno-Seal®goes on easier. If it is heated, it can then be applied with a paint brush and rubbed in with a rag. The varieties of application of Sno-Seal®are many. The best way to apply it is out of the can, rubbing the paste right into the leather with hands on a good, warm day. Do not bake the boots, but if it is a warm day, it would be helpful to at least have the boots warm. Avoid putting the treated boots into an oven to "bake" the Sno-Seal®on. I have found that heating the boot up slightly outside of an open oven door works safely. This is just enough heat (350°) to open the pores of the leather and let the Sno-Seal®penetrate.

*Shoe Saver®, a Dow-Corning product, can be used on the top portion. It is called a "silicone water repellent." The detailed directions on the bottle with its own applicator pad suggest several coats and tell how to apply.

*Ordinary shoe trees can be used in the boots when they are in storage to prevent their curling.

*On the trail, turn your boots upside down before you go to sleep.

Moisture will tend to settle in a boot left standing on its sole. Store the boots where they will be protected from rain, dew, frost. I have heard of people who take their boots into the sleeping bags at night with them, but I do not recommend it.

Packs

*The pack on your rack is the home
on your back.*

Chapter Three

That one day hike can be a special treat with no pack to carry. You travel light and unburdened. You can exult in Indian-like trail speed as you move rapidly on your hike. Returning downhill, you pace increases. With no pack jouncing around on your back, your fleetness helps you celebrate the released free-ness of yourself and the ever-abounding free-ness of the woods and streams about you.

Every hiker likes to travel this unencumbered way, especially on a well-known trail. It might be just a quick run up your favorite mountain and back again with no overnight planned. These occasional day trips are a welcome change from backpacking trips with several overnights.

Overnight means a pack. True, we have all seen hikers carrying duffle bags. Or else they've rolled up their food and extra clothing in a sleeping bag carried as a bedroll over the shoulder. A pack is essential and may be even more difficult to select than the right boots. Sometimes I think we tend to get too hung up on equipment here in America and lose sight of the fact that hiking and backpacking are meant to be a pleasure. I would rather see someone on the trail in sneakers and an inexpensive knapsack having a good time than a perfectly equipped hiker with the latest Kelty packframe having a miserable time. Still, I shall mention the optimum equipment for those who want it — or feel the need for it.

Just as the hobnailed boot has passed into oblivion in favor of various legged soles like the Vibram ® ; the backpack has undergone a tremendous revolution. Until fifty years ago, it was either a wicker basket with straps attached or a canvas tote pack with shoulder straps. Huge loads were carried in these packs and every now and then up in Maine or Oregon you will find a old woods-person still using an L.L. Bean wicker backpack. And even today you will see college students who work summers maintaining the string of Appalachian Mountain Club huts in the White Mountains of New Hampshire packing in equipment on packboards. You can lash almost anything to a packboard — even bags of cement — and it is very practical for carrying heavy loads. But for everyday backpacking, packboards are not used very often.

Just as there is a boot for heavy-duty climbing and a lighter boot for rock scrambling, there are varieties of packs. Most experienced hikers have a small pack or a rucksack for a brief trip. These are often called soft packs. Sometimes you are not going to be out overnight but do plan to have a mid-day lunch and perhaps take some photographs, so you will be carrying food, a camera and perhaps a few lenses, and of course that list of odds and ends we will get to later in the book — raingear, a compass, a first aid kit, or a snake-bite kit. Even an innocent day trip can produce a turned ankle, a scraped knee.

KNAPSACK AND FRAMELESS RUCKSACKS

For such a trip, a nylon or canvas knapsack is perfect. True, the pack sits directly on the back and in hot, sweaty weather it may be uncomfortable. Also with the load riding directly on the back, it is imperative not to have those extra camera lenses or a metal-boxed first aid kit packed close to the back. Storing of articles in such a pack where there is no daylight between back and pack requires more attention than with a packframe which rides away from the back. Sharp objects hardly noted the first half mile can suddenly begin to feel mighty uncomfortable. Best to have a poncho or an extra sweater next to the back.

One can easily carry up to twenty pounds in such a pack and in a pinch a sleeping bag can be tied on top to make a suitable overnight outfit. Many disadvantaged children from the city who get away for a few weeks at a summer camp cannot afford a frameless rucksack or a packframe; yet they shouldn't be denied that great pleasure of an overnight hike.

Many of these knapsacks today are made of nylon, which is a durable material, waterproof and lightweight. Canvas is also a popular fabric which tends not to be as sweaty next to the back as nylon. In fact, some soft packs have nylon on the outside of the pack and breathable canvas next to the wearer's back.

I know a person who purchased a **leather** rucksack in Innsbruck (a great place, by the way, to buy climbing equipment as it seems every Austrian has a pack of some sort) and has used it all over the world as it is extremely durable.

Many knapsacks do have a leather bottom for strength, or else a vinyl bottom. Virtually all softpacks sold throughout Austria have a heavier base as this is where much of the pack's wear and tear takes place. Sometimes these knapsacks may have a waist or belt strap which tends to hold the pack tighter and is especially helpful in moving downhill at a fast clip.

FRAME RUCKSACKS

One of the great advances in backpacking took place just before World War II with the advent of the framed knapsack — often called The Bergen, after the early models out of Norway. Essentially the frame pack has its knapsack attached to a sling or a frame, often of light aluminum, sometimes of wicker or (later on) fiberglass. The idea, of course, was to get the pack off the back slightly, allowing among other advantages, better ventilation. Fortunately, these frame rucksacks are still made in great quantity today. LaFuma in France alone must still produce thousands of these a week and they're seen the world over. They come in all sizes and are spacious enough to hold hiking gear for days — perhaps even weeks. Plenty of people have hiked the entire length of the Appalachian Trail stretching 2,500 miles from Georgia to Maine carrying a framed rucksack. These frame backs allow a greater weight to be carried than is conveniently possible in an ordinary knapsack, but in hiking uphill, such a pack does tend to make one lean forward a little to compensate for the weight which is lower on the back.

Frame rucksacks still have their adherents today, even in the age of the tubular packframe, and with good reason. They hold a lot of gear in a small place; for hitchhiking they are much easier to stash in a car than a packframe which takes up a lot of space. In air travel, breakage in cargo storage is less likely to happen with a rucksack than an tubular packframe. (Many airlines are paying thousands of dollars in claims on broken packframes). A rucksack's shape and length allows total head movement, while the packframe does not. This is one reason why climbers prefer the rucksack more than the packframe. Then, too, many models have provisions for lashing on extra possessions, including skis, to the outside of the packs. Since the frame rucksack rides slightly away from the back, objects inside the pack are not as likely to gouge the wearer's back. Low overhead objects can be avoided with a rucksack compared to the extending height of a packframe. Finally, unlike the knapsack, a waist strap is usually provided with a framed rucksack, which does give the wearer some hip carry with the resultant relief to the shoulders.

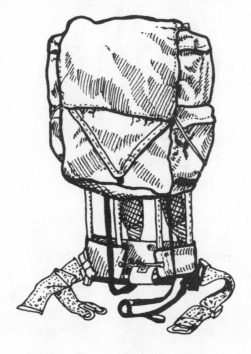

THE LONG CONTOUR FRAME OR PACKFRAME

The long contour packframe is a revolutionary aid. Its low profile and curved side members keep the pack's weight close to your back. It allows you to stand upright without the pack's weight pulling your forward or pushing you backwards.

Indeed, the landscape seems covered with packframes . . . and not just in the woods. Stand at any airport in Europe and watch the airliners from New York or Chicago unload. Every third person, it seems, has come to Europe with a packframe. Of these many will not hike in the Bavarian forests or the French Alps at all; they will use the eminently comfortable and practical packframe for bumming around Europe. For many travelers the packframe is their home away from home, their portable bedroom and kitchen, all there, right on the back.

This house on your back does have some very distinct advantages. The frame, which is made of tubular aluminum with side members and adjoining cross members, is the main support system of the packframe. Its shape is one of an "s" curvature which curves forward at the point of the shoulders and flares near the lower part of the back. Nylon or cotton cross straps are stretched across this frame and work to keep the frame off the back by hitting the highest parts of the back, the shoulder blades and the bench of the back. Shoulder harnesses or padded shoulder straps are attached to the frame which helps carry the load of the pack on one's shoulders. The waist strap is attached to the frame and is positioned around the waist resting on the upper bones of the hips. By tightening this strap in a proper manner the entire weight of the pack can be transferred to the hips. This transfer of weight takes a substantial part of the load of the shoulders. This transfer also puts the weight on the lower axis of the body (waist-to-legs), thus allowing the walker to stand upright. (And to think that several years ago many packframes were sold with the waist strap as an optional part). The combination of the "s" frame, holding the weight close to the back, and shoulder straps being alternated with waist strap helps relieve the weight pressure of numbed hips. Padded hip belts make carrying bulky loads a lot easier — if not almost more comfortable.

The advantages of a packframe can only be realized if it is fitted to the wearer. When was the last time you bought shoes without trying them on? When I say this, I can only visualize the multitudes of ill-fitting pack frames. A pack is as good as its fit. A manufacturer could make the "BEST" (in terms of quality) packframe in the world, but unless it fits you, it becomes useless.

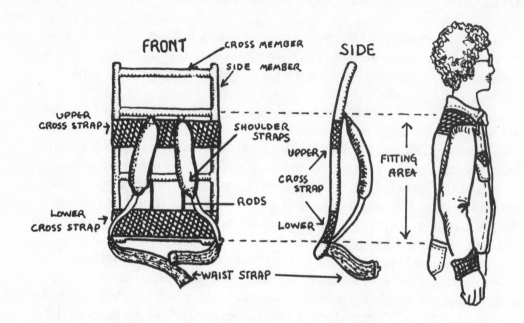

FRONT   CROSS MEMBER   SIDE

SIDE MEMBER

UPPER CROSS STRAP →

SHOULDER STRAPS

UPPER →

CROSS STRAP

FITTING AREA

LOWER CROSS STRAP →

— RODS

LOWER

← WAIST STRAP →

THE PACKFRAME'S FIT

Remember the "s" curvatures of the side members of the packframe? This curvature in length must match the shoulder-to-hip length of your body. For example: when the frame is too big for you, the frame curvature seems way out of proportion to your body. The frames come in a variety of sizes — small, medium, and large — with some manufacturers putting out a packframe that grows with the person. Occasionally there are in between sizes (medium and large) for difficult fits. The point is that sizing is important and if you are looking for a backpack store salesperson who makes the effort to fit you (size you) with a packframe you have just eliminated half the stores that sell backpacking equipment. Those who know packframes fit them.

It might not be a bad idea to measure the shoulder-to-waist area since body height sometimes has little bearing on how the frame will sit since there are long-legged and short-legged people. Consequently, I am a little suspicous of tables based on height which relate to the frame height. We often are advised that a person 5 foot 3 inches and under should have a frame height of 28 inches. This, of course, cannot always be true because there are short-waisted and long-legged people. I have a friend who is 6 feet tall who wears a medium frame (28"). When buying a packframe, it is not a good idea to rely on table and charts. An individualized fit from a knowledgeable salesperson will settle any doubts you have about what size you are.

The perfect fit only comes once out of a hundred times. Perfect fits, we do not hold out for, a good fit is what we are looking for. Here are some hints for you to keep in mind when purchasing a frame.

Pick the style of frame that you like and that meets your pocketbook.

The sales person will estimate what size you are. After this is done, try the packframe on. Weights (sandbags) should be used to give you the real effect of load bearing down on your back. Try twenty or thirty pounds to begin with.

Adjust the shoulder straps (tighten-up, loosen-down) so that the lower cross strap is divided in half by your belt line on your pack. Then check the angle of the shoulder strap, if it is too high above your shoulders (3") it is probably too big. If is too low (2") below your shoulders, it is too small. The shoulder strap angle should be (for most brands) level with the shoulders. If the shoulder strap level is too high or low, pressure around the neck and shoulder area will be felt after several hours of carrying.

The next step is to check the waist strap or padded hip belt. Since the weight is being transferred to the hip area, this is primarily where it should be carried (the hip bones and middle of the back). One mistake that I have seen is that people try to carry the weight on their stomach. The belt should be right in the middle of your hip bones. Put your hands on your hips before you apply the belt. Now, take the belt and place it on the hip area and give the belt a slight tug. This tightening will help keep the belt in place. The next step is to hunch your shoulders upward. By hunching the shoulders the abdomen is drawn inward; retighten the hip belt, then drop your shoulders. The packframe will feel light on the top with some sidewards motion. Tighten the shoulder straps (not too tight) to find your own preference for shoulder strap length.

Walk around the store as much as possible, don't just stand there. Let the salesperson know if any part of the fit feels peculiar. If you do not, you may be purchasing later headaches and pains.

Renting a pack, then buying it is one of the best solutions I have found when it comes to finding a true fit. Many stores deduct the price of the rental from the purchase price.

CARRYING YOUR PACK IN THE WILDS

Some of the following suggestions will help you not make the same kinds of mistakes I did.   **Starting out in the morning** — After one has eaten, the trail becomes the next attraction for the day. We have all heard of the waist strap and its advantages, but on a full stomach the two just do not mix. I suggest that you let your shoulders carry the weight for a while. Once you stomach has settled, use your waist strap.

SHOULDERS AND HIPS — Too many people overuse their waist straps. Let your shoulders carry part of the weight (25% of the time) and the waist strap (75%) of your walking experience.

CROSS COUNTRY TRAVEL — I have found that when you hike over rugged country, the shoulders can carry the weight better than the hips. If you apply most of your weight to your hips, you risk the chance of leg or ankle injuries from the unpredictable surface area of off-the-trail hiking. (The hip strap can be tightened around the waist to prevent the frame from swinging).

OVERHEAD OBJECTS — Since the packframe prevents one from looking up, the upper frame parts can be caught on tree limbs that lurk in dense forests.

FISHNET UNDERWEAR AND BELTS — Belts are usually worn to hold up one's pants, and they become a problem when carrying a pack. Sandwiched in between the waist belt and your skin, the belt only gnaws, bites, and rubs the area around the hip bones. Fishnet underwear can present the same problem. Try to avoid wearing a thick leather belt, and tuck the underwear away from your hip bones. It may be noted that fishnet underwear with padding on the shoulders is an unbelievable help.

After a quarter of a mile up the trail, it simply becomes a matter of individual physical strength and self determination with a little forward motion added. One may hike a short or long duration of time and distance. This is where the beauty of backpacking is realized: it is all an individual effort — that is what makes it all so pleasant.

AN IDEA ON PACKBAG DESIGN AND SIZE

The function of the packbag is still that of holding the equipment needed for wilderness travel. However in the design of some packbags, convenience in packbags and multiple pockets are sometimes confusing and only create disorganization. Even the packbag size, for the most part, has become somewhat larger, thus making the pack overburdening for those who decide to pack it to fullest capacity.

The beginning backpacker is faced with the problem of how many pockets and cubicles should the packbag contain.

Many of these pockets are created for convenience, which is fine for someone who has packed a pack. The problem is that the manufacturer assumes that the beginner already knows how to pack a pack, which unfortunately is not usually the case, and these conveniences only become burdens. So the beginners find themselves restricted by this design and resort to placing items in places where they fit instead of where they are needed. The main concern here is organization, not dividers or small pockets.

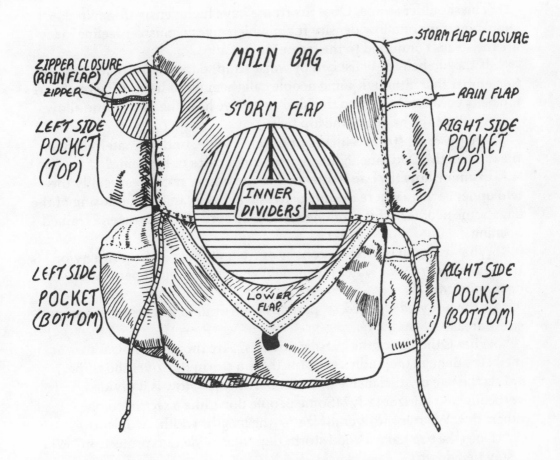

The size of some packbags has changed to the point that, for most people, they are generally too large. When packed to their fullest capacity, the walker is burdened by a pack that makes them a packer instead of a pleasure hiker. With this enormous weight the hike is no longer enjoyable because it has been turned into a physical fitness test. The size of the packbag dictates the size of load carried; a large pack is usually filled with a large load. Peoples' enthusiasm for comfort when backpacking outweighs their ability to limit themselves to just taking essential items. In the case where a packbag is packed with non-essentials, this extra weight is just unnecessarily hard to carry. Again, organization is the key word; if the packbag size can hold just essential items, it is more likely that the non-essentials will be left at home.

Essential items and a reasonably sized packbag are the basis of a lighter pack. Organization is what will bring these two together. The best way to start out picking the size of a bag and the number of pockets is by having some idea of what these essentials are.

Here are some additional points you may want to examine with the salesperson helping you select a packframe and bag:

* The shoulder straps. Does the frame have high density foam in the shoulder straps or a low density foam which gives a mushier feeling? How are the straps connected to the frame?

* Is the hip belt (or waist belt or waist strap) padded? Sufficiently wide? Remember that although some people call them waist belts, they really are **hip** belts because they fit on the hip bones. See how the packframe allows you to adjust the height of the hip belt.

* Are the cross straps 3 inches or 6 inches wide, or does material cover the full length? Does one tighten with turn buckles or by tieing?

* Examine how the bag is attached to the frame, noting especially the two upper corners where the most stress will be. Examine the closing of the bag. Some people prefer grommets and a tie cord. Others prefer a framed opening.

* What material is used — canvas or nylon taffeta or Cordura nylon? Is the bag waterproof or water repellent? What is the weight per square yard or running yard?

* Is the bag well stitched — perhaps even double stitches on seams and stress areas?

* What is the size of the outside pockets? Are the zippers plastic or metal (both have their adherents)? Is there a storm flap over the zipper?

* Is the bag divided inside into compartments? How is it divided, vertically and horizontally? (Some people don't like a sectioned bag; others do). What is the overall size — the length, width, and depth?

* Does the bag have a good storm flap to provide rain protection? Will it stay tied down?

As I said before, feel free to try a pack on in the store the same as you'd try on hiking boots. Tighten the hip belt sufficiently to see whether the frame appears to flow with the contour of your back. Perhaps at this point I should warn you, however, that there's tremendous controversy about the suspension system in packframes. A new system, known as the hip suspension system was introduced fairly recently. Magazines like **Wilderness Camping** and **Backpacker** Magazine are filled with pages devoted to the suspension system of various packframes. In general, the long contour frame adherents debate with the newer hip suspension system adherents. I don't know who is right, but a summary of the dispute is contained in several mountaineering supply catalogs, such as that issued by Eastern Mountain Sports. This particular retailer, highly respected in the East, feels that except for expedition work where heavy loads are carried over long distances uphill, the standard long contour frame and suspension (rather than the hip suspension system) offers the most versatile system for the majority of backpackers.

Here's a tip that may save you a lot of time and perhaps even money: study a mountaineering supply catalog before buying equipment.

Some of these catalogs are extremely detailed and even contain mini-essays on all aspects of equipment. Now that these catalogs have become 200-page, full-color books, they aren't always free, but a dollar spent for a good-sized catalog is a small investment in order to learn about the variety of equipment available. A good catalog will not only list specifications (tempered anodized aluminum 6061 alloy, 7.5 oz. waterproof Cordura, nylon mesh back bands, and so on), but will often state just what sort of backpacker the particular pack is aimed for. For example, here is a typical opening sentence from a current catalog describing packframes: "This item seems to fit the bill for people who want to get into backpacking without spending $40 or $50 on a pack and frame."

A SUMMING UP

There are those who feel that while the right equipment (together with its proper use) make backpacking relatively comfortable, it is possible to focus on equipment so much that the sheer enjoyment of the wilderness experience may be diminished. True, good equipment should allow one to concentrate on friendly animals, tender wild alpine flowers above timber line, varieties of fern in the lowlands — and the multi-shades of green there. But we must remember that long before the packframe revolution with its various refinements, people were going into the woods with what might seem today primitive equipment. Fur-traders in the west sometimes carried more than two-hundred pounds with a simple tumpline — a 2½ to 3-inch headband with long straps on either end which were wound around the bulky weight to be carried on the back. There were no shoulder straps whatever. Many canoe campers today still use the Duluth, a modification of this old method of transportation, and the packbasket (for all its inflexibility, fragility, and ability to irritate the back) is still seen in deep woods. (A tumpline can still be used with a packframe as an auxiliary support, but hardly anyone bothers.)

Don't feel you must have the ultimate, optimum equipment right away. Too many people think the most costly is the best — and that's not necessarily so. I have seen many backpackers who have bought a pack which is too big for their use. In many areas where there are a lot of hikers, used equipment — even boots — fetches a fairly good price and if you eventually feel your packframe isn't quite what you'd want for future trips, the chances are you can sell it to someone privately. A few mountain supply stores even allow trade-ins.

In my discussion of packs, I should have mentioned a very handy item — the belt pouch (hip-pack, fanny pack) which is also sold in ski shops. It's a wraparound belt with a built-in zippered pouch large enough to hold map, compass, and chocolate bar or two, some raisins, and a

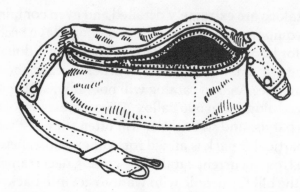

compact camera. It's amazing how much one can cram into a hip-pack and not feel any real weight while hiking through the woods or even scaling a relatively steep rock pitch.

I would not be overly concerned with the long and sometimes tedious arguments over various types of packframes which show up now and then in the excellent magazine **Backpacker** (28 West 44th Street, New York, N.Y. 10036). These discussions are really for backpacking aficionados, some of whom spend more time writing about backpacking than they do on the trail. In any **serious** expedition, or on a trip such as the Ryback brothers attempted down the spine of the Continental Divide (See **The Ultimate Journey**, by Eric and Tim Ryback, Chronicle Books, San Francisco, 1971), optimum equipment is just about essential; but for casual backpackers out to enjoy a few nights in the wilderness and perhaps see a deer or two en route, optimum equipment just is not that essential.

Perhaps I should add a word about children and backpacking. In a word or two: It's never too early to take a child into the woods. Sometimes infants are carried papoose-style into the woods, just as skiers will sometimes ski with a child on the back. As a child gets older, it can often carry its own load, preferably not in a too-large hand-me-down pack. Far from objecting at carrying a pack, the average child, imitative of adults, will **want** a pack to carry.

I don't think there's any minimum age limit in introducing a child to the woods — the sooner the better. We've all seen teen-agers who have lived so much in the city that they are afraid of strange noises or the darkness of the woods. Such unreasonable fears will be almost unknown to a child who has slept out under the stars (or even a drizzle) at an early age, with the friendly sound of a woodchuck nearby — or a porcupine eating away at the wood of a nearby tree!

Children are often delightful on the trail, pointing out things we take for granted so we see them once again, anew. I was hiking with a child once in lowlands when we came across a beaver dam. Now I've seen many a beaver dam, but this was Nonny's first. You should have heard her exclamations! Of course we lost half an hour from our scheduled trail time, but I can never pass a beaver dam now without thinking of her excited questions when she had seen her very first one.

PACKING THE PACK

Later on (when we discuss what essential items go into the pack) we can go into more detail about how to pack items into a rucksack or a packframe bag. However, a little of this material is essential now in selecting a pack because some people find they have too many (or not enough) outside pockets. (A photographer, for example, might want four or five outside-the-pack zippered pockets for accessories. Or they get a frame-bag combination and then discover later on they wish it hadn't been divided into so many compartments. Others would not be without a structured bag, with baffles inside and all sorts of compartments. It's all a matter of preference, but these are good considerations to have in mind at the time of purchase.

One might think that heavy items went into the bottom of the pack, with the lighter items on top. After all, this is the way supermarket clerks pack groceries. But the opposite is true: the heavy items generally go near the top, and also near one's back. Reason? It helps with center of gravity. Too much weight in the bottom of the pack is like having too much weight in the buttocks!

One warning: be careful of items with sharp corners because if they're jammed into a pack, sharp metal corners can gouge a hole in the nylon or light canvas material. Sometimes an item with a sharp corner (it might be a first-aid kit or a box containing a snake-bit kit) can be wrapped up into an extra sweater.

For really drenching rains, some people prefer a waterproof covering that is placed over the whole packframe bag. These rain shells may only weigh four or five ounces, but every ounce has to be considered when one is on the trail. Even a plastic garbage bag is useful.

Some people never do learn to adjust shoulder straps properly. Generally, these people have the straps too loose so the frame hangs too loosely. A good salesperson can demonstrate the adjustability of the pack. Most packs can be altered even more than a car seat which can be moved forward and backward and have the angle changed. Yet I have seen hikers locked into an adjustment which is not proper. The best packs come with printed instructions which I would read and absorb.

It is hard to resist the cliche that the pack is one's home away from home, but that's not a bad thought to have. Many a backpacker who became lost in the woods has been able to survive for days, even through blizzards, because the pack was at hand. Perhaps that is why when I hike I sometimes feel a sense of security, even comfort, in having the pack riding along with me. If I should break a leg or run into an unexpected, early-season driving snowstorm, I would know that I could survive. So in a large sense — frankly, in a **survival** sense — the pack is far more than merely a way of carrying possessions along. It may be far more life-supporting than imagined.

Chapter Four

Sleeping Bags

Wilderness bedrooms.

Backpacking, like life, is activity followed by rest. On a long trip, there is a cyclic rhythm: days of hiking through fern-filled meadows, crossing rushing mountain streams, slanting uphill on root-covered trails which angle back and forth across steep grades; then nights of rest — the quiet moments when the day's hike is over and a campsite has been chosen. After an evening meal, whether cooked or not, there are serene moments when darkness comes, birds quiet down for the night, and it is time to think of sleeping.

Of the four basic elements in backpacking (boots, pack, food, and sleeping gear), perhaps one's sleeping gear is the most important of all. One can tolerate a mild blister, accept a sore where a pack rubs too much, or even go days without food, but a good night's rest is almost imperative. Furthermore, there are plenty of lost-in-the-woods tales which confirm that a sleeping bag can save a life, since an adequate sleeping bag will protect one through mountain storms and snow, and many a lost backpacker has waited it out in the protection of a sleeping bag to be discovered later by a search party. Others not so lucky have left campsite (and sleeping bag) behind, wandered aimlessly about in the woods (sometimes in unknowing circles) and died of exposure. Sometimes when I am hiking alone (which I do not do very often and do not recommend), I feel that my sleeping bag is a kind of security blanket: If I should break my leg and be immobile miles away from the nearest road, I could get myself into it and wait through the pain for someone to come along the trail, especially since I always leave word of my hiking plans.

Already I have fallen into the trap of assuming the only adequate cover for a night's rest is a sleeping bag. Certainly the history of America expansion from east to west, across the Allegheny Mountains, the broad Mississippi, and into the Rockies, is not one of pioneers with prime northern goose-down sleeping bags. They used blankets and bed rolls. Under some circumstances today these are perfectly adequate. Many a parent has helped his or her youngster make a comfortable bedroll with a few old blankets and some large safety pins. True, a wool blanket may be heavy to carry and air may leak in and around the blanket pins, but the old-fashioned wool blanket may often serve adequately for a night's sleep, especially on a summer backpacking trip. I simply do not believe that the wilderness experience is open only to those with sleeping bags, expensive packframes, and Italian-made boots. Quite possibly a sneaker-clad youngster with a blanket roll may enjoy the woods as much as — or more than — the carefully equipped hiker who is so hung up on equipment that the whole idea of backpacking — the sheer joy of it — is lost.

In Mexico, even on cold nights, I've seen Indians hiking days to distant markets curled up at roadside in their serapes, sleeping peacefully. Give them a sleeping bag and they might feel restricted.

But is you are serious about acquiring basic backpacking equipment, a sleeping bag makes sense: the best of them are lightweight, provide warmth without weight, and are portable.

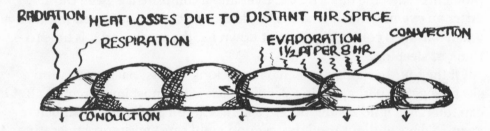

Perhaps I should not have said a sleeping bag provides **warmth**. In truth, it can only help the body retain the warmth which it is constantly manufacturing. Stripped to basics, then, a sleeping bag exists only to help retain sufficient body heat.

Humans lose body heat due to **convection** (windchill; movement of air carrying heat away from the body); **conduction** (loss of body heat by means of physical contact with cold objects — for example, snow cold rock, metal); **radiation** (unprotected head, arms, legs to which body sends heat directly — and heat is lost in open air); **evaporation** (The body's cooling system); **respiration** (inhailing cool air and exhaling warm air). I mention these items now because they will ultimately play a part in choosing the ideal sleeping bag.

Firstly, bear in mind how your body loses the greatest proportion of its body heat. Your body loses 50% of its body heat at 40° from an unprotected head. So, if a sleeping bag does not have a hood for head warmth, it defeats the purpose of keeping your body warm. (It may be a good idea to wear a wool stocking cap to bed).

Such an ideal bag will keep one reasonably warm at night, yet it will not be too heavy to carry and will pack or stuff easily. A costly bag made of the best down and suited for winter mountaineering may be unbearably hot on a summer hike and be unnecessarily heavy. Some backpackers like Art Harris, who helped me edit this book, have two down sleeping bags, one of which fits inside the other. Art swears by his Icelandic sleeping bags made in Glasgow. He has an Icelandic Special, a fine bag by itself and good down to slightly below freezing. Then he has a standard Icelandic "inner" bag. With the inner bag **inside** the Icelandic special, Art has slept comfortably at 0°F. In the summer, the "inner bag" used alone makes an adequate sleeping bag. This bag-inside-bag principle allows the user three temperature alternatives — either bag alone, or one inside the other.

The first thing a potential buyer of a sleeping bag should observe is (1) filler material, (2) construction, and (3) shape. The possible variety of each of the three will be mind boggling, but if all three of these aspects are thought of as a spare ⅓ of the overall sleeping bag, then one can choose the right one for her or his needs. The filler material cannot insulate properly without a proper construction, along with a shape that is not claustrophobia-provoking, but lightweight, non-bulky, and warm. As you read the preceding pages, keep in mind the vocabulary of sleeping bags. Once the lingo is learned, the purchasing game gets much easier.

SHAPE

The shape of a sleeping bag serves two purposes. The first is to have a shape that provides roominess for body comfort and secondly, to act as a barrier around your body to trap insulating air. The more roomy the bag, the less **efficient** it becomes. And the roomier the bag is, the more bulky and heavy it is. A sleeping bag with a large body contour may be comfortable to toss and turn it, but it defeats the purpose of insulation, because there will be too much air circulating around your body. A shape that is form-fitting to your body is good for heat efficiency but may lack body room. So, a sleeping bag should have a shape that is efficient heat-wise, and bearable to sleep in because it has some body room.

THE MUMMY SHAPE

The mummy shape (so-called because stretched out in such a bag, one indeed resembles an Egyptian Mummy) is quite popular, since most military bags have this shape along with a lower price tag is army surplus stores. The shape fits body contours more closely than a rectangular bag, it has less air space for your body to heat up inside the bag. But, it is known to many as the "claustrophobic special." A mummy bag frequently displays the following characteristics:

* Formed hood (or tie around the chin hood) which allows less air space around your face and body inside. Because of this shape, it is very efficient in colder weather, but too hot in warmer temperatures. This type of hood does act as a good pillow, if your head is outside the hood.

* Vertical envelope foot — restrains foot movements. Seems to make your feet "stand at attention" all night long.

* Half length zipper — since the zipper is located on the top of the bag, it makes the body more vulnerable to outside air circulation. In a 40°-50°F temperature, while the zipper may be opened, only the upper body will be cooled, leaving the lower half overly warm.

* Conformed shoulder and foot girth — which is very efficient, but takes some getting used to.

* Somewhat lighter than a similarly filled sleeping bag of rectangular shape.

* Less bulky because of its shape.

RECTANGULAR SHAPE

A rectangular shape bag, on the other hand, has more air space, thus making the body work just a little harder to heat up the extra cubic inches. Sometimes as much as a pound or a pound and a half may be added to the weight of such a bag because of its shape. Its characteristics are:

* Cut-off hood opening — by having this type of opening, air constantly circulates around your shoulders and head. Since this type cannot always be drawn up around the head to stop air circulation, it tends to be colder.

* Horizontal envelope foot — plenty of foot room.

* Full length zipper — the zipper usually follows the side and foot of the bag. It is good for cooling off when too warm,

but can be colder because of air coming through the zipper.

* Shoulder and hip girth are equal — giving plenty of room to turn over in.

* May be bulkier and not as easily compressed as the mummy bag.

* May be overall heavier than a mummy bag.

SEMI-MUMMY SHAPE

In between these two extremes, which admittedly I have over-simplified, is the semi-mummy shape sleeping bag. A moderately tapered, rectangular shape, not as form-fitting as the mummy. This compromise shape is used by most manufacturers today. It has a two-way hood with draw strings, which allows the sleeper in warmer temperatures to open the hood up for greater air circulation. This provides outside cooling air to cool off your warm body. In cooler temperatures, the hood may be drawn up around the head and face to cut off air circulation, which traps the air inside the bag, and allows the body to heat it up. The elephant foot, which is somewhat round, allows your feet to sleep in any configuration. A two-way full-length zipper located on the side of the bag allows two bags to be mated (more on this later). The two-way zipper enables the sleeper to zip the zipper up from the bottom for further air circulation or close it down in colder temperatures. There are many variations of the semi-mummy — from the "barrel shape" to an extreme taper — but most have a moderate shoulder and hip girth. A semi-mummy can be easily compressed and its overall weight (depending on filler) runs between 3 and 6 pounds.

Which shape to choose? Even among experienced backpackers there is some disagreement. Some people feel too constricted in a mummy bag. They feel they cannot toss and turn in it. To change position, they must roll over with the bag, consequently, they will take the extra weight of a rectangular bag because they feel less claustrophobic in it, feeling that they are able to have normal body stirrings, much as they do at home. And who is to argue with this? The idea of backpacking is to be comfortable, and if sleeping in a somewhat constricted sleeping bag seems so different from sleeping in bed at home that it feels uncomfortable and even prevents one from getting a good night's rest, then a compromise must be sought. A rectangular bag is similar to your bed at home, but weighs more. A mummy bag is lighter, but its shape has nothing to do with the shape of your bed at home. So, here possibly we can see why the semi-mummy is so popular. It's truly a compromise between the mummy and rectangular-shaped sleeping bags. And, what makes this compromise even better is that the semi-mummy comes in the same shape with many girth sizes.

To be sure you are satisfied with the shape of the bag before purchasing it, ask the salesperson for a personal demonstration. Many states allow the purchaser to slip inside the bag and try it out. Make sure you have at least a foot of space left at the bottom after the hood has been drawn. Test the zippers from the inside, and toss and turn a little to see if it meets up to your specifications.
GOOD LUCK!

TWO IN A BAG

I have seen two people sleep together in a normal-sized rectangular bag — almost an impossibility in a mummy bag. And there have been instances of lives saved when, on a mountain expedition, a sleeping bag was lost and two climbers shared the same bag through bitter cold nights. Many bags, by the way, are designed so they can be zippered to one another for couples. For example, there are semi-mummy-shaped sleeping bags with 70-inch zippers with two sliders, opening from both top and bottom. The bags also come with separating side zippers, both **left** and **right** side, and one of each is needed if the bags are to be zipped together. Any of these standard bags may be zippered together so long as a left-zippered and a right-zippered bag are used. I have gone into this matter in a little detail because one of the delights of backpacking is sleeping out under the stars close to someone you like — and by close, I mean in the same sleeping bag. As Trail Haus advertises, "Now there are mummy bags with room for mummy." Therefore, in choosing a bag, you might want to allow for bags which can be zippered together — now or later on! I would feel no embarrassment asking about this feature in a mountaineering supply store, for it is very common today. After all, why should a couple which sleeps together sleep separately when on the trail?

SIZE

In addition to the shape of the sleeping bag, one must consider size, for bags do come in different lengths — and in children's sizes. Some small adults might find a children's size adequate — and less costly. A child in an adult sleeping bag stretched out to its full length may be cold trying to heat all that space, not to mention the extra weight in backpacking.
Incidentally, a child's sleeping bag may have a later life of its own: many experienced adult mountaineers like to bivouac in a waist-length sleeping

bag (and a children's bag may be ideal) with a down and hooded parka to protect their upper torso. Climbers up the north face of the Eiger have been known to use this combination, for the half-length bag is considerably lighter to carry.

COMPONENTS

Before we discuss what seems to be the central question regarding sleeping bags — the material used for insulation — let us consider briefly some features of bag construction, for a poorly-constructed bag will allow cold spots to be created. To take an extreme example: at one time most sleeping bags had what is known as sewn-through construction. That is, there was plenty of insulation, but like a quilt, there were stitched seams every now and then to hold the insulating material in place so it wouldn't shift around. It turned out that, in truth, these bags were only as warm as their coldest spot — where the seams were. At such points, the bags were only one-quarter of an inch thick. All that fluff around didn't count for much, for the cold air leaked in and around those seams. One almost never sees sewn-through construction today except in very inexpensive sleeping bags, of which there are many on the market.

OUTER AND INNER SHELL

Looking at a bag, one sees at first the outer cover or shell. It may be made of nylon (ripstop or taffeta) and the weight is usually 1.9 oz. per square yard. This shell will be non-waterproof. If you are astonished at that, keep in mind that a thoroughly waterproof outer shell would be a disaster: it would not allow a person's body to breathe and, consequently, moisture would accumulate inside the bag and make the sleeper cold and moist. I have seen backpackers in perfectly good sleeping bags wrap themselves up in plastic "drop-cloth" sheet thinking they will keep all dew, moisture, and possible rain away from them, only to discover that their own body moisture accumulates since it had no escape route. Therefore, a sleeping bag cover must be breatheable, allowing perhaps 1½ pints of water to expel itself during an eight-hour sleep.

The inner shell may also be a nylon or taffeta ranging from 1.6 oz. or 1.9 oz. per square yard. Remember that the calendared material, giving the bag a wet look, does not make it more water repellent.

We should mention a problem which has actually had tragic consequences. There have been recorded deaths from people who had a sleeping bag cleaned and did not air it out before using it. Residual toxic chemical odors from the dry cleaning process were fatal.

ZIPPERS

There are advantages and disadvantages to zippers which is, perhaps, why some expedition parkas have both zippers and buttons. Some climbers shun zippers altogether, just wouldn't dream of having a bag with a zipper. Others, and these are in the majority, will put up with an occasionally temperamental zipper for all the convenience afforded. Not only can two bags be zippered together, as I mentioned, but individual bags can be easily ventilated. In a bag with a zipper which can be drawn from either end, one can let in air or close it off as one wishes. Some rectangular bags have a zipper around the head, side, and foot — in other words, around three sides, and these can be totally unzipped so that one has a flat blanket.

Obviously, the zipper must be strong. Despite the strength of metal, most quality zippers today are made of nylon or plastic as they seem to catch the fabric less, and are not susceptible to rust, and don't conduct cold as metal does. Look for a puller tab on the inside as well as the outside of the bag. The zipper made of Delrin® is a poor conductor of cold. A plastic coil zipper will not snag on the draft tube.

SLEEPING BAG CONSTRUCTION

The best way to explain the various methods of constructing a sleeping bag is by illustration. In the case of down bags, baffles are pockets that hold the filler material; in polyester bags, they hold the batting in place. Note the following:

BAFFLE CONSTRUCTIONS

sewn-through construction
(polyester or down)

laminated construction
(polyester or down)

triple laminated construction
(polyester only)

slant or off-set construction
(down only)

V-tube construction
(down only)

side block baffling
(down only)

A draft tube will run along the zipper inside the bag to prevent air from moving through the bag. This draft tube should extend past the end of the zipper at the foot of the bag and have some sort of over-lapping in this area. Also, look for stiffened material or webbing along the zipper side of the tube to prevent snagging by the zipper.

Examining baffles:

* Baffle length. Side block baffle stops movement of down or filler from the bottom to the top of the bag. (Usually it is not found in cheaper bags because it takes the manufacturer twice as long to fill the bag).
* Use your hands to determine which construction is which. Pull the upper-outer and inner shell apart. The direction in which your hands go will give you some idea of the shape of the baffling. A sewn-through bag is easily identifiable — most likely your hands will meet on the same stitch.
* There should be some sort of foot baffle system so that the pressure from the foot does not develop a cold spot.
* Note the stitching. Stress points should be back stitched, double sewn, with 8 to 10 stitches per inch (lockstitch).

THE FILLER

All sorts of material are used in sleeping bags. Some bags use cotton or wool scraps. Others use various synthetic materials which have little insulating value.

In the better-insulated sleeping bags, there are today two materials, each of which has its enthusiastic adherents. They are down and Dacron.

Dacron or Polyester Fiber

Dacron has several advantages. It is less costly than down, no animal needs be killed to acquire the insulating material, and the material tends to dry faster than down if it is wet. However, slightly more weight is needed to give the same insulating properties as down. A few years ago backpackers looked down their noses at artificial material in a sleeping bag. They thought only pure northern European goose down was sufficient, but now polyester bags are common. Issue #6 of **Backpacker** Magazine devotes pages to an in-depth evaluation of twenty-five leading polyester sleeping bags — indication enough, if any is needed, that the polyester bags have indeed arrived to compete with down. I should add as a postscript that there are also combination bags — made of both down and polyester. Since another advantage of polyester is that it doesn't compress as easily as down, REI and JanSport, among others, are making bags with the underside filled with polyester and the top with down! Foam bags are ideal for canoe trips or where much water may be encountered. Foam, of course, is heavier than polyester, but scuba divers use foam in their wet suits and a foam sleeping bag will retain 100% of its loft even when soaked. (Loft is displacement; the greater the loft, the better the insulation.) Perhaps that is why 'river trippers' have found these bags useful: they would seem to have limited appeal, however, to backpackers.

There may be a further advantage of polyester. The shell material (surrounding and holding in the insulation) need not be of such great importance. With down, the cloth must withstand the small quills associated with down; unless the material is downproof (and there are specifications for this downproofing) a quill might stick out, start a rip. The down would then tend to cascade out. With polyester fabric, the material tends to interlock with itself. There are no quills to penetrate the fabric and if a rip should occur, the material does not fly out quite the way down does.

Plumule

Feather

Down

A good filler material will bring about good loft which creates the air space which keeps the sleeper warm. Among natural materials, down is the most common for the following reasons:

*It is the warmest material for its weight and loft.

*Down is form-fitting and composed of individual clusters which are able to expand, contract, and move around to fill and shape any gap between the body and the down garment or bag.

*Down breathes since it is a natural substance; down's cellular structure absorbs and dispels moisture. Because air circulates through it, stale air does not collect; excess body moisture is carried away.

*Down has a certain resilience — down withstands an infinite number of compressions without matting.

*Down is light in weight due to the high thermal conductivity and high lofting. Much less weight is needed to keep warm than with any other material.

*Down lasts. With care, and cleaning, a down article can last a lifetime. For years, prime Northern European goose down has been the ultimate in sleeping bag filler, but the quality of European goose down has declined because, as the EMS Catalog states, "the farmers who raise it do not now, nor have they ever, considered it their major product." The geese, of course, are consumed as food and their feathers are purely a by-product. Since birds are now sold for food before full maturity, the goose down today is less good than it once was. What's more, the cost is greater.

Consequently, many manufacturers are now making a blend of goose and duck down. Duck down was one considered inferior, but improved treatment of the duck down as well as blending it with the more costly goose down has made a filler material which is not prohibitive in cost. And many people won't have anything except down, not only for its insulating values, but because it is soft, odor-free, and non-toxic.

Down material is regulated by law in various states, so look at the label.

Goose vs. Duck Down

Without going into a great discussion on the merits or faults of each, let us just say there are two sides. One side claims that AAA Northern goose down is superior because the goose, living in a cold climate, develops larger and fluffier plumage to protect itself from the cold. (But as we've already said, many of these geese are killed before full maturity.) Others claim that duck is a better buy because of its lower cost.

It might be better to label sleeping bags with what one ounce of filler will loft in cubic inches rather than simply stating what mixture of goose or duck down is contained. It might put the consumer's mind to rest once a universal testing method had been produced. By the way, the color of the down has nothing to do with its lofting ability.

You can examine the required bedding tag for the net weight of the bag (filler material) and the gross weight (overall weight). In general, down bags will scale in something like this:

$1\frac{1}{2}$ — $2\frac{1}{4}$ pounds of fill for a summer bag.
$2\frac{1}{2}$ — $3\frac{1}{4}$ pounds of fill for a winter bag.

ARTIFICIAL MATERIALS

People have discovered that artificial filler materials may have good loft, resilience, and be in many ways comparable to down at half the cost. Some respected artificial fibers used in sleeping bags today are:

Dupont's Dacron® Fiberfill II®
Eastman's Kodel®
Celanese Fortrel® - Polar/Guard®

ARTIFICIAL FIBERS

Some advantages of polyester fibers over down:
— Polyester fibers dry many times faster than down. The fibers also maintain excellent insulation when wet; unlike down, which absorbs moisture, polyester does not. So when it's wet, it will keep you warm.
— Since polyester fibers are comprised in sheets, they do not shift or "leak out" as down does.
— Polyester fibers possess a resilient springiness, which lets the fibers bounce back even after repeated compression. The ground's coldness is not felt, because cold spots do not develop underneath the sleeper.
— Polyester products are easier to take care of than their down counterparts. Frequent washings will not reduce insulation or harm the product. After a few washings the polyester softens while the loft increases.
— If the protective fabric tears, the repair can wait until it is convenient without loss of insulation.
— Polyester fiber products, if properly manufactured, will tolerate more abuse than down products.
— Polyester fibers are non-allergenic, odorless, and mildewproof.
— Polyester fiber products are considerably lower in cost than that of down.
— Overall compression in a stuff bag is one inch larger in diameter per pound fill than that of down.
— It takes approximately six ounces per pound more fill of polyester fiber to gain the equivalent of warmth to one pound of a good grade of down. Overall weight (gross) is about a pound heavier for polyester compared with down.

Comfort Ranges

There are cold sleepers and warm sleepers — and any couple with an electric blanket can tell you it is nice to have dual controls. For we all sleep differently, responding to temperatures in an individual way. It all has to do with one's metabolism, body weight, and the fats, proteins, carbohydrates consumed before sleeping. Also one must phase in the psychological factor. A World War II prisoner of war tells of forced winter marches when Allied prisoners were moved from one prison camp to another. At night, he slept by the side of the road with no sleeping bag — just a tattered blanket. He did it night after night and survived.

Sometimes people accustomed to sleeping in a bedroom where they don't even open the window at night suffer from a kind of psychological coldness when they are sleeping under the stars; they just aren't used to night air at all. Naturally, environment has a lot to do with one's comfort, also — whether it's a clear or cloudy night (a clear night may be colder); whether there is moisture in the air; whether there is much wind.

I would suggest you use the manufacturer's temperature ratings as a rough guideline only. Don't necessarily buy a bag because it seems to have a lower temperature rating. Some people think such temperature ratings should be eliminated altogether, for a customer may buy a bag supposedly good to 32° F and then find that he or she is just about freezing in the bag. Someone else in an identical bag might feel comfortable.

In examining a sleeping bag for purchase, you may discover more fill at the top than at the bottom. When lofting (shaking air into the baffles) a down bag, the bag should sink in the knee area, showing the buyer that a good percentage of down has been put in the torso and foot areas where it is needed most. Why not rent a sleeping bag before buying one? Many firms rent out backpacking equipment — a practical way to try a sleeping bag since such items are never returnable after sale. One night in a rented mummy bag might be sufficient to convince you it just is not for you — or that it is ideal.

If you like do-it-yourself projects (as well as cost savings from such ventures), you might like to buy a sleeping bag **kit** with instructions. Such a kit might save you as much as 40% of the normal price of a finished bag.

BAG LINERS AND BAG COVERS

For general purposes, a homemade cotton liner can easily be made for your sleeping bag. In fact, an old bed sheet can be folded vertically, then stitched at bottom and side. Presto — you have a sleeping bag liner which will take wear and tear off the sleeping bag itself and possibly make the bag warmer because one more layer of cloth exists to trap air. Of course a liner does add a little weight, and to some backpackers every ounce counts. Sometimes in very hot weather when the sleeping bag itself is just too warm and confining, one can shed the bag and sleep in the liner! It protects the body from insects and provides some (but not much) warmth when the morning chill comes along.

A fancier liner may be made by inserting a zipper along the side. Also one can sew in four tabs in the corners of the sleeping bag and the liner so that the bag and liner can tie to each other. However, I prefer not to do this because with tossing and turning during sleep, the tabs may rip from the sleeping bag, exposing the filling. I find it simple to stand up and pull the liner up around me before crawling into the sleeping bag at night.

Breathing covers for the bag may be purchased or made. One firm which sells a wrap-around bivouac cover for sleeping bags claims that the warmth of the bag is increased by the cover, but I think the biggest advantage is that the bag is protected from soiling or snagging. In warm weather one can also sleep in the sleeping bag cover itself, just as one can sleep in the liner. However, a backpacker's load may increase by as much as two pounds with both a liner and a sleeping bag cover and many hikers conscientiously limit the pounds they carry. Accomplished backpacker Ruth Rudner, who has written several joyous mountaineering books, carries no more than thirty-five pounds for a week or more. "If I decide on an overnight hike," she writes, "I can cut at least 15 pounds out of the pack." The weight, incidentally, **feels** a good deal less than it sounds, a small miracle which comes from modern, lightweight equipment.

WASHING THE DOWN SLEEPING BAG

Using an automatic washing machine does not hurt the sleeping bag as long as the process is not repeated too many times; repeated washings tend to remove natural oil from down.

Here are some precautions:

* Before washing, make sure there are no grease spots on the
  bag. If there are, the bag might better be dry cleaned (see below) or
  else spot remover may be tried first on the grease spots.

* Set the washing machine for a cold water wash and use a cold-water
  soap product.

* Wash the bag alone. Tape any metal zipper tabs.

* Stop the machine from time to time in its washing cycle and push air
  out of the bag, since air can be trapped in the baffles of the bag
  (causing the seams to rip).

* Rinse twice and spin twice.

* The bag may go through all the wash cycles, including the spin cycle,
  before it is dried.

BATH TUB WASHING

This method is preferred by many. Be sure all soap has been rinsed from bag.

POLYESTER BAGS

Polyester bags do not need dry cleaning unless there is grease on the liner. Normal machine or bathtub washing is all that is necessary. This washing actually improves the loft.

DRYING THE DOWN SLEEPING BAG

* When drying the bag, it **might** be better to use a commercial, coin-operated machine (with its huge 25-40 pound capacity) than the less-roomy home dryer. Most of these coin-operated machines have a thermostat control. Temperature should not exceed 100° F. Check the accuracy of the thermostat setting by doing a test run of nylon or elastic material and seeing both how quickly it dries and how hot it is to the touch when you remove it.

* A rubber sneaker or tennis shoe may be dried at the same time as the bag. The shoe will help to break up clumps of down and at the same time keep static electricity at a minimum.

* After drying, let the bag air for several days to make sure the filler has completely dried. It will take down longer to dry than some other matericals.

DRY CLEANING THE SLEEPING BAG

Finding a dry cleaning establishment which has dealt with sleeping bags before and uses petroleum-based solvents is not easy, but it is worth the effort, for some chemicals may harm a sleeping bag. (For example, some very strong chemicals may remove some of the oils from natural filler material like down.) A cleaner who does the work right on the premises would be my choice. Some dry cleaners have been known to refuse bags; others take them on a "no guarantee" basis. Bags with patches are especially vulnerable. Some chemicals used in dry cleaning are toxic. Therefore, as I suggested earlier, you will want to air the bag out at home and ventilate it thoroughly before using it.

STORAGE OF SLEEPING BAG

When in use, a sleeping bag may become wet or moist. If it is not dried before storage, moisture may mildew the material. Once mildew has set in, it is difficult to get rid of. In storing the bag, be sure it has plenty of ventilation. Hang it in a dry place if possible — for example, over a wooden dowel in a clothes closet. Some families prefer to lay their sleeping bags one on top of the other rather than hang the bags.

Except for fading the colors of a fabric, sunlight can not do a bag much harm. In Europe one sees bedclothes draped from balconies taking the sun and the air. After a long hike, I like to allow both sun and air to reach my bag before I store it until the next trip.

STUFF BAGS

The primary function of a small carrying bag called the "stuff bag" is to protect the sleeping bag, especially against abrasions, for the sleeping bag outer shell (made of lighter material) does not have an abrasion level as high as the 8 or 10 oz. material common to a stuff bag.

Strange as it might seem, it is better to stuff a sleeping bag into its carrying bag rather than roll it up. Stuffing is easier on the material and at the same time the bag may be made more compressible than by rolling. A stuff bag, which is much easier to clean than a sleeping bag, should be waterproof or highly water repellent for rain protection. True, some hikers prefer not to carry their sleeping bag outside, either above or below their bag on a packframe, but inside their bag. In such circumstances, the waterproof characteristics of a stuff bag are not so important, but stuff bag will still help reduce the sleeping bag to a compact shape.

GROUND COVER

A ground cloth or ground cover is practically essential as it is a barrier between the ground and the sleeping bag, keeping moisture of the earth from being drawn to the sleeping bag. A piece of a painter's plastic drop cloth would be perfectly suitable. A good size for this 3 or 4 mil plastic would be 5' x 7' allowing a little extra room on all sides. For the long pull the higher priced nylon tarp is ideal.

AIR MATTRESS

When the air mattress first appeared, hikers thought it was an answer to all their complaints. Lightweight and portable, it was blown up by the mouth at the campsite and was exceedingly comfortable to sleep on. No trace of twig or root penetrated the two or more inches of air on which the hiker slept. People who had never gone camping before began to change their minds and carried an air mattress deep into the woods.

After awhile, however, the air mattress lost some of its glamour. The best of them developed leaks. Sometimes, especially if they were not divided into separate air compartments, they were of no use whatever in the woods because of a leak. Now and then they'd go flat over-night — either a sharp rock or twig had done its work, or the valve leaked, or there was a tiny hole somewhere which had not been noticed before. Some backpackers claimed that when it got cold, all that air inside the air mattress got equally cold and sleeping atop an air mattress was like being on top of an iceberg.

PADS FOR SLEEPING BAG

Much more common today are lightweight insulating pads, either full or three-quarters length, used under a sleeping bag. Ensolite® (a rubber material; is a closed cell, non-water-absorbing foam pad which is ideal between the ground cover and the sleeping bag. It provides a thermal barrier between the body and the cold ground. Non-circulating air is one of the best known insulators. For insulation only, a thickness of 1/8th inch is sufficient. Any greater thickness is purely for comfort.

On frozen ground, the insulation provided by a pad is absolutely essential. Especially with down, the weight of the body compresses filler underneath one, but due to its closed-cell construction, Ensolite ® is not compressible. This is fine on the ground but not so great in a pack; consequently, most pads are carried outside a pack. Ensolite ® is sold in ½ and ¾ sizes (18" x 42" and 21" x 54") and in thicknesses of 1/ , 3/8, and 1/2 inch. Prices range from $5 to $12 depending on size and thickness.

Another material is Osolite ® or Superlight ® (as plastic material). It has the same function as Ensolite ® except that it is made from a different material. While it is less durable than Ensolite ®, it is much lighter — generally about half the weight and less expensive.

Foam pads of so-called open-celled furniture foam may also be used. They will, however, tend to soak up water and moisture if not covered by some type of waterproof nylon shell. The one-inch thickness, about the thinnest sold, may be too bulky for packing. However a foam pad can be quite comfortable. Often a suitable pad may already exist around the home, saving one the cost of buying something new for backpacking.

Note that some store-bought foam pads have very slippery covering cloth. This can be a great inconvenience.

Most people don't bother with a pillow, although inflatable ones exist. Some use their pack as a pillow; others use their stuff bag and stuff extra clothing into it.

Pleasant dreams!

Clothing

Glad rags, wilderness style.

Chapter Five

It is no exaggeration to say that proper clothing can make the difference between a comfortable or an uncomfortable trip. Sometimes the difference can be far greater — life or death. Reports of mountain accidents, carried in the back pages of most alpine and mountaineering periodicals, tell again and again of backpackers who started out in a summer sunshine-filled valley with shorts and tee-shirts only to run into violent winds or hail and rapidly-dropping temperatures a mere three hours later up on the high ridges above timberline. Without so much as a windbreaker or a sweater, these backpackers have rapidly lost their composure and panicked in the sudden storm. A night in such conditions among wet crags and boulders with no trees to lessen the driving wind and rain (or snow — even in the summer) has cost the life of many a backpacker. The White Mountains of New Hampshire now have prominently-displayed trail signs just as the scrub ends and the exposed ridges of rock begin. These signs warn hikers that even in summer weather, conditions can change quickly above timberline with almost no warning and that unexpectedly severe, almost winter-like weather can be a reality, even in mid-August.

Personally, I never like to be above timberline in the summer without protection against possible cold (a sweater or a down vest or parka), winds, and rain (a windbreaker, rain jacket, or poncho). I also like to have a cap because keeping one's head warm is not only scientifically sound, but makes me feel more comfortable, especially if the cap will pull down over my ears.

These same accident reports also tell another story: backpackers who carried extra clothing have been able to bivouac (in other words, wait out a night or a storm in some makeshift shelter, even if only under a rock over-hang) until the weather cleared or they were rescued. I can not emphasize enough the importance of allowing for harsh weather, especially at high altitudes, and even in summer weather. I belong, therefore, to the Be Prepared school of backpackers when it comes to clothing.

SWEATERS

Now this does not necessarily mean a lot of bulk or weight. That great wrap-around, belt-tied wool sweater made by Indians near Oaxaca, Mexico, may be appropriate on chilly mornings at Orr Springs or Big Sur, but is simply too bulky for the trail. Wool pullover sweaters, especially Icelandic sweaters with natural oils in the wool, are ideal for holding in body warmth. Ireland also sells magnificent, handmade all-wool sweaters. They are expensive, but if you don't mind a secondhand sweater, look through some of the barrels of "pre-owned" sweaters around the used clothing stalls on Dublin's Moore Street or in Salvation Army stores.

There was a time in America when for status one boasted about how much one paid for an article, but shortly after an inflationary economic crisis hit the United States, status was reversed: second-hand (or recycled) clothing was suddenly acceptable, especially if it could be purchased cheaply. Art Harris (who contributed to this book) sports a magnificent used Aran Islands handknit sweater which cost him an Irish pound ($2.34 at time of purchase) plus a modest dry cleaning charge. I see great turtle-necked sweaters at thrift shops and Salvation Army clothing warehouses. Once or twice I have seen genuine down jackets hanging on the racks next to high school band costumes. One can never tell what ideal backpacking clothing may be picked up for a song at a Hadassah Thrift Shop or a Junior League bazaar.

LAYERED CLOTHING

I also subscribe to the layered method of dressing because layers of clothing tend to hold in air. It is the same principle described in connection with a sleeping bag: with an outer cover **and** a sleeping bag liner, one is bound to sleep a little warmer. So, while the undershirt may not be a popular item on a college campus, I would recommend its wear for both sexes. It will absorb moisture, protect an outer garment, and provide one more layer to help trap air.

Do not misunderstand me: The backpacker should try to get by with as little weight in clothing as possible **without sacrificing comfort or ignoring the possibility of adverse weather.** I am not recommending one venture into the wilderness like a pack horse, carrying as much clothing as a cruise passenger. Besides, clothing is a highly personal item — almost a statement about one's self — and I would not venture to dictate what one wears. If you like to hike in overalls with shoulder straps or even a jumpsuit or warmup suit and find these convenient — fine. I can only suggest what — subjectively — I have found satisfactory.

For warm weather, I like to hike in shorts and either a tee-shirt or a tank-top. Even if it rains, I sometimes still hike in this simple dress on the theory that I'd rather get a little wet and keep the bulk of my clothing dry in my pack. I do not recommend this for everyone. At the first sign of wet weather, some people must outfit themselves in rain chaps, full-length poncho, and a rain hat. Recently when reading the detailed accounts of a number of hikers who have covered the length of the Appalachian Trail extending from Georgia to Maine (**Hiking the Appalachian Trail**, edited by James R. Hare, Rodale Press, 1975), I realized I am not alone in liking to hike this way **in warm rain.**

Fishnet underwear is highly recommended by many people. This fishnet material (very popular in Europe, especially Scandinavia) with large holes in the material acts as an air trap. Many skiers also extoll the virtue of this material (available as a jersey or as pants) worn under a turtle-necked shirt. There is good reason, for a layer of air is trapped near the skin. Thermal underwear, somewhat heavier, will serve the same purpose.

Some prefer to wear a turtle-necked pullover, nylon or cotton (nylon dries faster, but cotton feels less clammy when wet), over this underwear. Of course, in hot weather, a tight-fitting, neck-hugging turtleneck pullover can be uncomfortable. Others like a wool shirt because it offers so many combinations: it can be buttoned part way or all the way, or its flaps or tails may hang outside shorts or pants or be tucked in. Also, most shirts have good, button-closing pockets.

If one is allergic to wool, a shirt of a synthetic material or a chamois material may fill the bill.

Wool pants are preferred by some hikers. Most hunters seem to wear them, but they are not traveling long distances or staying overnight in the woods. Most backpackers find wool pants or knickers a bit too heavy. Of course wool knickers are very common in rock climbing circles.

DENIM

Considerable controversy exists over denim. Whether called blue jeans, dungarees, or Levi's ® (after Levi Strauss, a San Francisco manufacturer), this pant (or, if sawed off above the knee, this pair of shorts) has its supporters. I do find denim a slow-drying material if wet. Since dungarees are not always form-fitting, they can be uncomfortable on a long trip. A pair of Levis ® which will seem perfectly appropriate if one is lounging may turn out to chafe on a long hike. Still — a sizeable number of writers on backpacking advocate dungarees and they can't all be wrong. I prefer a good loose fitting pair of trousers. Normally, in backpacking the legs do not become as cold as the upper torso or even the arms.

Often, even in the summer, a lightweight down jacket is a good idea. Lately, polyester vests in the $20 range have been selling well. They keep the chest and back warm, yet are not so confining as a down jacket.

As one begins hiking in the cool of early morning, one may have a number of layers on — fishnet underwear, a wool shirt or else a pullover nylon or cotton jersey, a wool sweater and polyester vest or jacket! (Well, there may have been a frost overnight.) As the sun rises and it becomes warmer, layers can be shed. If one is hiking uphill and at several thousand feet higher altitude than at daybreak it suddenly seems colder, again on go the layers. Also when one rests, it can seem colder quite suddenly, so a layer may go on just for a rest stop.

SHORTS

For most summer backpacking, shorts or short dungaree skirts are ideal for hiking. Cooler than trousers, they do have some disadvantage: in heavy bug or mosquito season, they do not offer much insect protection. In wet or prickly undergrowth, they can be uncomfortable. Colin Fletcher, a sort of elder guru of backpacking, declares himself "a bigoted devotee of shorts." Fletcher, it seems, has his multi-pocketed shorts handmade in England (about $50). Several American firms sell walking shorts with several buttoned pockets and a built-in waistband (which means no belt, not always a comfortable item when worn with the waist-strap of a long contour packframe).

There is no need to discuss what one writer calls "distaff wardrobe." Everything I've said about clothing, with the possible exception of the short dungaree skirt, applies to both sexes. Once on a stretch of the Tahoe-Yosemite trail near Round-Top Mountain, I passed two women hiking topless in the sunny July weather, so even my references to hiking only in shorts and boots may be taken literally by both sexes. Besides, I don't think women need men telling them what special items (halter tops, and the like) they need to go backpacking. One of the great charms of Miriam Underhill's book, **Give Me The Hills** (Chatham Press) is her chapter, "Manless Climbing." Long before the feminist movement became a media event, Miriam Underhill was chafing at seasoned mountaineers who told her why a woman could never lead a climb. She then proceeded to lead the Grepon at Chamonix and followed that up in succeeding years with many "manless" climbs in the Alps, including the Matterhorn.

RAINWEAR

Backpackers respond differently to the rain. Some like to hike in shorts — or nothing at all — if the rain is warm, saving dry clothes for the day's campsite. Others get all gussied up.

Rain jackets are sold at any backpacking store. They have sleeves and generally a hood with drawstring. A lightweight nylon rain jacket which may be almost knee-length is the choice of many backpackers. A good lightweight rain jacket or parka may cost up to $20.

Others still prefer the serviceable poncho. Essentially a rectangular sheet with a hooded opening for the head, the poncho is less confining than a rain jacket and may be more comfortable in hot weather. It allows more air to circulate. In very windy weather, it can be tied around the waist to prevent flopping. Unlike a rain jacket with protective sleeves to the wrist, the poncho's arm openings do not provide as much arm protection, especially below the elbows. A good-sized poncho, however, will fit over a rucksack and sometimes even over a long contour packframe. By contrast, a pack is always worn over a rain jacket or parka. Naturally, there are advantages and disadvantages either way.

A poncho has several other virtues. It can serve as a groundcloth. If it has grommets in the corners, it can be used as a tarp. Two ponchos together form a makeshift tent or when the elements act up, one can just **crouch** down and cover with the poncho.

I would avoid the heavier rubber or plastic ponchos if my budget permitted, and use a lightweight nylon poncho. It will fold up as small as a washcloth and weighs only a few ounces.

If you really want to be protected, rain pants, or rain chaps are sold. The pants are more expensive than the chaps which are put on separately and tied to a belt or belt loops. Chaps are useless with built-in waistbanded trousers since they must be attached. Rain pants, on the other hand, have their own drawstring, like pajamas. I have known veteran backpackers who have never owned either rain pants or rain chaps.

The problem is well expressed by Colin Fletcher. In rainy weather one can either get all outfitted in rainwear and soak in one's sweat or let the rain come down on one's shorts and tank-top and soak in the rain. Many summer backpackers, especially in wilderness areas with the protection of trees, prefer to get a little wet en route knowing that dry clothes are in the pack. Like food on the trail, rain on the trail is handled according to one's preference and budget.

I shall not recommend a specific hat. Some want a broad-brimmed hat with sun protection. Others like a visored baseball cap. Some simply wear that all-purpose item — the bandana. I like a simple wool ski cap which will pull down over my ears, if necessary.

If your poncho, rain jacket, or down parka has a hood, you may not want a cap, but then again you might find it is warming to sleep in a cap. It also might be more comfortable since it gives a slight cushiony effect between head and improvised pillow — which can be anything from one's boots to a canteen! Ski shops sell ski mask caps with a slit or two for mouth and eyes. They often are long enough to offer neck protection, too. If money is no object, you can buy a balaclava helmet which offers — at least I'm told — good neck protection. If you look at old pictures of early climbers of Mont Blanc or the Matterhorn, you'll see many of them wearing balaclavas. I have one friend who hikes, rides horseback, plays backgammon, and, maybe even takes his meals, in a ten-gallon Stetson wide-brimmed hat. Who am I to tell him he should go out and buy a balaclava?

Not only do ski shops sell ski mask caps, they sell gaiters to be used from the top of the ski boot to mid-thigh. These nylon, zippered leg wraparounds protect the area between boot and ski pants, but they are ideal for hikers. Used between boot and trouser, they help keep out snow, rain, and small pebbles. They can easily be homemade and should be made of breatheable material.

BEDWEAR

Pajamas? I do not think they are needed. In fact any clothing salesperson will tell you the sale of pajamas is declining daily. Many backpackers — and not just those in zip-together bags — prefer to sleep nude just as they do at home. There's even a good reason: it is not sensible to sleep in clothing which may have become sweat-soaked during the day.

Others prefer to sleep with some clothing as they feel warmer in their bags. Those who hate to awaken in the cold morning nude and then dress (even if they dress inside the bag) may also wish to sleep with some clothing on. Here, again, there are no rules, only preferences.

It should be possible to go hiking without buying any additional clothing with the possible exception of hiking socks and raingear.

HIKING SOCKS

Two pair of socks are recommended. A synthetic dress sock may be used as the inner pair. Some climbers prefer silk. Then a wool sock may be used for the outer.

A good inner sock might be a pair of pure silk socks. They would be excellent for dissipating friction and allowing moisture to pass off to the outer sock. Janus Ragg socks are popular as an outer sock. They are ankle-length and 100% wool. Expect to pay several dollars for a pair of good wool socks. They are best washed by hand; if washed in a machine at the hot water temperature, they may shrink two or three sizes. While outer socks come in colors, I prefer a neutral gray. A pair of these socks will cost up to $3.50.

If you are hiking in knickers (which in certain types of weather can be very comfortable, but which tend to be too air-confining for milder weather) you may need knicker hose — a full knee-length sock — which may cost considerably more, up to $8.00.

The idea behind two pair of socks is that any friction in the boot will be minimized by having the socks rubbing against each other, (rather than against you) reducing friction and heat. Blisters are caused by heat, sweat, and friction. With a silk or even thin synthetic inner sock, sweat will be passed away from the foot through to the outer sock. In other words, the inner sock will act as a sort of wick. Also, two layers give a spongy base for the foot to rest on. An air space is provided under the foot so that every time weight is released off the foot, air rushes in to help ventilate. In cold weather, a dead air space is created to insulate the foot.

For years the wool merchants of Boston, at one time the wool capital of the world, claimed that wool kept one cooler in summer, warmer in the winter. Newer synthetic fabrics all but "did in" the wool merchants, but they were right all along. Wool is a marvelous material not only for climbing socks, but for much backpacking clothing. A wool sock, like many a wool garment, will keep the wearer warm even if the wool is slightly wet.

There are other inner socks that you might consider if you don't want a silk sock.
* Cotton inner sock, so-called athletic sock. It should have 10% to 20% Orlon to hold shape to the foot.
* Tube sock. A no-heel type of sock made of cotton with 10-20% Orlon ®
* Synthetic dress sock — made of rayon, Orlon ®, and nylon. A terry-cloth type of bottom helps cushion the bottom of the foot. Turn inside-out for more comfort and dryness.
* Fine wool sock (such as a Mojave sheer wool liner sock) — for those who don't mind having wool next to their skin. 80% wool, 20% nylon.
* A G.I. sock — 50% wool, and 50% cotton with nylon.
* Nylon dress sock — 100% nylon.

* A thin polyester-cotton combination with a dress sock and wool rag sock on the exterior. The foot portion from a pair of panty hose may be used in place of the inner sock.

OUTER SOCK

Some people prefer to have the outer sock with a small 20% mix of nylon for greater durability, and with nylon as toe and heel reinforcement.

The thickness of the sock depends on the users' preference, the type of hiking, the season of the year. A good combination for summer hiking is a thick outer sock with a thin dress sock for inner.

CARE OF SOCKS

When clean, socks function better. Some hikers carry as many as three pairs of socks, even changing socks every few hours on hot days and hanging their sweaty socks on the outside of the pack to dry en route. On lay-over days, socks can be washed and dried. Woolite ®, a cold water soap, can be used, but I do not think it is necessary to carry it along — any soap will do. Wool dries slower than nylon, but partially-dried socks may be tied to the pack and in good weather will dry reasonably well en route.

Detergents should be avoided with wool.

Socks should be washed daily, but many hikers go a week or more in the same socks. If you rub a candle on the heel of your sock you can save the heel from wear. Paraffin cuts down the friction.

ALTERNATIVE FOOTGEAR

Since I try to travel as lightly as possible, I am not in the habit of carrying along sneakers, moccasins, or sandals for use at the campsite. Sometimes, without socks, I clump around in my hiking boots, but some backpackers do like to carry along a change of footwear. For this purpose down boots (or"booties") are ideal. They can be worn around camp because they are soled and they can keep the feet quite warm if worn inside a sleeping bag. They weigh very little. A pair may cost from $10 to $20.

GLOVES AND MITTENS

Even in the summer, many climbers take along gloves or mittens for nippy mornings and nights. Later in this book when we look briefly at winter camping, we will discuss gloves and mittens.

Backpackers sometimes carry needle and thread to mend clothing which becomes ripped while on the trail.

THE LAYER SYSTEM

When dressing in the layered system, remember that dead air is an insulator and water is a conductor. By putting layers over each other, this helps set up this dead air space for insulation of the body. Regulation of cold can be done by adding layers, and shedding when it is too warm.

Avoid over-dressing, especially in cold weather. By having too many layers of clothes over the body when it is exercising, it creates an overabundance of perspiration. Since perspiration is water, remember that the thermal conductivity of water is 240 times greater than air.

Wet clothing only conducts body heat. Dry clothing is your best insulator. Carry a change of clothing, but try to avoid getting wet.

Clean wool has open spaces. When it is dirty or salty, dirt and salt substances fill these air spaces.

HANDLING THE ELEMENTS

ELEMENTS	ITEM USED	VARIABLES
Wind	Wind Parka or Lightweight Down Parka	In windy situations, use a parka as the external layer.
Wetness	Poncho or Rainsuit	These waterproof layers tend to be sweaty when walking. To prevent sweat saturation, remove some inner layers. (Jacket, sweater or shirt).
Coldness	Long underwear or fishnet Pants Shirt Sweater Wool Cap Gloves or Mittens	Adding layers — in cold climates or when less body heat is being generated by body movement. Shedding layers — in warmer climates, or when more body heat is being produced through exercise. Shedding also cuts down excess body sweat by allowing external air to carry away excess body heat. Trapped excess body heat turns to sweat which saturates inner clothing layers.

CLOTHING TIPSHEET

Clothing Material

Wool — Even if wool is wet it will still keep the body warm, because it is tightly curled. Its independent fibers do not absorb water. It traps dead air within itself and helps keep the body warm. Wool garments dry quickly, too.

Cotton — Cotton when wet will only draw heat from the body. Being an organic fiber, cotton is highly absorbent of water. The threads swell, putting water next to the skin instead of dead air.

Nylon — Nylon next to the skin can be very clammy because it does not pass water as well as wool. Since it is tightly woven material it has no dead-air capacity for warmth. It is generally used over an insulating material for a highly abrasive water-repellent or waterproof shell. Nylon garments dry quickly.

Down — Has good insulating ability (see sleeping bag section). Down takes a long time to dry.

Polyester Fiber Material — Used as insulation (see sleeping bag section). It will keep the wearer warm even if wet. Polyester fiber will dry very quickly.

Clothes for Backpacking
Clothes should fit comfortably, but not too snugly. Tightness tends to keep the blood from circulating and restricts movement. Loose clothing creates air circulation next to the skin, making the garment colder. Extremely baggy clothing gets in the way of the wearer.

Clothes should be rugged and be able to withstand heavy abrasion from rocks, and so on.

Pants — Lots of pockets for carrying odds and ends are helpful.

Shirts — Can be wool, cotton, but should have some pockets with closures, so nothing drops out.

BANDANA

I think the bandana is a great invention. This multi-purpose item can be a handkerchief, neck band, hat, forehead sweat band. Hikers who are awakened by early morning sunshine and want to sleep a little longer have been known to stretch a bandana over their eyes, thus making it dark again. In an emergency, a bandana can serve as a first-aid tourniquet. The bandana can also be a potholder. I cannot remember the last time I have been on a trail without at least one bandana.

Site Selection and Shelters

Chapter Six

The best in helter shelter and how to choose it.

One of the joys of hiking in Europe is that one can climb an Alpine peak and find a mountain hut offering food and overnight accommodations. Throughout the Alpine trail systems these mountain huts have been placed so that a hiker has only to carry personal possessions — no food, tent, sleeping bag, ground cloth, or pad, or stove. A day's hike apart, these huts are found at the highest elevation and in the most remote locations. Four or five languages may be spoken, but one thing is shared by all: a love of the mountain world of forest and rock and glacier.

In the United States only one similar chain of huts exists, and that is in the White Mountains of New Hampshire where the Appalachian Mountain Club operates eight mountain huts during the summer climbing season. Some of their huts, such as Madison Springs and Lakes-of-the-Clouds are above timberline; others, like Carter Notch or Zealand Falls, are set in deep woods miles from the highway. All are staffed, generally by college men and women, and offer breakfast, trail lunch, dinner at night, and overnight bunkrooms with blankets provided. The atmosphere is informal, with guests folding their blankets and helping the crew with dishes and table-clearing.

Except for the main hut at Pinkham Notch, right under the summit of Mount Washington, all these huts are a good hike in from the nearest highway. Like their Alpine counterparts, they have been placed a day's hike apart. An ideal eight-to-ten-day vacation would be hiking from one end of the chain to the other. The route covers remote forest land as well as the exposed ridges of the Presidential Range. Here, far above timberline, severe winds can be encountered even in the summer. But when one hikes through wind-whipped mist and suddenly sees the day's destination emerge from the mist, it is comforting to know one will be greeted in a warm, enclosed place where hot tea is offered before any registration form is produced.

For many people, backpacking without carrying food, sleeping bag, or any sort of shelter is ideal. True, on an August night there may be as many as a hundred people at the biggest mountain hut at Lakes-of-the-Clouds (which is not exactly a quiet wilderness experience), but many hikers prefer to let someone else worry about food and shelter and so these mountain huts are ideal. Information may be obtained from the Appalachian Mountain Club, 5 Joy Street, Boston, Massachusetts 02108.

In other parts of the country, a backpacker need not worry about shelter, for cabins and lean-tos are spaced a day's hike apart on many trails. For example, the Long Trail, which runs the length of Vermont from Massachusetts to the Canadian border, is equipped with shelter every eight or ten miles. Sometimes these shelters consist of closed cabins with a wood stove; often they are open-faced lean-tos which are also common in the Adirondack Mountains. Somewhere ahead, clearly described in the Long Trail Guide, will be a suitable shelter. In a rainstorm, these shelters can be exceedingly welcome.

Years ago, when most of these shelters were constructed, they were ideal. Set in deep woods, they were often remote from civilization, and seldom occupied. They were used by serious hikers. But as they became better known, summer campers and Scout troops began visiting them **en masse** (which they had a right to do). Also shelters which were within a reasonable walk from the highway became "townie hangouts" — groups of local people would carry beer and a portable radio in to these lean-tos for a night of revelry. Hiker and hedonist clashed.

Even more alarming: with everybody building campfires the woods surrounding these places began to look like Viet Nam in 1969 — the woods were scarred, denuded. Lovely birch trees had been destroyed. Garbage was strewn around; there were bits and pieces of glass, metal, plastic. Initials and inscriptions were carved into the lean-tos: KILROY WAS HERE. JESUS WAS A RADICAL. EL LOVES AH.

Frankly, these pristine shelters became a kind of wilderness slum. Most areas were affected: the Smoky Mountains, the Adirondacks, the Cascades — wherever, in fact, mountain shelters had been built. Art Harris recalls the last night he ever spent in one of these shelters at Lake Tear up on the side of Mt. Marcy in the Adirondacks. (It was here that Theodore Roosevelt, America's most mountain-loving President, was camping when he received news that he had to return to civilization to take the oath of office as President.) Art and his companion arrived before dusk, set the Primus stove to work brewing tea and then supper, and were snuggled into their sleeping bags talking in a sleepy, desultory fashion when they heard sounds, then saw flashlights. Emerging from the woods was a group from a boys' camp. Four hours later, after an enormous campfire, much singing, some fighting, and a lot of complaining, they were still tossing oranges at one another. Since then, Art has avoided lean-tos and shelters and taken his chances under the stars, in a tent, or (most common of all) simply under a tarp.

The best — absolutely the best way — to sleep is under the stars if the weather is right and the wind is not too high. We so seldom sleep this way that it seems unreal not be be gazing at a ceiling. As wonderful as the nights are under the open sky, the mornings are even more spectacular. Colin Fletcher put it poetically: "Without a roof, you wake directly into the new day."

Yes, there is the dew of a new morning; there are nighttime stirrings of animals which make some people anxious; there is always the possibility of a sudden weather change and precipitation, but I think the risk is worth it. So I have become something of a proselytizer, asking people, "Have you slept under the stars lately?"

The answer is almost invariably "No." Used to four walls, a floor, and a ceiling, most people feel insecure in the wilderness without something approximating their regular shelter. So we have people camping in noisy, crowded lean-tos when half-a-mile away there might be an ideal, quiet camping spot. We have people carrying tents into the woods so they may be surrounded on all sides by nylon, protected from the sky, moon, night air, animals.

Tents **do** have their place, of course. In extended mountain expeditions where there is snow, they are indispensable. In heavy insect country, they offer relief (although a hammock with mosquito netting might do as well). Good tents will keep out snakes and any curious animals, though **most** animals will keep their distance from humans. This may not include the porcupine, however, and some daring camp animals in search of food.

A tent does weigh something — several pounds for even the most lightweight tent — so carrying a tent along with a sleeping bag, a ground cloth, a sleeping pad, one's food, perhaps a stove, and personal possessions can add up to quite a few pounds. Often I find that wilderness backpackers like to begin with the security of a tent, then risk backpacking without a tent.

CHOOSING A CAMPSITE

A backpacker's necessities are simple: to stay dry, stay warm overnight, get a good night's sleep, eat well enough to be satisfied, get no blisters or backpack sores. For the Winnebago camper these comforts are almost assured, but the backpacker must make decisions which affect comfort — and the main decision, once out on the trail, is where to camp. Here are some considerations.

Comfort. Being comfortable can make a wilderness excursion so successful that you will want to return. A properly selected campsite may help fulfill one's appreciation of nature especially when you are fresh from a night of good rest. You can appreciate nature better if you have selected a good campsite. The next morning, you are not tired and your eyes are in tune with nature's displays.

Site Considerations. Protection from the elements.

The Wind. Wind chill is an enemy that one must always consider.

Any time I make camp, I check wind direction. If any major storm front is in the offing, I ask myself which direction will it be traveling? For example, on the West Coast the wind for storm fronts generally comes out of the Southwest. If these winds come, will there be trees or rocks to protect your campsite, or are you camped in an exposed area? When weather is fair, a natural wind change occurs. For example, where a mountain range has lower elevations (valleys) below it, the wind will travel down a canyon at night and up the canyon during the day. For **most** areas, this fact holds true. Consider this day-night change when you set up your tent. The more natural protection you have from the wind the better.

A 360° View of the Heavens. You are probably imagining being parked (camped)in a dense forest with no view of the heavens. The natural protection of the forest is the first concern; the stars come next (you will be surprised how many stars you can see from a path in the trees).

Rain, Sleet, or Snow. Harsh wetness can be one of the wilderness traveler's most formidable irritants. Use the natural protection available to counter the elements. I have set up my tarp tent in some horrendous storms and have slept through them comfortably because I let the trees protect me from the high winds and persistent rain.

The Site Environment. Nowadays, the "evolved" (in consciousness) backpacker is mindful of her or his impact upon the site area. If possible, one recycles or re-uses an existing campsite. (More on this later). Here are some of the typical wilderness environments that are encountered by backpackers nationwide:

* **Forested areas** aid campers by protecting them from high winds, stormy weather and hot days. When temperatures are cool, trees tend

to tame the wind and trap warmth. In fact, you can be much warmer sleeping under a tree than under an open sky (radiation of heat coming off the sleeper is trapped by the tree and is not dissipated skyward).

* **Meadow areas** are generally more exposed to the weather, especially dampness and cold. Meadow areas on a cold night can be 20° cooler because cold air settles where warmer air rises. On a windless night you will actually be sleeping in a lake of cold air. This settling accounts for heavy dew and frost in the morning.

* **Above timberline areas,** rocks and depressions can be counted on for weather protection. Considering wind direction and altitude is is important here. The higher the elevation, the lower the temperature reading (4° F change per 1000 ft. gained), plus there is a greater chance of wind chill and the prevalence of higher winds. During storms, the higher elevations are vulnerable to frequent lightning strikes.

COMFORT FOR A GOOD NIGHT'S REST

Water. H_2O has a lot to do with dehydration and wilderness cooking. So, in order to have a satisfying sleep, one must both eat and drink. If possible, urinate before bedtime. You will sleep warmer and you will not have to suffer a nocturnal "call of the wild."

Lakes, of course, are one of the biggest sources of a water supply. Try to make sure that both the inlet and outlet of the lake are flowing (this helps keep the lake flushed of impurities). If this is not so — or if you can't tell whether it's so — then water purification tablets may be in order. Also, avoid drawing water from swimming and fishing areas.

Streams are another source of water supply. Walk upstream and check things out. Considering pollution, the more white water in a stream or river, the more oxygen in the water (The chance of pure water is better).

Springs are a pleasure to draw water from. It seems sweeter and purer with every sip. Topographical maps or trail maps will give locations of springs in the hiking area.

Snow can be another source of water supply. The best time to collect snow-water is mid-afternoon till evening. (The snow's highest rate of melt is during the day). If one is in the colder climate with temperatures dropping below 32° F, snowbanks will not be melting. Anytime one travels in these above-timberline areas where water is not likely, water should be carried in your pack. Use this water by heating it up on the stove. Once it boils, add chunks of snow. This will help save the bottom of your pot from burning out. It is hard to boil snow by itself. (Snow is more oxygen than

72

water.)

Fuel for Fires. Cooking fires are becoming a thing of the past because of wood depletion. For more on this, please see Minimal Human "Impact" in this chapter.

Level Ground. If one is tired enough, sleep will come under the most uncomfortable circumstances. But, this really does not have to happen. Level ground with a natural "hip hole," head higher than the feet, or vice versa, can be found in many areas of the wilderness. Natural drainage will keep water from a rainstorm running away from you. Making a sleeping area a major construction project is definitely out! No serious backpacker levels a campsite or builds a platform with pine boughs or digs drainage ditches or improvises moats. Why bother? With all the natural areas available, who needs a destructive construction project? Pine needles or leaves can be shifted around to help level a "Bedroom platform."

Insects. They can be a discouraging factor when one is trying to get a few winks. Generally, try to be observant of their habitats. Mosquitoes live and breed where water is still or stagnant. Forested and meadow areas are typical mosquito lairs. If possible, camp by a stream (100 feet away), where air currents are more prevalent, or at the edge of the forest where winds are more brisk. (Mosquitoes have a difficult time flying in moving air.) When camping on a lake, select the windward end where mosquitoes and other insects will be carried away from you. Avoid vegetation such as skunk cabbage that attracts mosquitoes. Higher elevations seem to have less insects. The insect breeding season ranges from mid-summer to early fall.

After the first cold snap, insect populations begin to decline. Flies are attracted to latrine areas, dead animals, livestock and their droppings. If you can avoid such circumstances, do so. Ants live in colonies. Avoid setting up your bedroom area in such places. If possible, set your bedroom area up in one place, and your kitchen in another. This helps keep the ants and flies away from you at night.

Floods. Avoid camping in dry creek beds and depression areas. Flash floods and sudden storms have made some unaware backpackers aware of the flotation of their air mattress.

Rockfalls. Before setting up camp, walk away from the area and examine the cliffs and overhangs. Are there loose rocks, talus chutes above you? If so, consider moving your camp. Animals and people above you, or just nature, can dislodge one of those rocks.

Avalanches. Please see winter hiking, further on.

Deadfalls or Widow Makers. As you set your pack on the ground to set up camp, look above you. Are there dead branches that may come crashing down on you in the middle of the night? Two California Boy Scouts had a 200 pound branch fall in between them during the night;

73

luckily, no one was hurt.

Morning Sun. Some of us like to awaken with the morning sun. A personal preference, of course, but still a consideration.

Privacy. Very many times, seeing people on the trail all day is enough without sharing your campsite with them. With the crowding of many areas, you may find solitude only inside your tent. Select an area where you can obtain privacy and let others do the same. Recently, I selected a reasonably private campsite and was startled when a couple started setting up their camp fifteen feet from mine. Before objecting, I checked the rest of the campsites on the lake — all empty. So, politely, I confronted them and asked them to go to one of the better campsites in the area. (I personally described the virtures of each one). They left happily, and I thanked them.

SITE PREPARATION

Setting Up Camp. Though time may not be a major concern in the wilderness, allot at least two hours for setting up before the sun goes down. This gives hikers plenty of time to prepare themselves (bedding, dinner, and conversation) before hitting the sack.

A Campfire for Conversation. If you want an aesthetic fire, make sure an existing campfire circle is used along with a five-foot radius with dry grass and wood cleared away. Beware of overhanging branches and keep the fire to a low blaze (Less wood is consumed).

Draw Water. Shortly after choosing a campsite, it is a good idea to draw the water for cooking and begin dinner. While it is cooking, you can be setting up your tent or preparing your bedroom.

Nighttime Visitors. After a delicious dinner has been consumed, and all the cocoa has been drunk, then it is time to consider a "hanging" place for your food. Always assume that some animal during the night will want your food. The instant you do not assume this, your food will be gone, and I cannot begin to tell you how disheartening it is to watch a bear eat up five days worth of food right before your eyes.

Bear Bagging. Be sure to hang your food 100 feet or more away from camp. One backpacking couple I know of pitched their tube tent underneath their hanging food supply. During the night a hungry bear cub went directly to the food taking a beeline route through the tube tent, over the sleeping people, and up into the tree. So, keep your food away from your sleeping area. Here are some methods of bear bagging.

Climb the tree — climb at least ten feet off the ground and tie the food bag (your sleeping bag case will serve the purpose) at least three feet away from the trunk of the tree.

Hang the food. Take 50 feet of nylon cord and attach a rock to one end. Throw the rock over a high branch (a challenge in itself), then hoist the food up. Then, three to five feet away from the trunk, tie the cord off at least eight feet from the ground. Bears have been known to sever cords if they can reach it with their teeth. In heavy bear country, it is advisable to suspend food and pack between two trees. Avoid leaving food in your pack; in fact, hand your pack too. The pack may smell of food, and for some animals, that is tempting. If a bear does get your food, do not interfere. You can survive the loss of food more easily than a bear attack. I will state the obvious — **never sleep with your food.** Even long days without a bath will not repel a bear. (Many of the National Park information centers have a wealth of information concerning bears.

Other Furry Friends. Chipmunks, squirrels, raccoons, and porcupines (to name a few), have appetites too. So, hang your pack out on the smallest limb possible to discourage nocturnal visitors. Small animals are interested in your food in the daytime too, so hang it in a safe area when it is not being used. Despite the foregoing suggestions, if an animal of agility and climbing ability is sufficiently interested, there is little way of stopping them from getting your food.

MINIMAL HUMAN IMPACT

The wilderness experience is self-discovery for many backpackers. It provides that rare element — solitude — which in turn spawns tranquility, relaxation, and the ability to step aside and let the busy outside world go by. That is why so many backpackers treasure the wilderness and guard it jealously from the encroachment of the outside world. Besides offering an escape, however temporary from urban life, the wilderness can change people. It is a formidable "consciousness-raiser" in the best sense of the word.

It has been human destiny to dominate nature for so long that we forget that in earlier times men and women lived in accord with nature. Trees, plants, streams, and lakes were thought to have a "spirit" (animus) of their own. Humans lived with and shared their spirit with the spirits of forests.

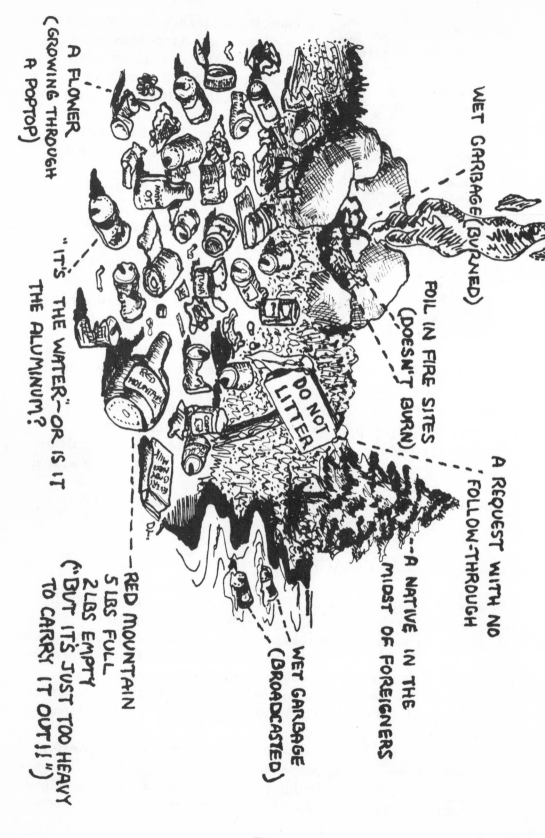

A FLOWER
(GROWING THROUGH
A POPTOP)

WET GARBAGE (BURNED)

FOIL IN FIRE SITES
(DOESN'T BURN)

A REQUEST WITH NO
FOLLOW-THROUGH

"IT'S THE WATER"—OR IS IT
THE ALUMINUM?

---A NATIVE IN THE
MIDST OF FOREIGNERS

---RED MOUNTAIN
5 LBS FULL
2 LBS EMPTY
("BUT IT'S JUST TOO HEAVY
TO CARRY IT OUT!!")

WET GARBAGE
(BROADCASTED)

76

Call it primitivism, if you like, but it may be this quality in a latter day primitive which can keep the wilderness experience reasonably intact.

The backpacker who thinks of herself or himself as a caretaker of the wilderness and "takes nothing but pictures and leaves nothing but footprints" will perpetuate the wilderness experience for present and future generations. You can perhaps glimpse the messianic fervor of the backpacker as caretaker.

Backpacking, as sport and recreation, has already attracted more than ten million adherents. With the campers, tourists, the wilderness is becoming crowded. Instead of barring people from the mountains and forests the National Forest Service and National Park Service have set new guidelines and instituted rules to curb the impact of people on the wilderness. Few of us like red tape but the permits required oftentimes by park and forest managements are crucial. The permits minimize the amount of impact and day use for areas within wilderness and park boundaries.

The following comments cover basic rules of courtesy to nature applicable both within areas under governmental aegis and areas of untrammelled wilderness.

Twenty-five people per party is the maximum number for park and forest areas. Large groups converging on the wilderness at one time have more impact than the same number would have over a period of several months.

"Caring" for the wilderness also means staying on trails. Cutting a switchback can start erosion that will last a lifetime. Where new trails have been laid out around delicate areas, like meadows, stay on the new trail. We have learned that in traveling cross country there is less impact if one walks the bare rocks and stream beds. These areas can withstand the impact more easily than meadows or forested sections. Boots can crush plants, grasses, and lichen that has taken nature years to create.

You can lessen destructive impact on nature by camping in designated campsites or by choosing used campsites. Keeping the campsite at least 100 to 150 feet from a lake or stream also minimizes pollution.

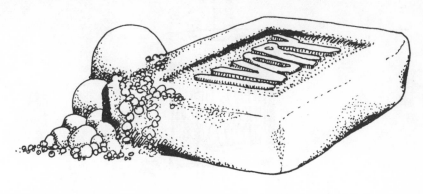

It is temptingly convenient to wash dishes, clothes, or yourself at stream or lakeside but we have learned about the harmful effects of soap mixing in the pure waters. Even the new bio-degradable soaps should not be mixed with the natural water. If you do all washing at least 150 feet away from the waterways you avoid polluting.

Using a portable stove and carrying your own fuel helps too. However, if you build a fire it is best to use existing fire pits and always keep the fire small. The warming, romantic campfire should only be built when wood is superabundant in the camping area. Forests depleted of wood lack the nutrients in the soil which feed worms and insects which in turn are eaten by birds and larger animals.

A "caring" backpacker leaves campsites cleaner than he or she found them. Wet food scraps and garbage are burned and the inevitable trash — tin foil, aluminum foil, plastic — is repacked for disposal at home. I even bypass the road and forest service trash barrel. I suspect its contents are often just dumped back into the forest.

The park or forest personnel often has set up facilities for the disposal of human waste. If not, one can use a cat hole, at least 100 yeards from any waterway. There, one can carefully burn toilet paper after covering excrement with soil. For the purist conservationist one can bring their used toilet paper home in a plastic bag and dispose of properly.

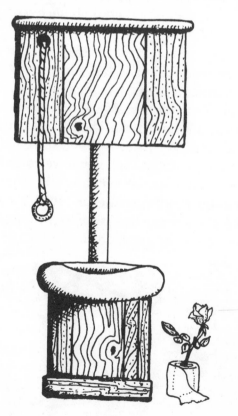

Unless you are planning a permanent residence in the forest Grizzly Adams-style, it is best never to cut boughs or limbs to provide bed or shelter. Digging tent trenches or leveling the ground is a sure way to leave camp scars. If you have selected an area with natural drainage, your impact on the forest is greatly softened.

Your reward for lessening your impact on the wilderness is a new vision, both inside and outside, that sets you **with** nature and not against her.

TENTLESS, TARPLESS CAMPING

Surely you have seen those Coleman advertisements showing a motor camper's campsite filled with folding chairs and tables, a two-burner stove, a lamp, a portable radio, a tent large enough for the New Riders of the Purple Sage and all their instruments, as well as assorted odds and ends — like pillows and metal coolers holding chilled beer and cola.

As a revolt against such overly-civilized motor camping, some backpackers are inclined to go the other way. They carry no tent, fly, or tarp, preferring to make-do in the wilderness. If they get a little wet, they get a little wet. Others go one step beyond that: they carry little or no food. When Art Harris was visiting me he met a man in Sacramento who worked at a health-food restaurant in Sacramento who could always find something to eat in the woods. A true stalker of the wild asparagus, he recognizes all sorts of edible plants and roots in the woods. can brew the most interesting teas from leaves and flowers found en route. The idea of confinement in a walled tent amid all that outdoors would go against Chris's grain, as it does many backpackers. Do not misunderstand me: there are times when a tent is essential; there are also people who will never be comfortable, physically or **psychologically**, unless they have the protection of a tent.

Some type of shelter is needed if you are going to spend time in the wilderness. It may be only a $2.00 tube or it may be an expensive mountaineering tent. I have experienced some very unpredictable snow storms in the High Sierra not in December, but in the middle of July. So, having good shelter can be critical. Some backpackers may make-do in the wilderness, but their knowledge is probably more extensive than that of the recreational backpacker. I personally find a wall tent quite confining. For others, a tent may be a necessity.

TARP TENT

I prefer shelters that are not only inexpensive, but also require a bit of a challenge to set up. For this reason, I prefer the tarp tent. Since it is lightweight and has varied shapes when erected, it can be set up custom made to the area in which you are camped. When you set up a tarp tent, check wind direction, natural terrain bedding, and protection available at the site. The tarp tent will give you protection against rain, some wind, and not make you feel as if you were sleeping in your bedroom at home.

The tarp tent is basically a single, waterproof fly used to protect sleepers from wind and rain. Often, a single sheet of translucent poly tarp (polyethylene) will serve adequately. There are several ways of setting up such a simple tarp tent. (One way is shown on page 80.) Grommets can be inserted at the corners and middle of the sheet and the tent can be suspended from trees or bushes using lightweight nylon cord. Adhesive tape grommets can also be purchased and introduced onto the sheet at various places. Much more common, however, is a simple invention, the Visklamp ®. This is a ball and clamp arrangement that works like a garter clamp. One can attach Visklamps ® (cost about 20c each) anywhere on the sheet of polyethylene and suspend the tarp tent with nylon cord. A similar product (only in plastic) consists of Versa Ties (a dozen sell for $1.50) which uses a disc and clip principle. Or a small stone or pebble can be bunched up in the corners of the sheeting and a cord tied (clove hitch) around the resulting bulges.

Of course one can buy pre-cut tarps with built-in grommets or with sewn-in tabs. Often a good-sized poncho will serve as well. Some tarp tents use a pole or two. Any good mountaineering store will sell tent poles, Visklamps ®, Versa Ties, Line tighteners, aluminum gutter-nails and lightweight aluminum skewers (for stakes), and so on. Instead of spending $100 for a tent, one can often erect a tarp tent for five or ten dollars, including money spent for cord, tarp, pegs, and Visklamps ®. Naturally a tarp tent is floorless — or should I say, the floor is provided by nature? A tarp tent is not much protection against insects or snakes, but it can be lightweight (1.4 to 3.5 lbs. without poles), and rain protecting. One never feels claustrophobic in such a tent.

Generally, these tarp tents are 7 to 12 feet in width and 11 to 12 feet in length, but a tarp tent is truly a do-it-yourself item and can be created in any size or shape you desire. Perhaps 2.2 oz. to 3.0 oz. ripstop nylon would be a more refined material than the polytarp and it may be waterproofed (K-koted ® or polymer).

Most ordinary polytarp is white, so your sideless tent will be light and airy. You can purchase a colored tarp tent if you want. Several mountain supply stores stock a "Bivouac Tarp" of 2.2 oz/sq. yd. ripstop nylon, with three grommets along each side and nylon duck used to reinforce each grommet. To give you an idea of size and price, the EMS catalog I have at time of writing offers an 8 x 11 foot bivouac tarp tent at $19 (weight 1.6 lb.) and a 12 x 11 foot model at $26.50 (2.5 lbs.). They also offer a stronger plastic sheeting than the polytarp — green on one side, white on the other. Here, again one may select on the basis of budget. Half a dozen Visklamps ® , some square footage of polytarp, a little nylon cord, a few tent pegs, and one has a roof over one's head at very little cost. Or pay a few dollars and have it all done for you — it would still be much cheaper than a walled tent.

One problem with tarp tents has developed in recent years: many backpackers regard these tents as disposable and have left the sheet of plastic in the woods. Plastic, an artificial product, will not return to the soil any more than a beer can will. Therefore, mountain supply catalogs are filled with little notices next to tarp and tube tents that read: "Please, if you buy a tube tent and use it — take it with you when you leave — If you plan to throw it away, that's fine, but throw it away, in a trash can, not in the woods. Thank you."

DIRECTIONS

1. Set your tarp tent up in your usual manner, but instead of using a tree for vertical height, use your pack.

2. Before tieing off the front part of the tent, insert backpack sideways, 3 feet back from the front edge of the tarp. Then tie off the front.

3. In the back tie a cord mid-way down the ridge of the tent, and tie it to a tree. (This will make the inside of the tent larger).

4. A 10' x 12' tarp in this combination sleeps two, (three in a pinch).

TUBE TENT

A tube tent is a circular sheet of plastic in the form of a tube. By using a cord as the roof beam, it is given an A-frame appearance. The cord is tied between two trees to hold the tent upright. Rocks or backpacking gear may be used to hold down the corners. The tube tent has one advantage over the tarp tent: It has a floor. But because the plastic is waterproof, condensation inside the tent is a problem, so both ends have to be left open for ventilation. The one-person size consists of a 10-foot circumference tube; a two-person tent would normally be a 12-foot circumference tube. The two-person tent always presents a greater condensation problem. These tents are generally ten to twelve feet long. A ten-foot length of tube tent material sells for 20c a foot. This 3-4 mil plastic material weighs about 3-4 oz. per foot.

Always, in **any** tent, but most especially a handmade tube tent, one must be aware of suffocation. It happens rarely, but it does happen. A cord holding the ridge line can snap, the sheet of polyethylene can collapse on sleepers. Normally, difficulty in breathing would awaken them quickly, but there have been instances of deep sleepers dying of suffocation when a tent, tarp, or plastic wraparound become so all encompassing that no air was allowed in. A candle burning in a tent with the ends closed off is a hazard.

Some mountaineering stores offer tube tents with mosquito netting at each end. Of course a floored tent with netting keeps insects and creepy crawlers at bay.

Both the tarp and tube tents are inexpensive, lightweight, more or less handmade, and not confining. Sometimes translucent (though not necessarily), they do not offer much privacy if one is camping along with others. For some people a true tent is the only way the backpacking experience will be a comfortable one. Also in certain situations (a winter camping, for instance, with snow — or the rainy season when a tent makes a lot of sense) a tent is almost a necessity.

Personally, I would experiment with these inexpensive shelters before I purchased a tent, for one can learn how much protection and privacy one wants. Also many backpacking aficionadoes never want to graduate to a store-bought tent; they feel that in their simple, inexpensive tarp tents they are closer to nature than in some tent manufactured in a tent and awning factory in Binghamton, New York.

If you are interested in a true tent, perhaps you can rent or borrow one first to get the feel of it, to see whether it seems too confining, too difficult to set up — whatever. But let me say at the outset — there is no perfect tent. If you make a tent waterproof, it will not breathe and moisture will form inside. If you make the tent of breathable material, there will be no condensation problem, but the tent will not be waterproof in a downpour. (This can be partly overcome with a waterproof fly above the tent — more about these fly covers in a moment.) If the tent is roomy, it may be too heavy to backpack.

I could go on like this with all sorts of qualifications. Recommending a tent to a backpacker is not unlike suggesting a car — personal preference plays an important role in selection. This is now especially true of tents which no longer come in one color — olive drab — but are multi-colored. One can choose the color of a tent, not only for aesthetic but practical purposes, for different colors give a different light inside the tent, and some colors stand out better in a snowfield than others. Green fits in pleasingly with forests, for example. Orange stands out.

Tent design is a subject in itself. They can be rectangular, A-framed, or octangular. They can be suspended by tent poles, cords, or lightweight aluminum struts. And just think of the variety of material: canvas, hardly used anymore because of its weight, has been replaced by many lightweight materials; nylon has virtually replaced long fiber cotton tents. Although nylon is lighter than cotton, it doesn't wick water in the same way cotton does. It is strong and almost mildew proof — perhaps its best features as tent fabric.

SINGLE WALL OR RAIN TENT

Many inexpensive tents (and some not so inexpensive) are single-walled tents. Many of these tents are made of one-layer coated nylon which is so waterproof that the tent tends to "rain" on the inside from condensation unless the tent is exceedingly well ventilated. A backpacker using one of these tents in mild weather and in a sheltered area will find the tent useful.

Some very inexpensive tents are made of highly inflammable material. Youngsters cooking in these tents or even lighting candles have been severely burned when the tent material caught fire. Sensitive to several TV reports on dangerous tents, the industry is trying to set up standards of flammability.

Material used in these walled tents may be K-kote ®, taffeta or ripstop nylon. With poles and pegs, a tent of this sort may weigh 4 to 6 lbs. Cost varies considerably. The popular Mount Marcy tent, manufactured by the Eureka Tent and Awning Company, currently retails for $45. The single wall, waterproof tent is more of a "backyard" tent than a true mountaineering or backpacking tent, but it is economical, roomy, and gives good insect protection.

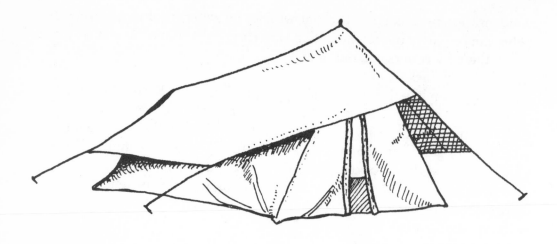

DOUBLE-WALLED OR MOUNTAINEERING TENTS

The basic difficulty with a single-walled tent is an inside-the-tent water problem. Water vapor inside the tent will condense on the walls, run down the sides and drip onto occupants and possessions.

The best solution to this is to have a breathable barrier roof and then suspend over it another roof of waterproof, coated nylon. In effect, one tent roof is suspended over the other. The upper roof is called the fly. Ideally, there is an air space of several inches between the two. Any vapor from inside the tent will pass right through the wall of the tent (since a breathable fabric is used) and is either evaporated or else condenses on the fly sheet itself, and then drips harmlessly to the ground. Sometimes this fly is attached to the tent, but generally it is separate and may be "rigged" or not as one wishes. In cold weather, the fly may be rigged closer to the main roof for warmth; in hot weather, a little distance between the two tent roofs will help. Actually, a double-walled tent will be cooler in the summer, warmer in the winter.

Wind is sometimes a problem, and a good triangular A-frame support system will insure maximum wind stability. A tent subjected to lots of wind should have shock cords on its guywires. It is well to pitch the tent facing into the wind if you wish to avoid excessive tent flapping, but for best protection against the wind pitching slightly crosswind is the best bet.

These low-profile, A-frame tents commonly come with a level roof line or else one which slopes from head to foot (and sometimes called a "low-ender"). Generally a two-person tent of this sort would weigh from 5 to 8 pounds, including the rain fly, poles, and stakes. For a two-person tent, the height might be three to four feet, the width four to five feet, and the length six to seven feet.

The floor material should continue up the side of the tent 10-15 inches. Some backpackers like to pitch their tent on top of a ground cloth to save wear and tear on the tent floor. Ordinarily, the inner tent will be of ripstop or taffeta nylon and water repellent (in other words, breathable) while the fly will be of similar material, only waterproof. Pegs will be stainless steel or aluminum, poles inner couplings aluminum tubing. Cost of these tents varies considerably, from $80 to $200. If you study a mountaineering catalog, you will see variations in these tents — some with tunnel entrances, other with a cook hole in the floor, still others with frost liners.

TENTING ODDS AND ENDS:

* When a tent has a tunnel entrance, it can be joined with another similar tent to make a totally weatherproof enclosure.
* Practice pitching a tent before going backpacking. The tent should be taut.
* Large family tents are not easy to backpack but are fun for a family which likes to be together. A family tent for six can weigh as little as nine pounds and cost $150.
* If you must roll up the tent in the early morning hours, make sure the tent is aired out before the end of the day. The seams take longer to dry. Avoid rolling up the tent with the stakes and poles, since sharp edges may rip the material.
* In pitching the tent, avoid excess strain on the guy wires and corners of the tent.
* In storing a tent, avoid mildew by exposing the tent to air circulation. If a tent got wet on a hike, erect it at home in sunny weather and sweep it clean before storing it for any period of time. Sometimes the seams may be painted with a seam sealant, a urethane-base liquid generally sold with an applicator tip.
* Most backpackers carry about fifty feet of nylon cord. It has a thousand uses (more of them later) but comes in handy with tarps, flys, and tents.
* There is no proof that aluminum tent poles attract lightning, but in a lightning storm it is not a good idea to be in a tent pitched right under a tree.
* Zippered doorways can jam in bad weather. Anyway, whether under stars or ripstop nylon, sleep well.

THE WEATHER AND YOU

Even though weather patterns may vary according to the area where you live, here is a checklist for predicting and recognizing threatening weather. It is a good idea to watch or listen to local meteorologist's predictions of future weather patterns. And, you can always consult the National

Weather Service by phone; a 24-hour tape recording is available.

If TV weather shows have not fully trained you as an amateur meteorologist, here are some of the important weather terms and meanings:

Low Pressure Area — Denotes fall in barometer. Storm activity likely.

High Pressure Area — A rising or stable barometer reading, usually meaning fair weather.

Major Storm Fronts — Usually beginning in late fall persisting until early spring (may happen in summer also).

Direction of Winds That Carry Storm Fronts — West to East, following the earth's rotation.

Rapid Temperature Change — Denotes some type of weather change.

Humidity Characteristics — Low pressure; high humidity. High pressure; low humidity.

NATURAL SIGNS

Because backpackers rarely carry barometers or radios for up-to-date weather predictions, one must rely on her/his own senses for in-the-field predictions and weather preparedness. Here are some time-tested weather maxims. (An excellent article on this subject is **Weather's Rhymes and Reasons** by David A. Elder, Better Camping & Hiking. Woodhall Publishing Company, May, 1974.)

Red sky at night,
Sailor's delight.
Red sky at morning,
Sailors take warning.

This familiar poem tells part of the story. A light red or rosy pink sky with no clouds means fair weather. If a somber red sky is streaked with clouds, winds, and rain may follow. When the sun shines through a cloud, the more spectacular the red color is, the more moisture and dust particles it holds, thus rain may be near.

The United States Weather Bureau recognizes over forty different cloud types. The important clouds for backpackers to recognize are Cirrus, Cirrostratus, Nimbus and Cumulus. An encyclopedia is an excellent source for learning about these weathervane clouds.

THE BACKPACKER'S NATURAL BAROMETER

Indications of a lowering barometer or low pressure:

* **"It Smells Like Rain"** — Have you ever said this and known why? Plants do have ordors, and with the combination of higher humidity and lower pressure, these odors become more evident.

* **Low Flying Insects** — Their thin and fragile wings are dampened by higher humidity and moisture. Their flying ability is handicapped by lower air pressure.

* **Perched Birds** — Their flying ability is also affected by lower pressure, and they seem to be waiting out the storm.

* **Sounds** — Seem to be more audible owing to lower pressure and higher humidity.

* **Trailing the Smoke from a Campfire** — A handy proverb is near:

If smoke goes high,
No rain comes by.
If smoke hangs low,
Watch out for blow.

If a strong wind is not present, high pressure is prevalent and smoke of the fire will hold a definite high course. When the smoke hangs low, carbon particles of the smoke are dampened by high humidity making them fall to the ground much faster. When this happens, the smoke hangs in a low profile to the ground.

Natural wind changes usually occur only with fair weather patterns (up the canyon during the day and down at night). Sporadic wind changes, with no special pattern day or night, tell you a weather change is brewing.

The wind's direction follows no certain pattern during the day or night. Also, a constant wind blowing from the (North), then changing to (west), then (southwest) is another inclement weather indicator.

These "natural signs" give you time to seek shelter. Thunder and lightning are, of course, great broadcasters of storms. When you see lightning, start counting one Mississippi, two Mississippi, and so on. When thunder is heard, stop your counting. Then wait, Lightning again. Start counting. The lower the count becomes, the closer the storm. If the count becomes progressively higher, you are saved. The storm is moving away from you.

Lightning can be a swift killer. It is unwise to stay in an exposed area. If you are the tallest object around, you risk being struck. It is also hazardous to be on a mountain peak or near an exposed large rock in an electrical storm. You should avoid forests with large (tall) trees because taller trees may be in a frequent strike zone.

Caves may be excellent for shelter from rain, but are dangerous during lightning storms. Rocks carry an electrical surface charge when struck and you might become the least path of resistance for that charge.

If you are trapped in an electrical storm, "get low." Do not lay down (this only increases your surface area to the ground). A crouching position is best, supporting your body on the balls of your feet. If rain protection is needed, drape your poncho over yourself.

If you are in an exposed area (meadow, scree slope, or mountain peak), seek shelter as quickly as possible. (In a small grove of trees for instance). When sitting becomes necessary, sit on your Ensolite®pad, boots or some type of insulator, and if your hair and eyebrows stand straight up on end, run like hell. The static electricity around you is developing into an electrical charge or strike.

Food and Stoves

*The art of the stomach
and how to serve it.*

Chapter Seven

Controversy existing over various sleeping bag insulating materials is nothing compared with contradictory views on backpacking food and preparation. For example:

* An increasing number of backpackers do not believe in trail campfires feeling they are ecologically wasteful and not very practical, anyway. They revolt against backpacking books which judge the worth of a woodsperson by ability to start a fire in the dampest weather.
* Despite aspects of modern civilization implied by small, portable stoves, backpackers often prefer to carry a lightweight stove and extra fuel, not only for convenience, but so they will not have to forage for wood to build a huge campfire.
* Among young people especially, the vegetarian way of life is growing. Vegetarians reading a backpacking book find almost nothing applicable to their lifestyle, for authors recommend beef jerky, dried meats, tuna casseroles, stews, meat bars, and the like, without once questioning the carnivorous diet. If a meatless diet is mentioned by one of these writers on backpacking, it is often done in a patronizing, gratuitous way in a few flip paragraphs. (Yet one finds on the trails a surprisingly large number of vegetarian hikers who eat no flesh at all; this **generally** includes fish, but not always.)

Since this is a people's guide to the wilderness, I feel I can not **dictate** food items, but only **suggest** here and there. I try to consider the economy-minded backpacker, so a total recommendation of sometimes expensive freeze-dried foods would be elitist. As backpacker Bob Zeuner, a young attorney, recently observed after several days on Vermont's Long Trail: "You can always tell the well-to-do backpackers by their food: they have all sorts of freeze-dried foods and powdered eggs."

But backpacking attracts people who can not afford freeze-dried or dehydrated foods. What's more, it also attracts people who do not even think in terms of **purchasing** food, but who have grown much of their food, or find it off the land as the Indians did before supermarkets or mountain supply stores with a selection of lightweight trail foods were known. It is a great experience for more traditional backpackers to meet at campsite some of these "unconventional" nutritionists (who really are not unconventional at all since they are only returning to the way things were some years ago) and observe them eating curley dock weeds they've gathered in a swampy meadow en route, spreading on their homemade bread a mixture of sesame butter, peanut butter, honey, miso paste, and powdered milk. And their dessert — a few hunks of a pressed banana. Wonderful!

NUTRITION ON THE TRAIL

I sometimes wonder why writers of backpacking books feel they must sermonize about nutrition to their readers who may have survived to middle-age knowing nothing whatever of protein, fat, or carbohydrates. I find it sad that so many Americans know so little about nutrition and I am even more appalled at how little some hospitals and school dietitians know about food. No amount of lecturing here, however, will accomplish much. People who become genuinely interested in nutrition gravitate to the ever-growing number of books on nutrition or else they discuss food in cooperatives or health food stores and truly "get into foods." Once you are "into foods," you can appreciate how superficial the food sections of most backpacking books are, this one included. I can only touch a few high spots as a basis for further reading (notice I said **reading** — which implies enjoyment and self-motivation — rather than **study**).

Most people who have thought about it realize that a balanced diet is composed of protein, fat, and carbohydrates. The protein is needed for "staying" power and maintenance of body tissue. Examples of protein-rich foods are: meats, fish, cheese, milk, eggs, nuts. From a money point of view, the soybean is perhaps the most inexpensive form of protein, and peanut butter is not far behind.

Fat, less easily digested, is necessary, too. On the trail, margarine is better than butter, for it keeps longer and is often fortified with vitamins. (Not many years ago, before interest in cholesterol levels of the blood, margarine was thought of as a poor person's food while more expensive butter was for one who could affort "dairy fresh creamery butter." Now there are $90,000-a-year MD's who, even at posh restaurants, request margarine rather than butter for their croissants!)

Carbohydrates, more easily digested, are used for quick energy. Examples are: sugar, honey, jam, candy, fruits, cereals, and some grain products. Again, an expanding awareness of nutrition has forced a re-evaluation of carbohydrates, especially in athletic training camps. Cyclists, long-distance runners, and swimmers are having second-thoughts about sugar, and some nutritionists and dentists are questioning whether we need any extra sugar at all. (See, for example, "Sweet and Sour: The Sugar Menace," by John Pekkanen and Mathea Falco, **Atlantic Monthly**, July 1975.)

Ideally a trail diet consists of these basic elements. Too often foods of backpacking are selected **only** by weight, convenience, and packaging which may lead to an inadequate diet. In the same way, off-the-trail foods are often selected only on the basis of taste alone, leading also to an inadquate diet.

In a sedentary job, many people maintain their body weight on 1,800 calories daily. (Like most of my statements, this is an **average** figure useful in making an occasional point.) However, take this average person away from desk, counter, truck, or prowl-car and put him or her on the trail carrying 35 pounds over eight miles of ascending and descending trails and what happens? A daily intake of 3,000 to 5,000 calories may be needed to maintain the body weight. Now a question arises here: does one **want** to maintain body weight? One of the attractions of backpacking is that all the exercise tends to reduce spare tires, flabby stomachs, and too soft buttocks. If one goes into the woods twenty pounds overweight and doubles the caloric intake because of physical exertion, she or he may finish a two-week trip tipping the scales at exactly the same weight. I am not suggesting that maintaining on the trail the same daily caloric intake of 1800 calories is necessarily a good or wise thing. But it might be a consideration if one wants to lose weight backpacking.

Some backpackers think nothing of going into the woods for several days with little or no food whatever! They will live off body fat, or collect wild berries en route, or pass through a meadow where the milkweed pods are ready for plucking and boiling, or just come to camp and meditate or smoke something, not necessarily tobacco, before lying around under the stars. How can I tell such people they should take into the woods salami sticks, cheese spreads, Bisquick ®, chocolate bars, potato flakes, and Rice-A-Roni ®?

Naturally, one wants to avoid starvation or dehydration. Lost hikers have been so weakened by days without food or water (or "Fuel" to keep going) that they have not had the strength to follow a stream to civilization or build an adequate shelter and wait for a rescue party. One also wants to avoid any trail illness. This can come about all too easily if one shifts diets too strenuously, eating on the trail foods totally different from those eaten at home. Diarrhea is uncomfortable enough when one is traveling alone and can be downright embarrassing when hiking in a group. It also dehydrates the body rapidly.

INDIVIDUAL FOOD OR GROUP FEEDING?

Whenever one reads of a mountaineering expedition when numbers of people are involved, food is invariably in charge of one person, who, after consultation, works out food requirements for base camp, mountain assault, and return to civilization. Generally, bulk food supplies are portioned out for portage among individual climbers or sherpas and all members of the expedition eat basically the same foods. An especially fascinating account of food used on the successful conquest of Mount Everest in 1963 is contained in the chapter "Food" by Richard Pownall in **Americans on Everest** (by James Ramsey Ullman and others, J.B. Lippincott, 1964). Even on this expedition, special consideration was given to the sherpa diet which differed somewhat from the regulation diet of expedition members from the United States of America. At high altitudes on this expedition, weight of food and calorie intake held precedence over pure foods of choice. Moreover, experience in previous expeditions showed that above certain heights, climbers' appetites underwent decided deterioration — sometimes no fatty foods could be tolerated, occasionally someone craved some exotic food. On that expedition, for example, Jim Whittaker, who now runs Recreational Equipment Inc., in Seattle (mountaineering equipment retailer and publisher of Harvey Manning's Backpacking: **One Step at a Time**, had a craving for tossed green salads among all the snow and bitter cold at Camp VI, high above the South Col. (For a partial list of food carried on this expedition, see Chapter 10, page 177.)

Obviously food needs for ordinary backpackers out to enjoy the wilderness experience are not similar to such an expedition, yet certain parallels do exist, especially the question of whether on a group hike individuals are to carry their own food, or whether food is going to be shared. There are obvious advantages either way. While it makes little sense to have six or seven people all preparing different foods at a campsite, neither is it sensible to determine that bacon will be served at breakfast and beef stew at night if several vegetarians are along. Such situations make me hesitant to assert dogmatically that food should be scheduled for a group, then broken down and packaged for carry. **Normally**, this is a good idea, with the inevitable compromises that must be made along the way. A white bread eater, for example, might not like the idea of all those loaves of Laughing Mountain Pumpernickel bread, and a Corn Flakes freak might never have eaten Alpen ® or Familia ® cereals.

In any event, about 4,000 to 5,500 calories per day should be allowed each person to be on the safe side. Many foods need to be repackaged to reduce volume, spoilage, and weight. Since cardboard boxes easily split on the trail, such items may be packaged in plastic bags. Hardly anyone except inexperienced hikers carry glass containers today, yet since there is an exception to every rule, I must mention Joe Holloway, owner of a health food store and an experienced hiker both in Japan and the United States, who always carries along a jar of honey well-wrapped in extra socks!

STOCK SUGGESTIONS!

Unless you prefer to live off the land, it should be possible to buy most of your trail needs at local grocery markets. Here are some ordinary store items which might be useful on the trail:

Various dried soups (Knorr ® and Lipton ® are two well-known
trade names); Bouillon cubes, veg broth
Potato flakes
Rice-A-Roni ®
Biscuits, Stoned Wheat Thins ®
Noodles, Spaghetti, Macaroni, Rye Crisp ®, Graham Crackers
Cheese
Powdered Milk
Beef Sticks
Salami Sticks
Instant Coffee; Cocoa; Tea
Fruit Sticks; Candy Bars
Raisins and other dried fruits
Powdered Fruit Drinks
Bisquick ®

Basic requirements for trail food would seem to be: not bulky, lightweight, easy to prepare, easily digested, nutritious, and tasty.

If it were not for the weight, canned goods might be ideal on the trail. After all, all one need do is heat up an already cooked canned stew and **voila** — a hot meal is ready. Unfortunately, canned goods have a number of disadvantages:

* Often they are heavy, containing a good deal of water.

* The cans do not compost and should be carried out of the woods again. (No fun with sharp edges and lids.) Buried cans will be dug up by animals.
* Cans are bulky, take up much space for content delivered.

Nonetheless, canned goods **are** convenient and occasionally on a simple, short overnight trip when a large quantity of food will not be carried, canned goods might be useful. I have seen experienced backpackers occasionally carry a tin of sardines or Nova Scotia kippered herring. Some brands of peanut butter come in cans. Peanut butter is not lightweight but packs a powerful protein wallop.

Glassware is not practical. Items which frequently come in glass containers should be repackaged, perhaps into plastic containers.

A health-food store offers more variety of foods for backpacking per square foot than any supermarket. Here one will find natural breads — in other words, breads made with stoneground whole wheat flour, soy flour, honey, cold-pressed vegetable oils, sea salt, and yeast. There are likely to be loaves of real Pumpernickel bread. Dar-Vida ®, a Swiss whole wheat bread and sourdough ryes are excellent. Here, too, ready to be repackaged, will be such things as sesame butter. A fine spread for bread can be made of sesame butter, powdered milk, and miso paste, sometimes called soybean puree. Miso has keeping power, is enormously rich in protein, forms an excellent base for soups, and is widely consumed by the Japanese in a variety of foods.

Who knows where the word **Gorp** comes from? Someone tells me it means "God-awful raisins and peanuts." Perhaps. At any rate gorp is carried by many hikers. Depending on one's taste, it seems to be a mixture of nuts, dried fruit, raisins, sometimes sunflower seeds. A few hikers put in M & M's ® ; other hikers consider candy and sugar to be dangerous foods, so nobody has a monopoly on what constitutes gorp. Since I live near the almond country of California, I think the almond belongs in gorp. Others like peanuts, salted soy nuts, Spanish peanuts, cashews, walnuts, pinenute, carob-chips, pumpkin and squash seeds.

A visit to a health-food store (perhaps one day all grocery stores will be oriented toward health, but I do not think I shall live that long!) will turn up many trail items. Offhand, I would mention these:

Dried coconut — May be used in dozens of ways, eminently portable.

Chia seeds — Eaten by American Indians years ago, still nutritious today. Small seeds, can be mixed with a variety of things, used as a cereal topping.

Honey in plastic containers — Several firms, including Paradise Valley Honey Co., Paradise Valley, Nevada 89114, package honey in plastic containers. Paradise Valley's honey is called Warm Gold. Unfortunately, it is expensive, but the container may be used again and again.

Soybean miso paste — Has a variety of uses, some already mentioned in connection with spreads for bread. Salty, so must be used sparingly. Can be mixed with chick peas. Some say it is an acquired taste.

Pero ® — An instant cereal beverage made from roasted and ground malted barley, chicory, rye, and molasses and manufactured by Unifranck, Ludwigsburg, Germany. (This product is somewhat similar to Postum ®, which contains wheat and bran.(The Pero ® cardboard containers with their metal screw-on tops, incidentally, are ideal to save as they make excellent lightweight containers for all sorts of foods.)

Dar-Vida ®. A nutritious Swiss whole wheat bread.

Roastaroma ® — A no-caffeine beverage for the trail. (Celestial Seasonings, Boulder, Colorado)

Bulgar wheat — A mixture of bulgar wheat with soy grits (10 parts bulgar wheat to 1 part soy grits) makes an ideal cereal-type food. With a mixture 1½ times solid to water, boil the combination, serve with honey, reconstituted milk — or mix in a powdered milk with the wheat and soy grits combination. This is a highly nutritious meal as the wheat and soy grits complement one another.

Backpack dinners — They are excellent! Made by Earth Wonder Inc. Blue Eye, Missouri, and Natural Food Backpacking Dinners, Corvallis, Oregon. Some examples: Hearty lentil soup mix, split pea-barley soup and Millet Stew.

Herbs — Many backpackers take along onion flakes, tarragon, oregano, and other spices. No reason a trail meal must be bland.

In the easily-carried paperback book **Recipes for a Small Planet** (Ellen Buchman Ewald, Ballatine Books, 1973) eight pages are devoted to lightweight, compact backpacking foods which avoid meats. Since little vegetarian food is available in freeze-dried form, the backpackers writing the section created their own simple basic foods and carried along small mixtures of spices to add flavor. Their method of operation — and one I do recommend — is to spend time at home preparing and packaging trail items with a view toward maximum usable protein — without neglecting flavor. For instance, if carrying raw brown rice (and entire Asian armies have existed for months on rice) they mix in soy grits before their plastic-bag packaging. Into granola or Familia ® (that marvelous Swiss cereal), they mix powdered milk so only hot water need be added out in the wilderness. Their weight parameters: 10 days of food for 2 people weighs in at 40 to 45 pounds. These backpackers feel that a meat-centered diet squanders the earth's resources and take as their text a sensible book by Frances Moore Lappe **Diet for a Small Planet.**

Some backpackers who are essentially in agreement with the Lappe philosophy, nonetheless, have reservations about rice on the trail. Any rice except so-called "minute rice" takes a long time to cook (unless one uses an ungainly pressure cooker) and may be impractical and wasteful of fuel.

Here are some suggested food items mentioned in the Ewald book:

Rolled grains-rye, wheat, bulgar, triticale
Raw brown rice with soy grits
Bulgar wheat or cracked wheat mixed with soy grits
Dehydrated potato flakes or macaroni with cheese and milk powder
Small beans like lentils, split peas, and mung beans which cook
    quickly
Grated parmesan cheese for various dishes, pasta, and the like
Hard cheese
Whole protein bread
Beanspred
Instant oatmeal
Protein cookies
Nuts; also mixed nuts and sunflower seeds
Dried fruit of all sorts

Finally, here is a typical on-the-trail lunch from the backpacking section of **Recipes for a Small Planet:**

Cheese and bread, dried fruit or protein cookies, peanut butter
and honey and (on the first day out) hard-boiled eggs.

Of course many foods are impractical on the trail because of spoilage problems. This is especially true of meat. But unless the weather is excessively hot or there are desert conditions, one can often use such items the first or second day. Thus, one sees people grilling hamburgers or sausages the first evening out or frying bacon the first morning. Some backpackers prefer an easy first-day's hike and a really sumptuous supper with special treats and perishable items which could never last beyond a day or two. One sees "first nighters" enjoying, with wine, fresh salads, corn on the cob (not too practical from a weight point of view, but probably fun, especially if the first night's camp is not a distant hike), fresh meats and cold cuts.

Sometimes these fresh salads can be enlivened by wild greens gathered on the hike in. Surely many backpackers are by now familiar with Euell Gibbons' book **Stalking the Wild Asparagus** (David McKay, 1962) in which he says: "A knowledge of wild food gathering can contribute greatly to our enjoyment of this back-to-nature movement. It can add new meanings to every camping trip." Gibbons mentions blackberries, crab apples, purslane, various sprouts, roots, and seeds. Many wild plants are sketched in the book so one can learn to identify them. As Gibbons points out, the American Indian foraged for food, found much to eat in fields, meadows, and along riverbanks. Arrowleaf, in fact, was the chief vegetable food of the Indian.

Such a philosophy — that food can be found in the wilderness — is fine, but I have four reservations: (1) One has to know what one is doing, as there are poisonous plants, especially mushrooms. (2) Many of Gibbons' foods are not prevalent in the mountains and dense forests, which are not good foraging places, but in woodlots, old fields, abandoned farms. (Every now and then, Vermont's Long Trail leaves the deep forest to cross some thirty-acre backwoods abandoned farm, for example, just south of Wallingford, Vermont, but otherwise you're out of luck.) This leads me to my third reservation: (3) Much of this food requires extensive cooking or boiling. Even simple milkweed pods. which I love to eat, requires several changes of boiling water to remove a slightly unpleasant taste. And, lastly, and most importantly (4) Excessive use of wild food will be as devastating to the countryside as deliberate destruction.

I do offer Gibbons' philosophy, however, to backpackers since a basic knowledge of wild foods can save a life. About thirty years ago a group of Boy Scouts were hiking on Mt. Katahdin in Maine. (This superb mountain has a distinction: its summit is the first place in the United States of America to receive the rays of the morning sun.) One of the Scouts became separated from the others. Search parties went out for days looking in vain for the lost hiker. More than a week went by and newspaper writers for the Boston papers which had been headlining the story of a lost Scout in the wilderness began to leave nearby Millinocket and return to Boston, for surely nobody could survive long in that "rugged" (a favorite newspaper word for almost **any** wilderness) terrain. But, incredibly, when most of the search parties had given up hope, the Scout emerged from the woods almost two weeks later. He had some insect bites, had lost a little clothing, but was otherwise all right: he had existed on stream water, wild foods and berries; he had never panicked and had followed a stream in its downhill run knowing that eventually it **had** to lead to a larger stream and civilization. The Scout was, in fact, so healthy upon his self-rescue that there were doubters who simply could not believe his story. I am not one of the doubters, needless to say.

I mention this story for there may be those who feel the Euell Gibbons approach to wild foods is totally impractical for backpackers, yet even a rudimentary knowledge of lichen, berries, and wood plants might well save a life. We are so accustomed to living off a supermarket that the concept of living off the land is alien to us — just as the supermaket was alien to American Indians.

FOOD ODDS AND ENDS

Before we move along to campfires and stoves, here are a few odds and ends:

* Dehydrated foods require cooking while freeze dried items require no cooking. You simply add hot water. Both are ideal trail foods because they eliminate water, the main component of food. However, they are somewhat costly. I have noticed that after eating these types of foods on a regular basis one can suffer from gas pains.
* Vitamin supplements on the trail are acceptable. Nowadays, nobody kids the hiker who insists on taking a 500 mg. tablet of natural Vitamin C rose hips three times a day. There have been so many studies extolling vitamin supplements that one just can not make hasty judgments.
* In hot weather, when sweating occurs, salt tablets may be beneficial, but I would think kelp tablets would be better. A 6.5 gr. kelp tablet (if you're not allergic to kelp) would supply more than the daily requirement of iodine. Potassium is also another body chemical that needs replacing after sweating. Dorancid is suggested. (Banana chips are a good source — as are dried apples.)
* Toasted wheat germ with dried fruits makes a nice trail snack. Dried prunes can be snipped and mixed with dried apricots. Bran Flakes can be added.
* A person who is addicted to fast-food outlets (in other words, a McDonald's, Burger King, or Kentucky Fried Chicken freak) is going to have an enormous adjustment to on-the-trail eating, whereas, a person who often eats so-called trail foods at home (as many health food aficionadoes do) is going to have almost no adjustment to backpacking foods. Any drastic change in diet can bring on problems, but I think the health-food person moving to fast-foods would be in more trouble than the fast-fooder moving to health foods.
* European dried cereals (especially Familia ® but also Alpen ®) are probably ounce-for-ounce better than heavily sugared American cereals, although this is a debatable point. I suggest you spend a little time in the cereal section of a supermarket reading ingredients on boxes. Most supermarkets carry Alpen ® since it is now distributed by Colgate-Palmolive Company, whereas, Familia ® is principally sold in health food stores. Familia ® has been a standby for hikes in the European Alps for many years.
* Some backpackers don't believe in meals **per se**, prefer to nibble throughout the day. Who am I to argue with them?
* The process of dehydrating foods is a well established custom. Freeze-drying is a newer, different process which involves removing water by drawing off ice crystals in a vacuum. Freeze-dried foods are especially good at high altitudes where cooking takes a longer time.
* Carbohydrates give immediate energy, but don't have much staying power, so be sure to get protein at every meal. Athletes who once

thought only of exercising, now are getting interested in protein intake. Several protein powders sold in health food stores make an ideal supplement; often they can be mixed into a nutritious and palatable drink. Brewers yeast is an excellent source of protein also.

* Be careful to maintain a good liquid intake while backpacking. This is so important I probably should repeat it in bold letters: BE CAREFUL TO MAINTAIN A GOOD LIQUID INTAKE WHILE BACKPACKING. True, too much water can sometimes slow one down — which is why soccer and football players don't drink copious quantities of water during a game — but if I had to choose between to little liquid intake or too much, I would choose too much. A vagueness, a foggy outlook can result from too little water in the body. Ultimately, dehydration can occur.

* In some cities — especially San Francisco — a "Chinatown" exists where grocery stores sell much more than chow mein. Many Chinese vegetables and soups are ideal for the trail.

* L.D.S. food storage stores are a good source of backpacking food. The wide variety of dried and otherwise easily portable foods available there have to be seen to be believed.

* On several occasions I have seen popcorn made out in the wilderness. It might be served as a dessert for those who insist on a final course. A chocolate (or better yet, a carob bar) eaten just before sleeping may assist the body in generating heat to keep warm. Carob avoids caffein which is contained in chocolate and some nutritionists feel chocolate mixed with milk harms the milk so that chocolate milk is not beneficial. I do not want to enter this dispute except to say that I have developed a taste for carob bars. Halvah is also a tasty, popular dessert or bedtime snack.

* Some people take with them an emergency food ration in case they are lost or must spend unexpected time in the woods due to weather or an accident.

* A recent product on the market is Morningstar meat-like products which contain no animal fats — in other words, no animal flesh. These look alike ham slices and sausages are made of vegetable protein, are not so perishable as meat, and are rich in protein. Some vegetarians are turned off by their similarity to flesh foods, but carnivores may find them a good meat substitute. In fact, with the high price of meat, textured vegetable protein products which resemble meat products are becoming more popular. Among them: vegetable patties which resemble hamburger, even a lookalike bacon. As these products become distributed by national companies into regular supermarkets (as, for example, Morningstar) the price becomes competitive.

* Why not go Italian one night (pastas, noodles, and macaroni are ideal on the trail), Chinese another night? Bamboo shoots anyone? I am serious, for these two national cuisines are both adaptable to the trail.

* In some ways, a main meal at night makes a lot of sense — one has something to do (all that meal preparation) in place of watching the evening news on TV. Yet, in many ways, a heavy meal at night is not sensible. In some cultures, the main meal is eaten at noon, followed by a siesta; then a work period in which some of the luncheon calories are burned off. Some backpackers prefer to do their daily hiking in two distinct segments: an early morning start, stretching up to a long, leisurely on-the-trail noon meal and rest followed by an after-noon hike ending somewhere just before dusk — in time to make camp, have a light meal, and turn in for the night along with the birds.

* One frequently reads of **pemmican** (see Chapter 10 for recipe) in stories of various expeditions, especially to the North and South Poles. Pemmican can be made at home, but it also can be purchased. It makes a highly-condensed, non-perishable food item; also, for its weight, an ideal emergency ration.

* Some writers on backpacking say that alcohol has no place on the trail. I do not want to be **that** emphatic. General Adolphus Greely's **Three Years of Arctic Service** noted that in the Lady Franklin Bay Expedition of 1881-1884, the General took along one hundred gallons of New England rum! "The influence of the liquor was undoubtedly beneficial, as it invariably tended to enliven the spirits and increase the cheerfulness of the men," wrote General Greely. He added a medical opinion: spirituous liquors may be of great use in small and moderate quantities, but exceedingly mischievous and pernicious in excess. On arrival in an Austrian Alpine hut, one may be served a **schnapps** made from the gentian flower. Neither will I sermonize about marijuana on the trail, but I would be less than honest if I did not confess I have seen more than one group contentedly sharing this weed out in the wilderness in the dusk of twilight. Of the two — alcohol and marijuana — there is no question which one is more portable, nor is there a question of which one is (at this writing, anyway) more legal!

* A variety of containers (plastic and aluminum) to transport foods are sold in mountaineering stores — even fancy gadgets for carrying eggs. Often with a little imagination one can do as well by saving certain food containers. For example, baking powder often comes in an easy-to-reclose can which can be used again and again for various foods. I have already mentioned the cardboard and aluminum Pero ® instant cereal container which can be recycled. A 35mm film container is excellent for condiments. The other day in a discount

store I saw small, sample-sized plastic containers of mouthwash for sale. Even containing the mouthwash, the plastic bottles with screw tops were cheaper than the similar plastic bottles purchased at a mountaineering store. Please do not misunderstand me: I am not knocking mountaineering supply stores. They offer freeze-dried foods, down sleeping bags, tents, long contour packframes — in other words, the very best to make backpacking truly a comfortable experience. If money were no object — and it **is** no object for many people — a camping supply store is ideal for **all** one's needs including food, shelter, bedding, clothing, footware — in truth, all one's needs are offered in such a store. However, there have been lots of articles recently which have stated that backpacking, like skiing, is essentially a middle-class or upper-class recreation and I feel this is emphatically not true. Consequently, I go out of my way from time to time to mention inexpensive substitutes for those who can not buy everything new in a camping store. Let us face it: there are many hikers who would not dream of using an old Rumford Baking Powder can to carry corn for popping, with a piece of masking tape reading "Corn for Popping" pressed over the words **Baking Powder.** But there are others who cannot imagine their budgets including the purchase of new containers when supermarkets are filled with containerized, overly-packaged goods.

One last comment on plastic bottles, make sure that you keep them aired out between trips. This cuts down on the "bottle odor" that can be smelled inside many a plastic bottle.

* I have already mentioned the necessity of daily water to avoid dehydration. Often guide books to trails (for example, the Sierra Club in San Francisco publishes a series of trail guidebooks, as does the Appalachian Mountain Club in Boston) tell where one may find water on the trail, whether spring or stream, and whether the water is likely to be good or not. There simply are no sure way of determining water purity short of laboratory tests. Sometimes water from a small spring may be better than water from a moving stream, although I think a cascading, rushing mountain stream would be **likely** to have excellent water — unless there are campers upstream who are throwing away their debris into the stream.

* A Chicago drug firm (Abbott Labs.) makes Halazone ® tablets for water purification. If in doubt a Halazone ® tablet may be dropped into a canteen of water — a tablet for a pint might be sufficient. However, Halazone ® Harris lived briefly in Mexico, he found out that one could lived briefly in Mexico, he found out that one could still catch hepatitis from drinking water which had been treated with

Halazone ® tablets. Iodine tablets leave a taste in water but are still more effective than Halazone.®

* Boiling water makes it safe, but ten minutes of boiling may use up a lot of fuel. At high altitudes, of course, boiling of water takes longer. Above 10,000 feet boiling is usually ineffective.

* There is a delicate balance between carrying too much water and too little. I have seen Boy Scouts all carrying what appears to be full canteens of water yet they are hardly ever out of hearing from a rushing mountain stream. The thought of all that weight being carried (in metal canteens, now almost passe) bothered me. Yet the other extreme is worse: a guidebook may indicate in advance that there are springs along the trail, so little or no water is carried. Then the hiker either cannot locate the springs (which are often slightly off a trail) or finds them inoperative. Or the streams have dried up — so it turns into a long, dry, waterless hike.

* Water is best carried in a lightweight plastic canteen. Some people complain water picks up the plastic taste, but I do not think it is noticeable expecially if the containers have been aired between use. Again, as with food containers, a budget backpacker can often find a suitable plastic container, even if it is a washed-out plastic bottle which originally contained Vermont Maid Syrup ® or an eight-ounce baby bottle.

* Children will often eat out in the wilderness foods they would not dream of touching at home. Perhaps it has something to do with the woodsy atmosphere and their spirit of adventure. However, two child-approved items are ideal on the trail: peanut butter and jam sandwiches. Don't laugh: a grilled cheese sandwich is easy to make on a backpacking trip and is an excellent food source.

* Some people who are great organizers like to plan all trail meals in advance, just as some househusbands and housewives like to plan a week's meals ahead of time. I have seen other backpackers who carry plenty of food and just play it by ear. Often they make out just as well. Generally, most backpackers like to have a simple breakfast which can be prepared in a short time (because mountain mornings are often nippy); others, used to a leisurely, full breakfast at home, like to continue the practice on the trail. Hiking in the early morning in the summer, of course, has an advantage: it is often a cooler time of day. Especially in desert country, mid-day heat can be enervating.

* Items like Rice-A-Roni ® (an 8 oz. package is supposed to produce six ½-cup servings) seem ideally packaged in the store, but cardboard can split in a well-filled pack. Most sensible backpackers do a lot of advance repackaging at home. Thus, Rice-A-Roni ® goes into a

polyethelene bag for lighter weight, less bulk, and strength. You may want to tear off the cooking directions from the box and insert into the plastic bag — and hope cooked cardboard does not end up in one of those six servings!

* Much has been written about the drinking cup. A certain cup known as the Sierra Cup (10 oz., stainless steel) is even something of a status symbol. Any cup will do.

* An ordinary 8 oz. baby bottle will be excellent for measuring amounts, and it has many other uses.

* In portioning food and cooking utensils among a group of hikers, avoid giving one person utensils and no food. Ideally, each person should be carrying some food in the event he or she becomes separated from the group.

* I like to tell people that for a group trip, the planning should start eight weeks before the trip and the food should be packaged and weighed a week before the trip, but for some, even such simple suggestions smack of regimentation. However, on a major hike I think an eight-week headstart with a practice hike thrown in is not a bad idea.

* It has been said that teenage boys have the greatest appetites, followed by men, women, teenage girls, and children in that order. Frankly, I do not know whether this is true or not or even what validity it has in food planning. Appetite and metabolism have always seemed to me highly individual things, having little relationship to sex or age, but I am willing to be corrected.

* On a group trip, the ideal weight per person per day might be 1½ to 2 pounds. Backpacking books always seem to state without question that men carry one-third their weight, women one-fourth their weight, and children one-fourth of their weight. Frankly, I think these "truths" handed down like holy writ may well be questioned. I am sure that mountaineer Ruth Rudner would question this. And Miriam Underhill recalls in her **Give Me the Hills** how patronizing men climbers were about the ability of women to carry loads, scale cliffs, and endure the elements. So many of these often-repeated assertions may be folklore, no more than myths. I do not, you will notice, present them here as **facts**, but simply as often-repeated assertions which might well be questioned.

* **Ideally,** water should be drunk frequently in small amounts. Of course this is not always possible.

* It is wise not to eat when exhausted. It might be better to have bouillon or tea or a cereal drink like Pero®, then later have a meal.

* The tortillas, a mainstay of the Mexican diet, is a food which is not too perishable and can be prepared on the trail.

TO COOK OR NOT TO COOK

Almost without exception backpacking books automatically assume meals will be cooked. As I have indicated already, it is possible to spend a week in the woods without doing any cooking whatever, and many of the foods I have mentioned are quite nutritious — even tasty — yet do not need to be cooked. Naturally, a person used to hot meals all the time is going to expect hot meals on the trail even if it means carrying a portable stove, fuel and cooking utensils.

So, before I automatically assume you'll be cooking in the wilderness, I want to make it clear that cookless backpacking is not only a possibility, but a sensible reality. Increasing numbers of backpackers munch their way along trails on bread, cheese, gorp, dried fruits, cereals, peanut butter, biscuits, wild berries, banana bars, coconut, sunflower seeds, salted soy seeds, carob bars, and so forth. I know a very literate backpacker who eats this way and with the weight saved (all those pots and pans, pot scraper, stove and fuel) carries instead paperback books. While everyone is fussing around trying to light a Svea stove, she is reading Anais Nin, munching gorp or eating a sandwich of whole wheat bread, sesame butter, and miso. Frankly, there is a lot less cooking going on in the wilderness today than there once was though a stove can brew welcome hot liquids in chilly fall and winter months. On a two or three day hike, even a person used to hot meals may welcome the saving in pack weight necessitated by cooking.

THE FRIENDLY CAMPFIRE

For years backpacking was associated with a roaring campfire. After a day's hike, one pitched a tent or stretched out sleeping bags in a lean-to and then immediately searched for wood. Many a backpacker carried a belt hatchet; others carried an axe or a small saw into the woods. Soon a wood-devouring campfire would be underway, almost as though it were a ritual, a necessary part of backpacking. Isn't this what one comes for — the blazing fire in the middle of the woods, the snapping of burning wood, flames licking along pine or birch logs?

Naturally, the campfire was used for cooking. Huge pots were suspended above the fire and Scouts roasted marshmallows and hot dogs in the open flames. But the campfire was more than blackened pans and pots of stew: it was central to the wilderness experience. Backpackers sang around the fire, or told ghost stories, or played the harmonica (probably the most portable musical instrument of all). Facing the fire, face and chest could seem scorched while the back could be chilly, but it did not matter: the campfire mystique prevailed. From starting the fire (sometimes without matches) through blazing inferno to dying embers, the campfire was as much a part of backpacking as boots, knapsack, compass. No trip, even on the desert, seemed complete without a campfire. Wasn't this the way pioneers lived long before Coleman ® stoves had been invented?

Naturally, it followed that backpacking books were filled with advice on how to build a campfire and what woods to burn. Scout manuals advised scouts how to rub two sticks together and get a spark which would ignite tinder and eventually produce the desired blaze. Writers told how to strip saplings to suspend pots; the green wood, they pointed out, wasn't likely to burn as easily. And every book warned: be sure your campfire is out when you break camp.

Nowadays some books are still filled with this campfire lore, but most outdoors writers have had their consciousness raised. Not only did the campfire sometimes start a forest fire, it used up so much wood that commonly used campsites looked positively denuded. Builders of fires who once got their fall-down wood a few yards from a lean-to found themselves foraging with axe deeper into the woods. for every available **stick** near the campsite had long been burned up. The President of the Smoky Mountain Hiking Club recently described a trail shelter on Mt. Le Conte as "so littered, over-used, and trammeled that it is very depressing to visit and see the gross abuse natural beauty has suffered." Art Harris can attest to the devastation wrought at two of his favorite places in the East: Hermit Lake at the base of Mt. Washington's Tuckerman Ravine and the Chimney Pond area of Maine's Mount Katahdin, northern terminus of the Appalachian Trail. As recently as 1961, the guidebook to this area of Maine wilderness advised campers that "Firewood may be obtained from the forest; only dead trees may be cut."

Today, all this has changed, not only at Chimney Pond and Hermit Lake, but in national forests all over the United States of America and in Canada. At first, one had to obtain a campfire permit from a ranger. Now, in most forests, campfires are banned altogether. They just did too much ecological damage in a small concentrated area, turning a woody campsite into a blackened, open "wilderness slum." In this ecological age, the campfire has gone the way of the pine bough bed. Yes, on beaches sometimes driftwood will be turned into a campfire, but a campfire was never that efficient anyway: it blackened pots and made a lot of work either cleaning pots or cleaning whatever the blackened pots came in contact with; there was no easy way to regulate the flame and much of the time the fire was flat out; in rainy weather hours could be spent nursing a fire along, drying wood, and trying to get water to boil amid smouldering wood; smoke not only lofted skyward (leading firetower observers to believe a forest fire was underway), but, with windshifts, blew into the face of backpackers; there were accidents with sheath knives and axes; there was often an interminable wait upon setting up camp before the first bubbles of boiling water emerged from a suspended pot for tea or bouillon; there was no easy way to brew a simple cup of tea or Pero® at lunchtime because fire building was such a project; arriving tired, wet and cold at a campsite meant an immediate major effort: hunting for wood and getting a fire going when one was tired and just wanted to relax and have some hot chocolate. And there were also several major forest fires which started from dying embers left behind by backpackers. True, some forest fires have been beneficial to forest life, but many have not — especially those which got out of control and burned homes, logging camps, and hunting lodges.

Now, as a result of outright bans on campfire in some places, as well as environmental considerations, such fires are almost passe today. Somehow, backpackers have found that the wilderness night can be enjoyed without a massive blaze of wood. They have even taken to hiking with foods that need no cooking. But the major change has been the widespread use among ordinary backpackers of what has been for years a standard mountain expedition piece of equipment: the lightweight stove.

PORTABLE STOVES

The small, portable, lightweight stove fueled by kerosene or white gasoline has long been a part of climbing expeditions. With it, one could brew hot tea or soup during a brief lunch stop, cook inside a tent, or cook far above timber line where no wood for a campfire existed. Weighing around a pound (a few over two pounds), the stove functioned in the rain, at high altitudes, and (with a proper windscreen) in gale force winds.

Once used exclusively by trained climbers, these lightweight stoves began to be attractive to backpackers who neither wanted to build a campfire nor consume a non-cooked diet. Before long the Primus 71-L, formerly seen on the ridges of Annapurna, was a familiar sight in the Cascades, the Smokies, the Green Mountains. In a word, backpackers had discovered the enormous convenience of carrying their own lightweight stove — even if the mere idea seemed contradictory with the back-to-nature movement. There was, they admitted, a certain irony in abandoning the campfire and bringing into the woods a metal stove imported from Sweden, along with a supply of white gas or kerosene, but what convenience! And no need to carry an axe and strip the woods.

Today stoves are carried by walkers of all sorts who have found that a wilderness campsite at night can be ever more enjoyable without a blazing fire at the central point. Now, with supper easily cooked over the stove, they rest afterwards, aware for the first time of night noises, the dark and soothing quiet of the woods. A new esthetic experience has replaced the once venerated campfire. Besides, most people are used to cooking on a stove and are unfamiliar with cooking over a campfire.

We can dismiss rather quickly several stoves which are not truly suited to backpacking and move along to the endless debate over various stoves and fuel. Sterno stoves are not practical because of their weight and the long time it takes to get any real heat. Heat tablets fall into the same category. A pure alcohol stove, such as one sometimes sees in fancy restaurants were there is tableside cooking, is quite safe, but not really very efficient. A new "Zip Ztove" which is designed to burn charcoal, twigs, or pine cones is lightweight (14 oz.) but uses batteries (which do not function well at low temperatures), has geographical limitations (what about finding fuel in the desert or above timberline?), and above all disturbs the natural floor of the forest, for in some ways pine needles and cones are more important to the ecological chain than downed woods. Needles, of course, protect the young trees and pine cones hold the seeds.

Thus, we are left with portable stoves which burn the following fuels: kerosene, white gasoline, butane, and propane.

Of these fuels, butane and propane are the most convenient. Stoves using these fuels start instantly and can be restarted with no problems. There is no messy pouring of gasoline or kerosene, no flasks of fuel, no worrying about pressure build up — and almost no danger. True, there are **disadvantages** which we shall discuss on page 108, but many backpackers who find kerosene and white gas stoves somewhat temperamental (they **can** be difficult to start) endure the disadvantages of cartridge stoves because of their convenience. I know when I acquired my first Bleuet, I was astonished at its simplicity. I could take it out of my pack, turn a valve, light a match, and have water boiling withing ten minutes for a trailside cup of tea. Only later on did I learn to balance its great convenience with some of its shortcomings.

Kerosene is a widely available fuel. In fact, it is obtainable in all parts of the world, even in places where white gasoline might not be available, although white, unleaded gasoline is fairly common now in the United States of America and Canada. Gasoline stoves are generally prohibited on small boats, but kerosene, which is not nearly as volatile, is regarded as a relatively safe fuel for the galley of a schooner. It will not explode as easily as gasoline will, having a higher flash point. (An eighty-person mountain hut in the Eastern mountains was burned down when a member of the hut crew was transferring gasoline for a generator from one container to

107

another; the gasoline somehow exploded and in no time the entire mountain hut was swept by gasoline-fed flames.) Kerosene, at this writing anyway, is still one of the cheaper fuels, while gasoline prices, at least in the U.S., Canada, and Mexico are rising sharply.

In backpacking stoves, kerosene is burned in its vaporized state unlike traditional kerosene stoves with a wick. So these stoves require some sort of priming, usually from alcohol or an alcohol paste. Untreated kerosene is more smelly than white gas, but because of its safety margin **vis a vis** white gasoline, it is favored by some backpackers who would not dream of owning a white gasoline stove. It also is effective at high altitudes and low temperatures.

White gasoline is more explosive, more volatile than kerosene. This very quality makes it handy for backpacking stoves which tend to ignite more easily and seldom need (as kerosene stoves sometimes do) **pumping** to help fuel get to the burner. Gasoline is a cleaner fuel, too; pots don't blacken up as they do with a wood fire and as they sometimes do (to a lesser extent) with kerosene. The fuel does not smell; if you spill a little on your sleeping bag, for example, it almost acts as an odorless dry cleaner. For its weight, white gasoline is an enormously efficient heat source.

In many ways, the white gasoline stoves are easier to ignite, for one can use a tiny bit of the white gas fuel itself for priming. If you have ever noticed on a list of backpacker "must carry" items the word eye-dropper and wondered why one would carry an eye-dropper into the woods, let me explain: with an eye-dropper, one can extract a few drops of fuel from the tank of the white gas stove, set it afire atop the stove and soon generate enough heat so pressure problems are taken care of; then the white gas is ready to burn. Open the valve at the right moment and the white gas, in its vaporized form, burns. In other words, a white gas stove is easier to start than a kerosene stove — though neither fuel is as convenient in starting as butane or propane. White gas, however, is in many ways a dangerous fuel and there have been accidents not only on the trail, but in transporting the fuel, pouring it from one container to another, and so on.

Now all these portable stoves, whether fired by butane, white gasoline, or kerosene, have certain disadvantages: when cooking in a group, the stove is often too small for the amount of food involved. Neither is it practical to place a very large pot on top of the small stoves; in fact, such a procedure can send heat back into the stove causing dangerous overheating.

Without exception, these portable stoves come with detailed directions on starting, maintaining, and repairing. Often these directions are printed in four or five languages, so it would not serve much of a purpose here to go into excessive detail on the mechanical operation of these stoves unless one acquired a second-hand stove with no directions. What is more, each stove seems to have its own characteristics and blanket instructions would not be all-encompassing. One or two general observations may be made for white gas stoves, currently popular — although butane stoves are increasing their share of the market:

STARTING A WHITE GASOLINE STOVE:

Be sure stove is level and valve is off. With an eye dropper, extract some gasoline from the tank and immediately replace cap and screw it on tightly. **Then** squeeze some gasoline from the eye dropper into the so-called "spirit cup" **below** the burner head. Light this gasoline and let it burn. Use ribon or optimus gel for starting stoves in cold climates. As it burns, the resulting heat builds up pressure in the tank below and heats up the gasoline to a vaporizing stage. After fire has burned out, open the valve. Now light the gasoline vapor which should be coming out of the burner tip. With a clean burner (all stoves comes either with self-cleaning devices or a cleaning needle), one should shortly get a hot blue flame. Wind protection (or a good wind-screen) is important; otherwise, the flame may be blown out or else the fire will be inefficient.

I cannot emphasize the stability of the stove enough. Once a dinner is spilled on the ground, it is hard to enjoy. However, avoid putting the stove in too much of an enclosed space which may hasten overheating of the stove. Before backpacking, you can check out the stove's stability on level ground with various-sized cooking pots. Obviously too large a pot not only contributes to overheating, but to the stove's imbalance. Out on well-established trails, an abandoned campsite will often work well as it should have level ground and protection from wind. It is important to have an adequate windscreen. Some stoves (like the Svea 123, Optimus 99, Phoebus 725, and Optimus 80, or the Primus 71-L) come equipped with sufficient wind screens. Some other stoves, such as, the Bleuet S-200, do not come with windscreen. Lightweight portable windscreens may be purchased separately, or made by hand.

Here are some odds and ends regarding backpacking stoves:
* Butane stoves may be compared with the familiar L.P. (Liquified petroleum) stoves common throughout the country. The **principle** is the same, although butane (rather than propane) is used on most backpacking stoves, because propane, stored under higher pressure, requires a heavier cannister. Butane is almost seven times as expensive as white gas to operate, per gallon. Butane stoves, however, have one thing going for them: they are lightweight and easy to start.
* "White Gas" is not to be confused with "lead-free" gasoline as lead-free gasoline may have additives. White gas stoves are affected by

109

temperature; most snow campers have been known to sleep with their stoves in the sleeping bag to keep them warm so they will start easier in the morning. From an ecological point of view, white gasoline is transported by the backpacker in a reusable aluminum container, whereas butane cannisters cannot be reused. (Ideally, they should be packed out of the woods; buried they can be dug up by animals. Unburied, they are a simple eyesore.) White gas, highly volatile, must be kept away from open flames. Smokers beware.

* Europeans seem to purchase more kerosene stoves than Americans, even though the stoves generally weigh in at a few ounces more than the white gas stoves. (Sometimes just a pump makes a weight difference.) White gas is not common is Europe.

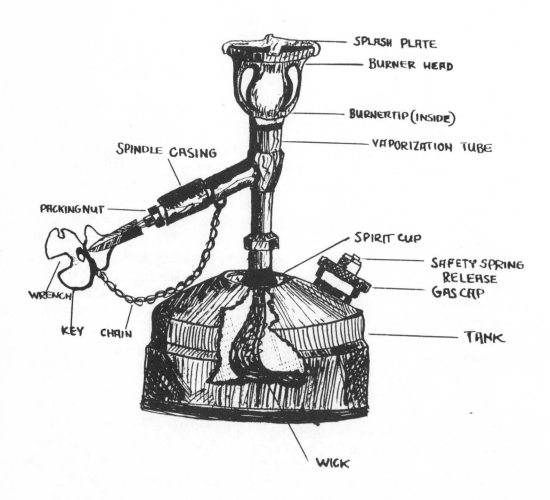

WHICH STOVE TO BUY?

Some popular stoves are these:

Butane and	Bleuet S-200 (still the biggest seller)
	Optimus 731 Moustrap (liquid-fed cartridge)
	Gerry Mini-Stove (liquid-fed cartridge)
Propane Stoves	Primus 2361 "Grasshopper" (a propane stove)
	Primus 2255 "Ranger" Ministove (using propane)
White Gas Stoves	Phoebus 725 (My first stove. Very stable although slightly large.)
	Optimus 80 (formerly called the Primus 71-L)
	Svea 123 (Had small sales in the United States until Colin Fletcher sung its praises in backpacking books.)
	Optimus 99
	Optimus/Primus 8-R
	Optimus/Primus 111B (one model burns white gas; another model burns kerosene)
	Optimus 80
	M.S.R. Mountain Safety Research Easy starting.)
Alcohol Stove	Optimus 77-A (Although alcohol is not as efficient a fuel, it is safe and the stove itself weighs less than comparable gasoline stoves. Easy starting.)
Kerosene Stoves	Optimus/Primus 111-B. (One model burns white gas; another model is adapted to kerosene)
	Primus 100

Often I am asked not only to recommend which type of stove to buy (For example, kerosene, white gas, butane, propane, or alcohol-fed stove), but what particular model to buy. Unlike some writers of backpacking literature, I do not like to make **specific** suggestions. If you have come this far in the text with me, you may have noticed I have not recommended any special sleeping bag, tent, make of boot, or parka. And I am not about to recommend any particular stove. The best I can do is point out advantages and disadvantages of each. Naturally, the terrain you will travel and the climate encountered will be factors in your decision, as well as the length of time you will be traveling and the amount of fuel required. (Obviously on an extended trip, butane cartridges could present a weight and disposal problem. In fact, one is not always sure with a Bleuet stove whether the present cartridge is full, half-full, or nearly empty, so it is possible to start brewing tea and discover that a new cartridge is needed before water will boil.) Some hikers who do not do much cooking but like hot tea or instant coffee now and then might prefer the Optimus 77-A, an alcohol stove. It is lightweight, convenient, safe, and might be perfectly adequate for a trip of a week or less. Others feel that because of their efficiency, white gas stoves are the only sensible trail stove. Temperature may also be a factor, for I have discovered that butane-fueled stoves do not work as well in very cold weather; they also work less well when the cartridge is nearly empty. I would like weight, pot ring size, stability, and price would all be factors.

There is one other consideration which I am hesitant to write about in detail — boiling time. While it is a consideration as anyone who has waited for a sterno stove to boil water knows, there is wide discrepancy in the quoted times. A backpacking magazine will quote the time required to boil a quart of water at sea level on a particular stove; the manufacturer's catalog description will quote another time. Then along comes the delightful Colin Fletcher conducting his own at-home experiments and getting still another set of figures.

In general, the white gasoline and kerosene stoves will boil a quart of water inside of ten minutes — often around four to seven minutes. There is no doubt whatever that the butane-fueled stoves take longer — as much as ten to sixteen minutes depending on the pressure of the cartridge (i.e., how full of fuel the cartridge was).

In terms of convenience, the cartridge stoves are superior. Easy to start, quiet burning, fairly safe, heat controllable, lightweight, they are ideal. They are more costly to operate, however, and have problems inherent in their cartridge design — discarding empty cartridges, availability of cartridges, and less good operation with a nearly empty cartridge. (There is a litter problem among litterbugs, but even an experienced knapsacker doesn't like to tote along two or three empty metal cartridges.)

In terms of economy, gasoline stoves win hands down. Even using Coleman Appliance Fuel or Camplite white gas as sold in discount stores, the cost of operation is still considerably lower than with a butane stove. White gas, however, is not as common in Europe where kerosene is much more readily available. Although kerosene is smelly, there are various deodorized kerosenes which cost slightly more. I think there is a slight trend now toward kerosene stoves as a safety measure.

Just like some skiers who have a pair of downhill skis and a pair of slalom skis, there are elitist backpackers with several stoves. They might use a convenient Bleuet on a short family-type trip and use a white gas stove on a long trip or mountain expedition.

Backpacker Magazine in their No. 15 issue (Summer 1976) announces results of stove testing in "Backpacking Stoves I — How Safe Is Your Stove?" The stove accidents described are ghoulish but the magazine makes the important point that stoves can be as dangerous as guns. The danger of all portable stoves, whatever the fuel, cannot be emphasized enough. A momentary carelessness can mean the destruction by fire of a valuable tent (never use a stove in a tent even if stove openings are built in), sleeping bag, even personal injury.

UTENSILS

Some stoves come equipped with optional cooking pots which fit in with the stove. (See, for example, the Sigg Tourist Cook Kit to be used with the Svea 123-U. The Svea 123 comes with a tiny pot with a handle which can be attached. Frankly, the pot is so small its use is limited, but it **is** handy.) Before running out to purchase a fancy Swiss-made lightweight kit of nesting aluminum pots with lids (and you will find such articles at a backpacking store), why not see what you have around the house, perhaps left over from scouting days? Obviously, a lightweight utensil is more desirable than something heavy, but this is just common sense. The so-called scout individual cooking set which consisted of a frying pan, plate, covered pot, and a cup which nested in a single compact unit is a very common item — so common I've seen a Mirro unit tagged at 50c at a garage sale! This kit generally sells new for about $5. It can be used as it is, or just part of the unit can be taken along. Again, it depends on the sort of cooking you do.

Any camping catalog will contain pages describing utensil sets, plastic and aluminum cups, pot grippers, plastic egg carrier, plastic containers of all sorts with screw tops, and open mouthed plastic bottles of every conceivable dimension. One can also buy knife, spoon, and fork sets, but an old kitchen spoon and a half-discarded knife seem to work as well. A fork may not be necessary at all, although eating a salad with a spoon isn't all that convenient!

A relatively lightweight (well, something over three pounds) pressure cooker is available. Obviously, fuel can be saved with a pressure cooker and it could be convenient in a base camp. I do not think I would want to carry it across the Knife Edge of Katahdin, however.

A few years ago a friend at Swissair gave me a genuine Swiss Army knife. Few gifts have ever delighted me more. It spreads cheese, cuts French bread, opens cans, serves as a screw driver, corkscrew, and file. I could go on and on. I find it more versatile than a belt sheath knife and lighter in weight.

Waterproof matches are sold, but wooden matches can be dipped in nail polish, cut down to size and fitted into a plastic or metal 35mm. film cannister where they will be almost waterproof. Salt and pepper can be carried — if they are needed at all — in small envelopes, although small containers are preferred by some people. Some nutritionists frown on

American usage of sugar and salt and would discourage backpackers from taking either into the woods. As I said earlier, kelp tablets may be better than salt tablets when it comes to excessive sweating. Most herbs and condiments — well, in fact, most food — can be carried in polyethylene zip lock bags which generally work out better than containers. (A collapsible water container is often a convenient trail item, especially if — as it **should** be — the kitchen is removed somewhat from a source of water.)

I would not presume how to tell people to wash pots and pans except to hope they don't use streams too freely so that campers downstream are the victims of an upstream kitchen. Incidentally, I am told that a blackened pot is not such a bad idea — it helps the pan absorb heat more easily, but of course a sooty pot can rub off on other items in the pack if it is not protected. Wash 'n Dry "towels" or nylon scrub pads are strong and work well on pots and pans. Naturally, a biodegradable soap is preferable. Some soaps come in a toothpaste-like tube which is a great convenience.

Lately lightweight Teflon ® frying pans have appeared on the market, with a detachable handle. Grilled cheese sandwiches (and clean-up afterwards) are a snap in these Teflon ® skillets. Just as at home, the least pleasant part of an evening's meal is the clean-up. If you simplify utensils as much as some backpackers who carry only a cup and spoon, it may not take long to do the dishes. Then it is time to let the coolness of evening sift into camp. As the birds quiet down and darkness comes, one's sleeping bag seems about as good a place as any to be — even if the wristwatch says only 8:45 PM!

There are moments when I am hiking alone when I wake up at some unusual hour — say 2:30 AM. It is cold, the stars are out, there is no sound of civilization — no jet overhead nor sound of tractor-trailers in valley highways; only myself and the wilderness. Sometimes, at such quiet moments, I reach out of my sleeping bag (without actually getting out of it), start water boiling on a lightweight stove, and eight to ten minutes later half sit up in my sleeping bag drinking sleepy time tea. Ah, the comforts of home up in the High Sierra! Marvelous!

Traveling

On the trail.
Perils and pleasure.

Chapter Eight

Walking is such a natural exercise that it does not require a "how-to" handbook. Many well-meaning writers on backcountry hiking cannot resist the temptation to instruct readers how to walk — how many miles to cover per hour, how many rest stop to take, and exactly how you should pace yourself. These writers are not content unless they are telling you **everything.**

Experienced backpackers and hikers have developed many helpful tips on hiking that are interesting. It depends on you. How many miles do you want to cover? What kind of pace is most comfortable as you travel a wilderness trail?

Well, hiking is not military marching. It is a highly individualistic recreation — which is its great virtue. I have no quarrel with those who spend all day long doing a fairly short and level stretch of wilderness trail. En route they may have identified ten or twenty birds, looked at an assortment of ferns, and watched chipmunks for half an hour. Others like to sit at trailside (if it is not buggy!) and experience the remoteness or silence of the woods. Other hikers stop to eat wild berries, collect geological samples, or photograph a startled deer. Thankfully there are simply no rules beyond common sense.

Common sense dictates that one allows enough time to reach a destination before sundown. Common sense dictates that in group hiking the pace be a compromise between eager beavers up front, cruising along flat out, and the unhurried cadre at the rear. But beyond these parameters, what is there to say about an activity which is so highly subjective?

Some hikers have adopted what they call the "rest step," especially on steep terrain. You simply pause a second after the foot is advanced; with the weight on the back leg, you skip a beat, then advance the rear foot. Try to set up a constant and rhythmic breathing pattern. Sometimes singing to yourself can encourage this inhale-exhale pattern. In movies of high-altitude climbers, this sort of somnambulistic stepping may sometimes be seen.

Most guidebooks not only describe trails in detail but list distances, elevations, and average times. For example, the Appalachian Mountain Club **White Mountain Guide** says that it is 9.3 miles from Kancamagus Highway to Desolation Shelter and suggests the average hiking time is 4 hours and 40 minutes. Obviously, this is a fairly level walk, for in other places the book lists climbs of half this **distance** which require more **time**. Most guidebooks have worked out a formula taking into consideration distance, terrain, and elevation to arrive at their suggested elapsed time figures. Some climbers find the figures conservative; others have to keep moving right along to come anywhere near the approximate times. It hardly takes more than one or two hikes to realize where one fits in with these suggested times.

Since hiking is such a natural activity involving little more than ordinary common sense, I feel many of the following observations may be patronizing. You have permission to skip along through them rather quickly. If you find something you didn't already know, I will not only be surprised but delighted. Perhaps this section could be called **On The Trail Hints**:

* Jumping rope is an excellent body and leg conditioner for hiking. So are bicycling and jogging. Olympic skiers who live in the Alps often spend their summers hiking; the two sports, one for winter and the other for summer, complement one another. Some of the same equipment can be used in each.
* Reports of mountaineering accidents often mention that hikers, having left desk jobs and driven a long distance to the trail, were out of condition for loads being carried and terrain encountered. If one gets tired during downhill skiing, a warm lodge is nearby with hot chocolate or chili. Hiking in the woods is a different matter, especially in cold weather when one becomes chilled while resting. Practice hikes are common before serious mountain expeditions and not a bad idea for novice backpackers.
* Backyard camping, especially if you have a new tent or sleeping bag, is a sensible way to have a shake-down. Previous experience at erecting a tent in a backyard can come in handy trying to erect a tent when you are tired and the wind is blowing.
* Avoid the temptation to begin a hike at a fast pace. Children who have been cooped up in a car for a long drive love to race into the woods and start out on the trail at a blistering pace. Often all this accomplishes is to build up an early and unnecessary sweat. Tell the children one more time about the tortoise and the hare.

* A child or an adult in good condition should be able to work up to ten or twelve miles a day of backpacking although the distance may be sharply reduced if the terrain is rough or steep. Winter hiking is something else. Sometimes the snow is so deep or the trails so icy it takes an incredible time to cover what is in summer a short, pleasant distance.

* There is a certain point — different for each person — when the pack is just too heavy for the body. Most people carry too much most of the time, although not always enough of the right things. No two people agree on what is right and wrong. Michael Abel says in his **Backpacking Made Easy** (Naturgraph, 1972): "The use of a FLASH-LIGHT is considered the criteria which separates the old timer from the young whippersnapper. The old timer would not be caught dead with one." Yet there are backpackers today who regard a flashlight, extra batteries and bulb as absolutely essential. (When carrying the flashlight in your pack, do not forget to reverse the batteries so it will not turn on accidentally and leave you stranded when you really need it). Another backpacking book which I shall discreetly not mention by name shows a hiker's pack being filled with such items as canned fruit cocktail and spaghetti sauce. Talk about needless weight! Experienced backpackers are like experienced tourists — they seem to be able to function better each trip and their luggage gets lighter and lighter! Generally, but not always, the hiker with the grossly over-weight pack is the inexperienced hiker who believed all those back-packing books and took along everything they suggested, sheath knife included. I have seen hikers carry into the woods citizen's band radios. I suppose if one got lost, a CB radio might be helpful, but there is a limit to what one can carry. Some potential backpackers take only one hike and stay out of the wilderness forever — the pack was too heavy, the sleeping bag did not keep them warm, they could not tolerate trail cooking — who knows? Often, I think, an overweight pack is the biggest cause of dissatisfaction.

* It helps to have the hands free when hiking. In other words, do not carry articles by hand or keep hands in pockets. Being able to grab a tree or a stump when one starts to fall is often the difference between a nasty bruise or none at all. Loose, rocky terrain is often hard to navigate. In wet weather, exposed rock above timberline can be a slippery surface. Sometimes in windy, wet weather, a hiker will half crouch going down wet rocks. There are some trails so steep that you sometimes have to pull yourself uphill by side-of-the trail scrub or rock.

* Many hikers like to rest with their pack on rather than go to all the trouble of unbuckling a packframe and taking it off. There is a psychological matter here too: the pack often feels twice as heavy

117

when you hoist it back on your shoulders if you have had it off awhile. (Why do baseball players swing two bats at the on-deck circle?) You can find places to sit down and rest the weight of the back on a log, stump, or rock without actually taking the pack off your shoulders. Leaning over with the pack on can have the same effect. But do avoid excessive sitting down. It only makes it harder to get up, plus it tightens your leg muscles.

Naturally a full rest stop (with raisins, carob bars, protein cookies, beef jerky, and perhaps even a quick cup of tea from the stove) is different; the pack comes off. Three types of rest stops can be combined for variety. On a very steep pitch, a rest stop of ten to twenty seconds may be sufficient to keep one moving along well again. In winter, long rests can be hazardous: days are shorter and colder, the pack is heavier with winter clothing and snow saws, water is more of a problem and so is dehydration, the water in a canteen may be frozen, as may the on-the-trail sandwiches.

* Writers on backpacking disagree on many things (I disagree with one writer who scorns guidebooks entirely), but on one point we seem to be in universal agreement: early morning is a good time to hike. Few backpackers would dissent because in the woods they tend to wake up so much earlier than at home. Awake, restless, they soon prepare breakfast. When that is finished, the watch still may show just 6:45 AM. So it is a good time to hit the trail. Hikers who wait around for the dew to disappear or the sun to warm up their moist groundcloth miss the best time of day. Besides, if one hikes from, say, seven to 11 AM, there will be time for a long, leisurely lunch and maybe even a siesta.

* Many areas have hiking clubs. This is a great way to buy used equipment, get advice from more experienced hikers, meet other backpackers, take part in practice one-day hikes, and work up to more strenuous backpacking. The Sierra Club on the West Coast and the Appalachian Mountain Club on the East Coast are two clubs with many activities and active local chapters. Some have their own wilderness cabins for members. The East Coast has more to offer in the way of facilities than the West Coast. Nearly all have scheduled hikes with a leader throughout the year. I cannot recommend these clubs enough. Besides, they all take an active part in fighting to preserve the wilderness environment against trail bikes, fast-food stands, highways, and excessive use.

* Both of the clubs I have just mentioned publish guidebooks to various trails. A guidebook consists of detailed descriptions of trails with indicated mileage and elevations, location of springs or camping sites, and explanation of trail intersections. Often an Eastern guidebook will describe a lean-to or cabin — whether it is an open or closed shelter,

how many persons it has bunks for, whether there is a dependable source of drinking water nearby. Most guidebooks also contain an emergency first-aid section. Some even mention flora and fauna you might find. Without exception, guidebooks contain excellent fold-out maps, generally based on topographical quadrangles which show contoured elevations. But nothing can replace a topographical quad sheet which shows the entire (15 minute map showing 17 x 22 miles) area instead of one specific hike or trail route.

Some backpacking purists claim that only maps are necessary, that a guidebook tells you more than you will ever need to know and lessens the joy of self-discovery. Whenever possible take along a guidebook, preferably an up-dated one. Trails are sometimes relocated and maps are not as up-to-date as a trail description. Clubs often publish an annual take-along **addendum** which gives up-to-the minute bulletins on trails. Heavy spring flooding, for example, may have devastated a trail; a fierce winter storm may have caused blowdowns which have not yet been cleared; a trail which proved just too soggy going through a marsh may have been totally re-routed to avoid swampy land; a prominent trail sign at a critical intersection may have been ripped off by vandals, or shot through with bullet holes, or used for campfire fuel, and not yet replaced. Such items often will be in a guidebook or one of its annual additions and few of these points will show up on a map.

Guidebooks also allow one to select a climb from an aesthetic point of view, for trail descriptions are so detailed they give the arm-chair hiker an advance feel for exactly what is in store on a certain trail. A guidebook will mention whether the trail slabs over open rock ledges or whether it meanders through dense conifer-filled woods. Sometimes a few sentences will do the trick: "During the season, these exposed ledges are filled with blueberry plants." Or: "In the col are two cold mountain lakes. The upper one is reserved for drinking water, but the lower lake is excellent for swimming. At the southern end of the lake is an unusually flat rock ideal for sunbathing." None of this subjective material would appear on a map. In this way, a guidebook helps attract hikers to little known, off-beat trails. Personally, I have often been lured to a particular mountain trail by a small guidebook detail — an unexpected woods waterfall, a still-standing steel firetower with a spectacular view, an abandoned lumber camp deep in the forest.

Even on a familiar trail, I can sometimes lose my bearings. The guidebook is sure to tell me where I am and how far I have to go: "Leaving the heavy spruce, the trail zig-zags a rocky ledge, then enters scrub pine for a quarter-mile flat stretch leading to a stream half a mile from Carroway Shelter on the height of land above the stream." There is hardly a trail-filled section of the country for which a guidebook does not exist.

Even a guidebook of trails in the Midwest exists. Despite my often-expressed respect for the budget backpacker, I endorse the concept of trail guidebooks.

   * Even with a guidebook, it is often difficult to remain oriented on the trail, especially if hiking in an area where old logging roads (which resemble trails) or animal runs intersect the trail. Trail intersections are expecially difficult places if a sign has disappeared; in winter, snow may cover up a sign. People have become lost in relatively simple ways: they have mistaken a logging road for the main trail and gotten lost getting back to the main trail. (Too often impatient, they try to cut through the woods to find the trail rather than carefully retrace their steps back to the point of error.) Others have simply gone off the trail for toilet, gotten mixed up in direction, and suddenly found themselves hopelessly turned around. The most frequent cause of a lost person is a group which separates. Sometimes a hiker who is interested in photography or else is simply a slower walker will say cheerily, "Go on ahead. I'll catch up to you." Whenever I lead groups of hikers, I try to keep the group together at all times, even if it means a slower pace than some might like.

   Until recently, many trails were marked with an axe blaze on a tree. Then somebody began to realize these blazes were not healthy for trees, so trails are often marked by splashes of paint, or by small trail signs — sometimes a small tin emblem attached to a tree, and occasionally by cloth tied to trees. Above timberline, trails will be indicated by painted markings on rocks. Sometimes a cairn (a pile of rocks) or trail duck is used. Winter hikers prefer cloth strips tied on trees where trails signs would otherwise get covered by snow.

   Even a cairn may be buried in snow. Since many types of trail indicators are useless in the winter, one must occasionally fall back on common sense and a good sense of direction by using map and compass.

   Trails are frequently maintained by local mountain or hiking clubs, sometimes with an assist from the Forest Service. Much trail maintenance is done by volunteers. That huge, fallen-down tree which has been recently cleared away from a trail may, in fact, have been cut and pushed aside by a city accountant and a dentist on a weekend of volunteer trail clearing. Because of high water and rushing streams which may be difficult to cross in the spring, much trail clearing is not done until early summer. I have actually turned back from an attempted climb in the spring when a river was just too torrential to cross. (I went up and down its banks for more than an hour trying to find a safe crossing and gave up. Perhaps I should add still another common sense platitude: it is not sin to turn back — the literature of mountaineering is filled with the writing of still-living climbers who had enough sense to turn back.) There are signs at timberline in the White Mountain National Forest which read: "The area ahead has the worst weather in America. Many have died there from exposure. Even in the summer, turn back **now** if the weather is bad."

Bushwacking or cross-country hiking is finding your own route in a trailless area. If you have a compass, a map, reasonably good weather, and know what you are doing, bushwacking can be enjoyable, for it is truly more of a back-to-nature experience than walking along well-trodden trails where one may find a Hershey candy wrapper at any moment. Bushwacking or cross-country hiking is not for the unguided novice, however. It is an easy way to get lost, but of course not every place we want to go has a trail! This type of travel is best learned on an excursion when experienced compass and map readers are along to lead the hike.

* I have never used a walking stick or walking staff, but some hikers do, including experienced alpinists. They claim it is handy for crossing streams or for pushing through tall grass to send snakes scurrying away, and that it can even serve as a tent, tarp, or fly pole, perhaps.

* Many accidents on the trail have been caused by the reluctance of a party member to speak out about discomfort for fear of spoiling the good time of others. Not everyone can be in top shape. I urge members of hiking groups to speak out frankly about their condition. If one feels faint, needs a rest or a drink, is feeling dehydrated or light-headed, I say, Speak Up! Too often a hiking party will get deep into the woods before realizing a member of the party is too weak or ill to go on, or turn back. False pride can lead to unnecessary problems. For example, a hiker may feel a blister is developing. A

ten-minute stop in which adhesive tape or moleskin was applied might prevent a real blister which would spoil or cancel altogether an extended hike.

* If you cannot find a guidebook for the area you are planning to hike in, try to get good maps. Get the topographic quadrangles issued by the United States Geological Survey, or Forest Service maps which are sometimes available free from Ranger Stations. The Survey maps perform well in showing contours and elevations, but I question their updatedness. Forest Service maps are up-to-date but I am appalled by their inaccuracies. Mountain and trail club maps remain as the most reliable guides.

U. S. topographic quads may be ordered from Washington, although most states have retail outlets for the maps. Retail outlets sell the maps for $.25-.50 more than the Government sells them for. An index of maps is available free from the U. S. Department of Interior, Geological Survey, Reston, Virginia 22092. Mention the state of states you are interested in.

* Often a trail which zig-zags up a slope in a series of switchbacks will have an informal, straight-line shortcut for impatient hikers. I never take a party over these shortcuts. They are not only steeper, but from an ecological point of view, they are harmful, especially in rainy season, for the natural run-off from a zig-zag trail is destroyed and the shortcut becomes a stream, sweeping along rocks and small boulders and causing damage to the original trail, carefully laid out with a view toward preserving the forest during spring runoffs.

* As good as jogging, rope jumping, and cycling are to condition a person for hiking, I doubt if there is better preparation than practice hiking with a pack, even if it is through Golden Gate, Rock Creek, or Central Park. Consider the elevation when you practice. When the 1972 Olympic Games were announced for Mexico City, athletes knew right away there would be a problem of altitude. No matter how well they trained at lower elevations, it would be an enormous adjustment to run an Olympic Marathon at Mexico City's high elevation. So they trained at sites high up in the mountains or on a high plateau or in Mexico City itself. Too often a backpacker who functions well in a seacoast city will wonder why he or she is feeling slightly woozy three days later while climbing. Ideally, you need several days for the body to become acclimated to the higher altitude. Take it easy the first few days, (Skiers often notice this more than backpackers because a ski lift may deposit them on a 11,000-foot summit less than twelve hours after leaving sea level).

ANIMALS, BIRDS, INSECTS AND SUCH

To me, one of the joys of backpacking is to come across a surprised deer in a mossy clearing, to descend from height of land and discover, when the trail levels out below, a beaver dam, or to see a chipmunk scurrying off into the brush. I have seen a giant moose standing in the Montana wilderness, and I found this experience almost spiritual.

Once, coming out from the woods near Tuolumne Meadows in the Sierras at dusk, I came across a bear with its cubs. I will admit, I started producing lots of lactic acid in a hurry, but eventually the quartet wandered off in the night, and I made my way to the highway to drive back to Sacramento.

One learns, in time, about animals of the woods. The porcupine cannot **shoot** its quills in the manner of "Catfish" Hunter throwing a pitch at the plate, but its quills can be bothersome if you (or your dog) get close enough. The porcupine loves salt and will search for it throughout the night.

* Some hikers take dogs into the woods with no trouble. I know one hiker whose dog just seems to exist on a day-by-day basis waiting for the moment when he'll accompany his owner into the Sierras. Some dogs, however, can keep a group of backpackers awake all night, for they are not used to the dark or the smells and sounds of wood animals scurrying around. More than one backpacking trip has been disrupted when dog and porcupine tangled and dog yelped at its newly-acquired, painful quills. Dogs sometimes "run" deer, also. Other dogs have accompanied their owners over all sorts of terrain and in the most remote woods without difficulty.

In general there is nothing to fear from animals of the woods. The fox at night, the moose crossing a stream, the surprised groundhog, the sunbathing snake — all want to avoid a confrontation and will run, bound, or slither away. Yes, there **are** exceptions, generally in areas where black bears have been fed by tourists. In all honesty I must report that a bear has been known to maul a sleeping hiker. (In bear country, I like to sleep some distance from my food supply.) I suppose such an attack is statistically as rare as a shark's attack on a swimmer, but I would be less than honest if I did not admit it **is** a possibility. (Adherents to the walking staff or stick claim they sleep with it next to them, ready to fend off any curious animals, but I imagine they seldom use it.) The best preventative against the bear is to be sure there is no food around to attract. Unfortunately, well-used campsites, particularly lean-tos and cabins which have been used by a succession of hikers, not all of whom have carried their garbage back out to civilization, do attract bears who have learned to look for food scraps.

* Chipmunks, rabbits, and squirrels are all clever and go after the strangest things. Miriam Underhill tells how she took supplies into Zealand Notch one winter on a toboggan. After an overnight inside

123

the hut, she discovered the next morning that the toboggan ropes had been will chewed by some nocturnal animal — probably a rabbit.

 * In the Sierras, I saw a few timber rattlesnakes. We kept a respectful distance from one another. The rattler, of course, is a poisonous snake, along with the copperhead (found more often than one imagines, especially in the Smokies).

 * Snakebite is extremely rare and sometimes occurs when a hiker is teasing a snake, poking at it with a stick or otherwise annoying it. Many snakes like to sleep in the daytime — be especially alert around ledges and in tall grass. Snakes will try to get away if they hear someone approaching. The best advice I can give if you see a snake is to stand still a moment; ordinarily, the snake will move away. If suddenly surprised (or teased), a snake will **attack.**

Every state has venomous snakes except one. A few thousand rattlesnake bites are reported every year, with very few fatalities. (This is compared with approximately 1500 fatalities every year from bee stings.)

Some bites are harmless, but one never knows. Therefore, to be prepared carry a Cutter Snake Bite Kit (about $3.00 and weighing one ounce), or a Welshgard Snake Bite Kit (double the price). Unfortunately some people do more harm than good with these kits; they overcut around the wound which causes excessive bleeding, or they cut across the tendons in the hand. Properly used, these kits should prevent any lethal dose of poison, but snake-bitten people are often their own worst enemies: they panic or go into shock or race around instead of being calm. Few snakebites are fatal — very few — but they can be if not treated properly.

In places like Texas and Arizona, some backpackers prefer a high boot (a Gokey boot) which reaches almost to the knees, for they feel secure against bites on the calf. Most snakebites are on the lower leg, but can easily occur on hands and arms if a snake is handled. Some hikers are blissfully unaware that there are poisonous snakes in North America and pick up snakes or play with them. I give all snakes a certain distance when I can, even though most snakes are, of course, harmless.

 * Insects are a problem. I have never cut a trip short because of insects, but I have seen some hikers do it — especially when black flies or mosquitoes are out in force. Cutter makes an effective insect repellent. I would avoid aerosol can repellents on a hike — but then I try to avoid aerosols at all times. A cream or liquid repellent is easier to carry and more ecologically safe than aerosol sprays. There are legends about a product called Fly Dope. (Sometimes it is called **Woodsman's Fly Dope.**) It consists of mineral oil, rectified oil of tar, citronella, pennyroyal, camphor, and oil of bay — and is a highly effective product. It smells terrible and stains clothing dark tan, but helps keep insect at a distance.

Here, for what it is worth, is a recipe for homemade fly dope called Pinkham Notch Fly Dope. (Pinkham Notch is at the foot of Mt. Washington):

  3 oz. Pine Tar
  2 oz. Citronella
  1 oz. Olive Oil
  1 oz. of Pennyroyal
  1 oz. of Creosote
  1 oz. Powdered Camphor
  1 tube Carbolated Vaseline

 The summer catalog of L. L. Bean, Inc., (Freeport, Maine 04032) offers an Australian style bush hat called **Bean's Allagash Hat** with a mosquito net carried in the deep crown. In buggy territory, the net comes down to cover the face and neck, held in with a chin strap, gloves may seem like a winter item, but when the black flies, chiggers, and mosquitoes are thick, they can be a comfort. People who are allergic to bee stings generally know about their condition in childhood and learn to take precautions. A paste of baking soda or mud can alleviate the pain of a bee sting.

 * Snowmobilers versus cross country skiers, trail bikers versus back-packers — it seems that outdoor groups line up as opposites, each disliking what the other stands for. Tolerance flies out the window. Snowmobilers claim they can go into the deep woods to rescue hikers, or leave food for starving deer, yet a cross country skier does not like to come across snowmobile tracks or hear, in the remote woods, the unmuffled sound of a roaring snowmobile. So it is with hikers and hunters. Most game hunters are in the woods not for aesthetics: they are there to kill deer and in the process they have been known to kill innocent hikers. Annually, they scare lots of hikers out of the woods. I know an experienced backpacker who hangs up his rucksack (he wouldn't dream of owning a new-fangled packframe) when hunting season starts. No matter how brightly he is dressed, he feels he is not truly safe in the woods. Besides, the whole hunting ethos bothers him; he gets "bad vibes" from the woods when hunters are stalking deer. I know another person — a woodsperson she calls herself — who spent such a stressful fall day on the Long Trail with the sound of firearms puncturing the quiet that every fall she writes a letter to the newspaper saying what a shameful practice hunting is and that hikers carrying cameras feel unsafe in the woods with gun-toting hunters roaming around. I do not wish to become embroiled in this controversy, but I must admit it is difficult to do any serious hiking during deer season. I **will** go on record, however, as being emphatically opposed to those people who take guns into the woods to shoot squirrels, groundhogs, rabbits, and other woods animals for

"sport." Some sport! They also take pot shots at tin cans, trail signs, or whatever strikes their fancy. Ugh . . .

* Innumerable first-aid books are available for advance study; some pocket first-aid books are light-weight enough to be packed along. Here are some common emergency problems in the woods:

Cuts — from knife or axe

Blisters of the feet

Bruises — from falling on a trail

Burns — from stove or camp fire

Frost bite

Hypothermia (a drop in body temperature — more common than thought in all seasons of the year)

Insect bites

Snake Bites

Sunburn (especially on high ledges in summer when one under-estimates the strength of the sun)

Sprains

Dehydration

I recommend the American Red Cross First Aid Book (Doubleday). It goes into detail about treatment for sprains, fractures, shock, fainting, and other basic problems. However, I would like to brush over quickly several of the above problems because they are quite common among backpackers:

* **Blisters** can usually be avoided (See Chapter 2 on Boots), but if one suspects a blister is starting, immediate aid should be given. Moleskin is ideal with pieces of adhesive tape holding the moleskin in place over the blister.

Some backpacking books suggest a blister should be punctured right away before applying any tape or moleskin. However, conditions in the woods are not too antiseptic, so it may be better to see if it can eventually be made to disappear on its own. If it must be opened and drained, soap and water should be used first. If alcohol is available — even in a flask for drinking! — it can be used. A needle or knife blade can be used. Either can be sterilized with a flame. Dressings should be applied. A blister which becomes infected is far worse than an ordinary blister and can spoil a trip.

* **Hypothermia** has been called "the hiker's hazard" or "killer of the unprepared." Essentially it is the rapid lowering of body temperature. It can happen in a wet rain or in above-freezing temperatures when a hiker feels chilled. Unfortunately, too many backpackers die of hypothermia. When five members of the Sierra Club were hiking on California's Mount Ritter, a surprise storm came up; four of the five died of hypothermia.

Normally the body temperature is, as we know, 98.6, but to maintain that, the body must produce heat. When heat **loss** is greater than heat

production, this dangerous ailment can take over. Heat loss can be brought about in several ways: **Radiation**, especially around the head. At 40° F., nearly half of the body's heat is lost through the top of the head. At -5° F. the figure is nearer three-quarter's of one's heat production. **Convection.** One often hears about the wind-chill factor, for air movement takes away heat. **Conduction.** When one sits on or touches a cold object, heat is drained away. **Respiration.** In the winter, this is more of a problem as exhaled breath carries away moisture which the cold, dry inhaled air can not replace. Under these circumstances, dehydration can also be a problem. **Evaporation:** One sweats to keep the body cool. Perspiration acts as a conductor and conducts heat away from the body. The real villain is rain and wetness, for water conducts much more heat than dead air. United States Navy tests show that a nude person in 32° F. water shows signs of body temperature lowering within just five minutes. (A nude person in a room controlled at 32° F. would not feel the effects nearly so fast.)

When, because of a variety of these heat losses and exhaustion, a hiker becomes chilled, shivering starts; often the blood vessels contract which reduces the flow of blood to extremities and skin. The body temperature can fall alarmingly fast and a hiker may become confused, even unconscious. The December 1974 issue of **Appalachia** tells of two New England victims of hypothermia. One, a winter climber on Mt. Katahdin, died. The other, a Connecticut woman, recovered because of unusually good first-aid. Her narrow escape is almost a classic hypothermia case, so let me abridge the account:

> Patty Dougherty was part of a novice hiking party of four men and three women who drove a long way from Connecticut to the White Mountains. With only a small breakfast, they started around 10 AM to climb up to Madison Springs Hut from the valley. The day (August 17) was warm and sunny, although rain had been predicted for the afternoon. Each hiker was dressed in shorts and shirt, but all carried extra clothing in the pack.
>
> By mid-afternoon, Patty felt a little weak and dizzy, but kept going with the group. The sun disappeared, clouds swept in, the temperature began dropping. At 3:45 PM in the small scrub near timberline, she sat down complaining of nausea and weakness. Rain began. One woman remained with Patty and others hurried to the hut a quarter-of-a-mile away to get assistance. Soon Patty started to shiver. Being covered with a poncho did not help. As wetness and cold began to seep into her, she slipped into a hypothermic state. Soon members of the hut staff reached her, found her unresponsive to questioning and uncontrollably shivering with the cold. Her temperature

127

already read 95.6 — in just twenty-five minutes she had fallen into hypothermia. Fortunately, her illness happened close to the Madison Springs Hut where she was taken, wrapped in blankets and sleeping bag. At the hut, she was undressed, wrapped in hot blankets, massaged, and given hot tea. Thanks to prompt and knowledgeable help, she soon came around. But as **Appalachia** reported: "A long drive, inadequate food, harder than anticipated hike and a change in the weather brought on a hypothermic condition in a very short time. As with most hypothermic cases, the event occurred in temperatures consistently above freezing . . . Until she collapsed, no one realized that anything was wrong."Had the incident occurred a few miles from the staffed hut, the results might have been quite different.

Treating hypothermia is mostly common sense — recognizing its symptoms as soon as possible (Patty's symptoms were classic), then getting the person warm. Sometimes this requires drastic, but life-saving methods, such as stripping a conscious victim of clothing and getting him or her into a sleeping bag quickly — sometimes with another person so the body heat of another person will warm the victim. High energy foods and warm liquids are good. Often on a small party one must make an agonizing decision: whether to stay with the victim or go for help. In the Sierra a hiker left his companion on the trail leaning against a tree while he went for help. An hour later when he returned, he was dead. (A good discussion of hypothermia may be found in **The Outdoorsman's Medical Guide**, By Alan E. Nourse, MD, Harper and Row, 1974, or Dr. Theodore G. Lathrop's **Hypothermia, Killer of the Unprepared.**

The body operates off the same fuel supply for both heat production and physical mobility. If one's "fuel supply" is already on empty, and not replenished, the body becomes physically exhausted. Then, in a heat loss situation (water and wind), the body is more apt to fall into a hypothermic stage. "Shivering," for instance is the body's natural response to staying warm. Physical movement, can exhaust the body if food (carbohydrates or proteins) are not being ingested. A person can become a victim of hypothermia in a relatively short time. The combination of more heat loss than heat production, and further onset of fatigue, fear and panic, all are part of exhaustion.

Obviously, one of the risks of hiking alone is that there is no companion to help in such an emergency, especially on a sparsely traveled trail. Wool clothing may help — it tends to keep one warm when wet, whereas a cotton sweat shirt, for example, will cling to the body keeping a layer of water next to the skin. The layered system of dress also may protect against hypothermia. In an emergency, a victim may be taken into a tent which can sometimes be heated slightly with a portable stove or with a candle. (Be careful using a candle inside a tent, expecially an inexpensive tent which may be only slightly flame retardant or not at all. In most instances the fabric will burn if in direct contact with the flame). Never force food or drink into an unconscious person. The conscious victim of hypothermia, however, will respond somewhat to high-energy foods and hot liquids. The old remedy of administering alcohol is dangerous; it may give the illusion of warmth, but alcohol is a depressant which will slow down the body's heat production process.

Ironically, there have been a few instances where hypothermia actually saved a life. Once a young boy was finally rescued from an ice-filled lake into which he had fallen; everyone thought he was dead as he had been submerged a while, but at a hospital he survived because, the doctors said, the frigid water had plunged him into a sudden hypothermic state which had allowed his body functions and oxygen supply to "coast." Before I leave the subject, however, I do want to emphasize that hypothermia is not a winter climbing illness; it can occur during all seasons — even, as with Patty Dougherty, in the middle of August in New Hampshire.

* Further details on first aid in the mountains will be found in Chapter Nine of this book.

LOST IN THE WOODS

No morbid curiosity impels me to read the accident reports in various alpine journals; I read them because I learn from them, just as an airline pilot can learn from reading of airliner mishaps. Excluding reports of winter climbs (winter mountaineering is a highly specialized activity) there is a consistent pattern to summertime accidents: inadequate knowledge of terrain to be hiked (reason enough to consult and carry a guidebook), poor physical conditioning, inadequate clothing, reluctance to turn back when things are not going well, underestimation of the fury of mountain weather in mid-summer, and loss of direction in the woods . . . or worse, loss of the trail in the clouds above timberline with no way to get a directional orientation.

It is easy to go astray. I have been lost myself and managed to do it several times quite easily. Sometimes I have been daydreaming and got onto a side trail, perhaps an abandoned stream bed, and suddenly realized I was seeing no more trail markers or else the trail would come to a dead end. At other times in swirling clouds above the timber, I haven't sighted the next rocky cairn through the mist, and I have wandered off to one side or another. Fortunately, I have so far always followed my own advice ("Stay cool!") and have stopped to reason where I might be. Invariably, by retracing steps, I find my way back again to the security of a marked trail.

Yet a surprising number of people **do** panic, often when they are less than a hundred yards from the trail. Instead of calmly assessing the situation, trying to orient themselves by elevation of land, stream bed, or ridge, they have hastened to catch up with their party and nervously bushwacked off in the wrong direction. A few minutes later they are hopelessly lost.

Sometimes a group will split up, though not be design. The leader knows where they're headed and when coming to a trail intersection, takes the correct turn. But a tag-along bringing up the rear, tired and talking to himself ("Why are they hiking so fast?"), may take the wrong turn and be hiking on a trail which, in nine miles, might reach Desolation Valley! In leading camping groups, it's a good — maybe even **essential** — idea, to have a leader at the front and a co-leader bringing up the rear, but this, like most mountaineering advice, is just common sense. Even so, parties split up, a city person with little country know-how will get separated from the group and too often **panic**.

Actually, if you are hiking with a full pack (sleeping bag and food) there is no need to be alarmed; you have brought your "kitchen" and "bedroom" with you. Even if you had no food, there should be little concern, for a reasonably healthy adult can go at least thirty days without food, and often longer. (Water, however, is an essential.)

SURVIVAL IN THE WOODS

At first, you do not realize you are lost — the trail must be right over there, beyond that boulder. But once you are there, the forest looks just as tangled and nothing resembles a trail. So, therefore, it must be in the opposite direction, down the ridge a way, beyond that huge tree lying on its side, its roots unearthed. But no, that is worse: the woods are thick with thorny brush; no trail here either.

The heart pounds a little faster, you are breathing hard now. You call out, "Hey, you guys!" and only the usual noises of the woods are heard. Then you stand nervously still to listen: perhaps if you are quiet enough you can hear the rest of the group with their trail jokes about how they hope to find a Carvel Ice Cream stand around the next switchback. But there are no voices of people anywhere, not even sounds of cars off in the distance. No jet overhead — as if that would do any good. There, amid the needled floor and the towering conifers, you wonder for a moment if you are lost. That seems impossible, for only a few minutes ago you were on the trail.

You wander around a moment, adrenalin pumping, and discover what **must** be the trail: the bushes seem to part, the trail leads in the right direction. Cheered, you set out to overtake the rest of the group before your body — that is, assuming the sun is out: an easy way is to note the direction of shadows cast by trees. Also, with a rough estimate of shadows cast by trees. Also, with a rough estimate of the time, one can determine the points of the compass. Even without knowing north or south, you can at least travel in a consistent direction this way and not get turned around in a circle. To be even more precise, you can determine the time (or estimate it based on the lunch stops), correlate that with the sun, and get a rough idea of direction. Since most novice backpackers are not conscious of the sun in their ordinary day-to-day existence (only knowing whether it is "out" or not), an estimate of direction will be very rough, based, perhaps, only on the concept of the sun rising in the east and setting in the west — but my point is this: even a rudimentary sense of direction is better than none. Besides, the mental exercise in figuring all this out is productive, taking your mind off thoughts of panic.

It would be ideal, at this point in time, to have a survival manual with you, but who carries a wilderness survival book into the woods? The classic, by the way, is Bradford Angier's **How To Stay Alive in the Woods** (Collier Books, 1962). This book deals mostly with summer conditions, however. A more comprehensive manual which includes mention of winter and desert conditions is **The Survival Book**, by Nesbitt, Pond, and Allen (Van Nostrand, 1959). Newer books include **Outdoor Survival Skills** by Larry Olsen (Brigham Young University Press, 1974). Even with a long-ago reading of one of these books, you may recall some tiny piece of information which would make survival easier. Perhaps you recall that moss is more likely to grow on the north side of a tree (not really true, of course); or you recall how a rudimentary sundial or suncompass may be made; or you recall how fish may be caught with the hands or a bent paper clip; or how, in the desert, a sheet of plastic may be rigged in a scooped-out earth bowl to generate water. Colin Fletcher has an excellent description of this on pages 131-136 of his immensely readable, sometimes chatty book **The New Complete Walker** (Knopf, 1974).

There are few hard and fast rules, but I have already hinted at one: don't abandon your pack. As heavy as it may be, keep it with you. Without extra, warm clothing, you could get wet from precipitation or perspiration and, when the temperature dropped at day's end, become a quick victim of hypothermia. It is no fun to bushwack around through heavy vegetation with a pack, especially a frame pack whose top may catch in low-hanging vines and branches, but the pack is a necessity.

Eventually, of course, you have to decide whether your aim is to find the trail again and catch up with your party of whether your aim is to find your way out of the woods. Fortunately, most backpacking is done in hilly, even mountainous terrain, so finding your way out of the woods is often as simple as finding your way **down** to a highway via slope of land, they know you are missing; you'll certainly say nothing about it when they ask, "Hey, where were you? Did you stop for a beer?" But the false trail goes nowhere, except to a patch of briars. Slowly the realization comes: you are lost.

In such a situation it is hard **not** to panic. The fact is, most novice backpackers **do** panic, and no admonition of mine **not** to panic will help much. I am not ashamed to admit I have had a few close calls in winter. Frankly, in the summer I do not have that much concern, for by now I am at terms with the summer woods and know how to survive a long, long time. But winter is something else: dandelion greens are not that easy to come by, nor is rock lichen, and temperatures can drop alarmingly fast once the sun sets.

Almost without exception, the people who survive being lost in the woods are those who use that supreme survival tool — the brain. Using up a great amount of their energy, people will dart around thinking the trail **must** be right around someplace. Sometimes, to facilitate this frenzied search for the elusive trail, they will take their pack off, set it against a tree, and never see it again: their survival tools (canteen, sleeping bag, food) also become lost, and their dilemma has now become more complicated: half an hour later they can find neither trail nor knapsack! Now, they are truly lost in the woods in shorts, a tee-shirt, and hiking boots.

It helps to have a map in your pocket. That is where I carry my map — I like to have it right with me rather than in the pack. With a map, especially one showing contoured elevations, you can often find your way back to the trail with a little effort. The dotted line indicating the trail will be shown as black against brown contour lines, the blue lines of streams. Supposing you recall having stopped for lunch beside a brook between two high ridges half an hour ago. Chances are you can find the exact location on the map, for the stream will show as blue and the two high ridges, one on either side of the blue-marked stream, will show up in density of contour lines. (I am assuming everyone knows how to read topographic quads. Fortunately the directions are printed on the reverse side of these maps, and many grade schools teach topographic map reading in geography rather than insist students memorize imports and exports of Brazil.) Then, allow a little distance for post-lunch hiking and determine approximately where you went off the trail. That, at least, is a start toward orienting yourself.

By examining the slope of land (or climbing a tree to get a view of the terrain), you may be able to make a calculated guess in what direction the trail lies. Even if it means bushwacking for what seems an interminable distance, you should intersect the trail — that is, **if** you can go in more or less a straight line. That is not hard with a compass, but difficult without, unless you can keep the sun's position more or less at the same angle to fall of stream. Many a lost hiker, like the Boy Scout in the Los Padres National Forest, finds the way out of the woods following along a stream because **ultimately** most streams lead to a recognizable place, or a piece of civilization.

Incidentally, some hikers carry a whistle (not unlike a basketball referee's whistle) with them at all times: its shrill, high pitch can be heard at much greater distances than a shout. The standard S.O.S. distress signal is three blows on the whistle, wait a few minutes, then send three more blasts. It is quite possible for hikers to be separated by more than a mile and find each other through the sharp, woods-penetrating whistle whose sound can be pinpointed more easily than the shout, "Hey, you all."

If you have retained your pack, you can make the best of circumstances wherever you are: you should have your sleeping bag (even if someone else is carrying the tent), food, and warm clothing. You can rig up some sort of shelter near a log or a boulder or a ledge overhang and wait for the next day. Naturally, the edict against campfires does not apply in an emergency. In the daytime, smoke from an emergency campfire may even pinpoint your location. If lost without a pack (perhaps it was just a day hike with only a belt pounch or fanny pack), an emergency campfire will dry out clothing and keep one from freezing. Survival manuals contain detailed description on how to start a fire in the woods with or without matches, in rainy weather and dry weather. Bradford Angier, for example, devotes two chapters to the emergency woods fire — how to find kindling or tinder, what woods burn best, inflammability of evergreen twigs, starting a fire with bow and drill or striking a spark. But let us hope that you have remembered to carry matches (heads dipped in nail polish) in a small 35mm film can.

Thirst can become a problem, a much more serious problem than hunger because dehydration is much more quick to set in than starvation. In fact, I do not recall ever reading an account of a backpacker starving in the woods. I do read of them going into hypothermia, drowning trying to cross a stream, or becoming dehydrated, so thirst and warmth seem to be the two problems. Of course, the need for water intake can be reduced by cutting back on exertion, but these words are almost pointless, for the lost hiker is going to exert plenty. After a while, however, it makes sense to travel in the non-hot times of the day and conserve energy. Both smoking and alcohol can contribute to dehydration. (Perhaps the only advantage the smoker has is that he or she is likely to be carrying matches!)

Water can often be found hidden in lush areas of vegetation; sometimes willows mark a moist spot. Rain water — from several previous days — may be found in curious places — a natural bowl in a rock, for example. In an emergency, you my decide **any** water is preferable to none. Moisture collects on a groundcloth; there may be dew on the morning grass. In other words, while there may not be a spring with water coming up pure from the earth, there may be sources of water which you would ordinarily overlook.

After all, survival in the woods is a matter of dealing with circumstances by adaptation. If hungry, no reasonable nourishment can be refused: lichen, wild turnips, pawpaw, wild raspberries, wild cranberries (though bitter tasting), elderberries, wild onions, miners lettuce, nettles, dandelions. There are other fine sources of protein which we may gag at when contemplating: frogs (the legs are considered a delicacy in many fine restaurants), insects (the **thought** of eating insects bothers most people, but tinned chocolate-covered ants are also an expensive delicacy). Actually, many of us have food prejudices. At one time, nobody ate the tomato — it was considered strictly ornamental. While Americans eat corn, most Europeans consider corn food for cattle and are astonished when they come to North America and see cloth-bibbed restaurant patrons nibbling away at corn cobs smothered with salt and butter.

So as far as I know, I have never eaten flesh from bears, porcupines, beavers, or snakes, but all survival books tell how to capture these and prepare for eating. Grouse and birds also supply protein in an emergency. In fact, as Nesbitt-Pond-Allen say: "Anything that creeps, crawls, walks, swims, or flies is a possible source of food." Their book has an excellent section on building simple snares or traps for small wood animals. In fact, I would suggest that somewhere along the line the serious backpacker might read one or more of these books filled with sensible suggestions on how to survive in the woods. Shelter and water are the crucial essentials for survival. It could be dangerous if the person lost expended great amounts of energy searching for food expecially in cold climates. Better to conserve vital energies by remaining as immobile as possible. Body fat can sustain your life for up to 30 days and replace the presence of food.

Still by reading the survival books, one learns what to eat when the problem arises. When I became stranded once, for 10 days, I really had little knowledge of survival foods, but to keep my mind occupied, I observed what the wildlife around me was consuming. This was a great lesson even though I never have gotten a chance to practice it since.

Finally a word about search parties. Often a lost hiker will be a day ahead of the search party who discover signs of a rudimentary campsite with footprints which match the sort of boot the lost hiker was wearing, but there is no sign of the hiker nor any indication in which direction he or she might have gone. Sometimes a search party will say, "If only she had stayed in one place we could have found her." That is because the search party generally starts looking from about the place of disappearance, fanning out in different directions. A boy was lost in deep New York woods, having wandered off from a hunting lodge in the Adirondacks.

Searchers kept finding evidence of his presence as the days went by, but could never find the boy. What happened to him is a mystery to this day, but had he stayed in one place for a day or two, he might have been found.

I am not saying there is a rule cast in concrete: stay in one place because there is not. There are times when finding your way out of the woods is a relatively simple matter. But there are other times, especially in flat areas of deep forest, when staying in one place and awaiting rescue might make more sense than wandering erratically, leaving tempting, but uncertain, clues as to your movement. Eventually, most search parties join hands in sweeping woods, calling out as they move along in a line, so that it is difficult **not** to find a person who has not wandered miles away.

I hope you are never lost in the woods, but if it happens in relatively mild weather and you have your pack with you, there should be no real concern: it might even be an experience which will cause you to make the front page of the local paper and be the subject of conversation for a few days when you return to work. And when you have done it once, it is much easier to cope with any future "lost in the woods" experiences. It might even be possible after that to practice what all the backpacking books proclaim: When Lost, Keep Your Cool.

Winter
Camping

*A look at the snug life
. . . below zero.*

Chapter Nine

Winter hiking can be enjoyable, but in Canada and in most of the United States, it is a recreation which should only be undertaken initially with an experienced winter guide or instructor, let's face it: in the summer, anyone can go hiking in the woods with just a hazy notion of the principles of backpacking expressed in this and other books. True, one could become lost, as a seven-year-old Knoxville boy did in the Smokies in 1969, never to be seen again. But the chances are the summer hiker will experience only occasional discomfort — insect bites, sore muscles, a few blisters, and maybe a sleepless night now and then. This book is designed to eliminate — or reduce to almost zero — even these small irritants so that wilderness backpacking can be reasonably comfortable.

Winter backpacking, as I said at the outset, is altogether different. To be comfortable (in fact, to **survive**) much more attention must be paid to detail, top-notch equipment, and the fury of winter weather — even if it seems mild and pleasant in the valley. While summer hiking is for everyone — adults and children with the most inexpensive equipment including bedrolls and sneakers — winter hiking is almost a specialty, like white water canoeing. It would be foolish for me to "democratize" winter hiking and assert that any combination of wool blankets will do just fine or that one does not need fancy fiber fill polyester or expensive goose down sleeping bags or a $150 mountain tent or good down parka. Not so, for when it comes to winter, there can be few compromises. The "best and the lightest" philosophy — and hang the cost — may mean the difference between death and survival. For even experienced winter climbers have become frostbitten, overly-tired in swirling snow, and have lost their lives despite good equipment. A snow avalanche, for instance, can easily wipe out several hikers in a few minutes.

If winter hiking is so specialized, you might wonder why I have even mentioned it in this book. Why not simply dismiss the subject with a neat sentence like this: "Winter hiking is so serious and fraught with such peril that I'd suggest you read a book like Raymond Bridge's **Snow Camper's Guide** (Scribner's, 1973) before you even think of **winter** hiking?" The simplest answer is that even a three-season hiker can run into unexpected winter conditions. For instance, it has snowed every month of the year on Mt. Washington, New Hampshire and in the Rockies. Unexpected late-spring storms have surprised High Sierra hikers who thought they were going to have a joyous, spring romp through budding trees — but ended up coping with eight to ten inches of heavy, new snow. Hikers who never thought of snow blindness, a trail that wasn't just plain earth, or converting snow to drinking water have often been surprised. Sometimes they have panicked. So a brief chapter on winter hiking seems appropriate. Who knows, your autumn leaf-checking hike may turn into a winter hike miles away from your parked car which may not even have its winter anti-freeze? If you want to skip along to the final chapter and save this one for later, be my guest.

HAZARDS OF WINTER BACKPACKING

Most hazards of winter camping can be overcome with the right equipment and its proper use. It may seem simplistic to add "and its proper use," but there have been instances when hikers with the proper equipment abandoned it in face of a blizzard in an effort to escape downhill away from the force of the unexpected storm. Here are some of the hazards of winter camping:

- boots frozen stiff
- sleeping bags damp and inadequate for minus 25 degrees F.
- hands so cold that touching metal tears off flesh
- camera shutter inoperative; lens frozen on one f. stop
- toes numb, frostbite
- canteen and food in pack frozen
- snowblindness from dazzling sun reflected on snow
- snow unexpectedly deep and no snowshoes
- snow cave built (inadequately) for protection collapses

137

- no kindling or wood easily available for warming or cooking fire if portable store inoperative
- wind strong enough to blow down tent
- windchill factor adds to severity of temperature
- ice crystals form on eyelids and moustache
- visibility almost zero making trail following (hard enough in winter when white blazes don't mean so much) nearly impossible
- altitude sickness (at 10,000 feet the air has 1/3rd less oxygen than at sea level — and with less air pressure, the reduced oxygen is not so easily forced through lung walls)
- snow avalanche
- car battery frozen when hike ends
- car buried by snow plows

COOLING POWER OF WIND EXPRESSED AS "EQUIVALENT CHILL TEMPERATURE"

WIND SPEED		TEMPERATURE (F)																				
CALM	CALM	40	35	30	25	20	15	10	5	0	−5	10	−15	−20	−25	30	−35	40	−45	−50	−55	−60
KNOTS	MPH	EQUIVALENT CHILL TEMPERATURE																				
3 - 6	5	35	30	25	20	15	10	5	0	−5	−10	−15	−20	25	30	−35	−40	−45	50	−55	−65	−70
7 - 10	10	30	20	15	10	5	0	−10	−15	−20	25	−35	−40	−45	−50	60	−65	−70	−75	−80	−90	95
11 - 15	15	25	15	10	0	−5	−10	−20	−25	30	−40	−45	−50	−60	−65	−70	80	−85	−90	−100	−105	−110
16 - 19	20	20	10	5	0	−10	−15	−25	−30	35	−45	−50	−60	−65	−75	80	−85	95	−100	−110	115	−120
20 - 23	25	15	10	0	−5	−15	−20	−30	−35	−45	−50	60	−65	−75	−80	−90	−95	105	−110	−120	−125	−135
24 - 28	30	10	5	0	−10	−20	−25	−30	40	−50	−55	65	−70	−80	−85	−95	−100	110	−115	−125	−130	−140
29 - 32	35	10	5	−5	−10	−20	−30	−35	−40	−50	60	−65	75	−80	−90	−100	−105	−115	−120	−130	−135	−145
33 - 36	40	10	0	−5	−15	−20	−30	−35	−45	−55	−60	−70	−75	85	−95	−100	−110	−115	−125	−130	−140	−150

WINDS ABOVE 40 HAVE LITTLE ADDITIONAL EFFECT.	LITTLE DANGER	INCREASING DANGER (Flesh may freeze within 1 minute)	GREAT DANGER (Flesh may freeze within 30 seconds)

DANGER OF FREEZING EXPOSED FLESH FOR PROPERLY CLOTHED PERSONS

After this dire listing, you may be ready to throw another log on the fire, put a Chuck Mangione LP on the turntable, and settle down to read the evening paper knowing that hell has no fury to equal a winter storm in the mountains. You will let the mountains, in their eternity, cope with winter.

Yet there is something about winter backpacking — a certain winter mystique — which defies description. The conifer branches heavy with snow, animal tracks in freshly-fallen snow, the surprising warmth of a snow igloo or snow trench, the expansive whiteness of a snow bowl — these only hint at the experience of winter camping. True, the skier, born to a high summit via chairlift or gondola, occasionally experiences some of this joy, especially early in the morning before ski trails are crowded, but he/she is never far from hot chocolate, baselodge, chili, or a warming hut. Skiing just isn't the same. The Nordic skier, on thin cross-country skis comes closer — but he/she is out for the day only — or a few hours. The **real** winter backpacker intends to set up camp before dusk, cook **inside** the relative warmth of a snow cave, and sleep the night through — even if the clear night air drops well below zero. Somehow, in such an environment, people feel **tested**. If there is no longer any more challenge for some in summer backpacking, there is always a challenge in winter — especially in most of Canada and northern United States. Yet, even these geographic guidelines are elusive, for I have scraped snow off my car in San Francisco and have seen substantial snowfalls in the higher regions of the Los Padres range. True, in some desert regions of America's southwest, winter is mild, but leave those desert towns and churn up into the mountains and you will encounter snow.

There are certain advantages to winter backpacking, the most obvious one being lack of crowds. Those once bulging lean-tos filled with Scout troops are now abandoned even by most curious animals who are hibernating. Not even the Forest Ranger has been by to check on things since hunting season ended. Heavily-travelled summer trails are clear of hikers; candy and cigarette wrappers are mercifully covered with snow. When you do have that rare occasion of meeting other winter hikers, an almost instant camaraderie is set up — like two trans-Atlantic air seat-mates suddenly discovering that each is a chess aficionado, a practitioner of TM, or a student of TA.

No porcupines gnaw at latrines or logs, clever mice don't chew into a knapsack for lemon drops or oatmeal, and snakes are not about to slither into an occupied sleeping bag to get warm. (When this actually happened to a summer hiker, he remained absolutely still a long time until he was certain the snake had gone to sleep at his feet. Then he made a quick exit from his bag before the snake became fully awake!) As I say, winter hiking has its own mystique, and if you can get away from snowmobiles, enjoy.

Some winter hikes are possible in ordinary boots, especially if there is little or no snow at low elevations. A walk through such snow is only moderately different from spring-summer-fall hiking. Many who do not actually hike in the middle of winter find they can get a head start on three-season hiking by starting out in late winter with snow without waiting for the sun to melt all the winter snow. Even in late spring, it is possible to find patches of snow in the deep woods at high elevations. But when you sink too deeply into snow, you need either cross-country skis or snowshoes.

HIKING IN

It is even more important to stay together in winter than in summer. A leader (assuming there is a leader — many hikers are understandly put off by the concept of a leader; it reminds them too much of their work!) should not lose sight of the last person. Pace and rest breaks are also more important than in summer; a too-long rest break in winter can result in a chill. If in good physical condition, it may be better to keep going steadily, even if the pace seems slow. If possible, it is better not to sweat too much in winter hiking; this can be controlled by taking off and putting on garments. Sweat which may evaporate easily in the summer does not so easily evaporate in the winter. Wet clothing which later freezes is a real winter hazard.

SNOWSHOES

It has been said many times that one great advantage of snow shoes over skis is that one can learn showshoeing in about ten minutes and snowshoeing can be lots of fun.

There are scores of patterns of snowshoes; each Indian tribe had its own pattern. Even today, different sorts of snowshoes are available based primarily on conditions under which they'll be used. Snowshoes vary in upturn of toe, length, width, general shape. In general, the larger the webbed area is, the more weight the shoe will support. Such shoes are also used in areas where lots of fluffy snow exists. As the shoes become wider, they are a little more awkward to control (because humans walk with their feet fairly close together.) A snowshoe with a tail may be good on the trail, but in some ways it makes for less maneuverability. A hiking showshoe may well have an upturned toe which is easier to handle, especially in showshoeing down a grade.

Here is a general outline description of various snowshoes. While **any** snowshoe will support you on the snow, you might as well get a pair suited to you, the terrain and snow conditions you will encounter. Whether you use old Army surplus trail shoes or newer, aluminum Black Forest types, you probably will be able to get around, rawhide to snow.

Snowshoes pre-date skis and quite obviously snowmobiles. Let us consider some basic shapes:

The individual shape of each type of snowshoe has a specific characteristic, usage, and weight support, or flotation on the snow.

* **The Bearpaw** or Trail Shoe 12″ x 34″ — one of the shortest types of snowshoes found. Its usage is for greater maneuverability and less flotation. It is very difficult to break trail with a pair of Bearpaws since they lack a curved toe. When the Bearpaw is used in backpacking, the user usually follows behind the leader, and has the advantage of walking on an already broken trail. The Bearpaw will support up to 125 pounds on most normal snow packs. NOTE: Snow conditions vary so much that this weight support is only an estimate. Remember, also, that if you are carrying a pack, this must be included in the total weight.

* **Green Mountain Bearpaw** 10″ x 36″ — The Green Mountain Bearpaw is a longer version of the Bearpaw. This stretch-out length and narrower width makes this shoe an excellent all-round backpacking snowshoe. The toe has a slight upturn, which gives it moderate trail breaking ability. Its shape has good maneuverability around trees and a stable climbing ability. Since the Green Mountain Bearpaw has a greater length than the Bearpaw, it has a much larger surface area, which gives it better flotation. The weight support runs up to 200 pounds.

* **The Maine** 9″ x 30″ to 14″ x 48″ has many sizes. This type of snowshoe has a tail; width exceeds 10 inches. The tail is mainly a form of construction. It serves one useful purpose in the snow; acting as a rudder, it helps keep the body of the shoe running in a straight direction. It also takes some weight off the shoe since the shoe does not have to be lifted fully off the snow. Since the width exceeds 10 inches, for people with a shorter stride, a straddling step has to be used. For those with a longer stride, a heel and toe union between the trailing shoe (toe), and the leading shoe toe (heel) can be developed. The Maine has little toe upturn which gives it a limited trail-breaking ability. Because of its shape and length, the Maine is not as maneuverable in smaller areas, but is great for general showshoe touring. Since it has a wider width and tail, the flotations vary. The weight support runs up to 125 pounds.

* **The Michigan** 13″ x 48″ to 14″ x 50″ — Generally has the same characteristics and usage as the Maine, but it comes in larger sizes which gives it a greater flotation ability.

* **The Cross Country** 10″ x 46″ — The Cross Country has the toe of a Green Mountain Bearpaw and the tail of a Michigan. It is generally used for cross country traveling with maneuverability, and the toe has a good upturn for trail breaking. It also has good sliding characteristics for coming downhill. The weight support can run up to 175 pounds.

* **The Alaskan Trailshoe** 10″ x 56″ — One of the longest shoes

manufactured, it has a long upturned toe with a slender tail. It is generally used in open terrain, since its length gives it poor maneuverability in small areas. A taller person has a much easier time maneuvering them since their height is in proportion with the shoe's length. Someone under 5'5" will find the Trailshoe somewhat harder to handle. Since the toe has a long upturn, trail breaking and sliding down hills can be accomplished quite easily. Its overall length and width gives it weight support up to 175 pounds.

* **The Black Forest** 10" x 45" — One of the greatest breakthroughs in the showshoeing industry; its aluminum construction makes it lighter than wooden shoes of its size. The Black Forest shape provides that of the Green Mountain Bearpaw but with a longer length. This shoe is excellent for overall maneuverability and climbing in any area of the snow country. The toe has a long upturn which gives it an easy trail breaking ability. Because it has a longer length than the Green Mountain Bearpaws, it has a flotation factor that runs up to 250 pounds.

* **The Plastic Snowshoe** 12" x 30" — The Plastic Snowshoe, in the smaller size, is generally used for emergency purposes only. Because of their flexibility and slickness on the snow, they are generally not used in a backpacking situation. (Sometimes called Snow Treads.)

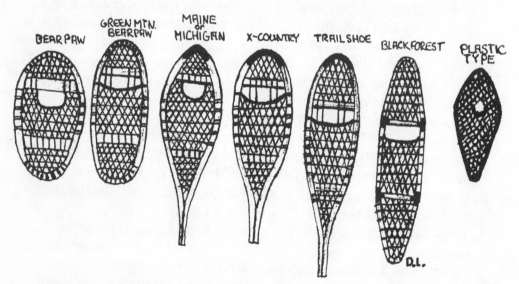

Snowshoe Size — The size depends on:
* The height, stride, and weight of the individual
* Load carried
* Snow conditions
* The terrain to be traveled.

A smaller or larger size depends a lot upon the usage. Snowshoes such

as Black Forest, and Green Mountain Bearpaw only come in one size.
Their size, however, can be used by many different sized individuals.
* A longer length gives a longer surface area for sliding and flotation;
  inhibits overall maneuverability, because of its length.
* A wider width gives a larger surface area, but interrupts a normal
  walking stride by making the individuals straddle their legs. Maintaining this position after several miles tends to make one somewhat
  uncomfortable. A width that exceeds 10 inches usually has this
  straddle characteristic.
* A width that is 10 inches still has good weight flotation and edging
  control. A length which is between 36 and 45 inches can still be
  maneuvered in areas that are encountered in backpacking situations.
* The weight depends, of course, on the size of the shoe and the material
  it is made out of. One pound on your feet is worth five in your pack.

BASICS OF SNOWSHOES

Snowshoe basics:
* Toe cord — this is the hingeing point of the walker's foot, and also
  where the snowshoe binding is attached.
* Center of weight of snowshoe — located 2/3 of the length of the shoe
  from the tail or heel of snowshoe. (When balanced at this point, this
  shoe should fall back letting toe of snowshoe lift and the tail drag.)
* A rigid snowshoe has better flotation than a flexible one. Also, when a
  snowshoe flexes or bends underneath the foot, more effort is
  involved in taking the next step.
* A tail on a snowshoe (example: Alaskan Trail, Michigan, and Cross
  Country)
  Advantage — the snowshoe trails in a true position because the
  tail acts as a rudder.
  Disadvantage — gets in the way when maneuvering in smaller areas
  (obstacles and terrain).
  The tail has no bearing on the snowshoe's flotation or weight
  support ability.
* No tail (example: Bearpaws, Green Mountain and Black Forest)
  Advantage — better maneuverability
  Disadvantage — the snowshoes don't run quite as true as a
  Trailshoe, partially because of shorter length and no tails.
* Turned up nose of snowshoe vs. a flat shoe. Less effort has to be given
  to each step with turnup since turned up portion will stay above
  surface of snow (depending on weight and snow conditions). A shuffle
  step can be used where as with a completely flat shoe the shoe has to

be lifted out of the snow and thus more effort is expended by the walker.

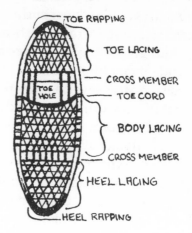

EXAMINING THE SNOWSHOE

* The frame — wooden snowshoes use white ash because of its straight grain for strength and relative lightness. Aircraft aluminum is used in the aluminum snowshoe.
* The webbing
  Rawhide — referred to as gut, it is stretched in the toe, heel and body areas of the snowshoe. An excellent material as long as it is maintained.
  Neoprene — a rubber strip with fiberglass sandwiched in between the two layers of Neoprene, which has great strength and durability.
* The toe cord or master cord should be well wrapped to prevent binding wear. A coating of finishing resin can be used on both nylon and rawhide toe cords to protect them from such wear.
* The toe and heel ends should be well wrapped to protect the ends of the snowshoes from excessive wear.
* The toe hole allows the boot to dip forward into the snow.

GENERAL MAINTENANCE OF SNOWSHOES

* Wooden frames require a coating of spar varnish to protect them from wetness.
* Aluminum frames require little maintenance.
* Rawhide webbing — There are military snowshoes that were built in 1943 that are still being used today by avid snowshoers. Rawhide has an esthetic look to it, but requires the greatest amount of care. The rawhide must be coated with spar varnish (marine varnish) to protect

it from wetness. Once rawhide gets wet, it will stretch and rot. Even when a new pair of rawhide lacings are purchased, they should be coated with varnish before using them. This type of webbing should be varnished after every trip to prevent it from rotting and stretching. These applications also help keep a smooth surface on the rawhide which prevents snow buildup.
* Neoprene webbing — A new type of webbing which requires little maintenance. No coating of varnish is required except on the wooden framed snowshoes. One thing to watch is the fiberglass ravelling from between the neoprene. To prevent this, hit the webbing with the flame of a torch; this will singe the excess fiberglass off.
* Nylon webbing requires a heavy coat of finishing resin to keep from wearing and breaking.

SNOWSHOE BINDINGS

Bindings hold the foot to the snowshoe.
* Materials used include
  Neoprene — neoprene with fiberglass sandwiched in between requires little maintenance and does not stretch when being used.
  Leather — requires waterproofing with either oil or Sno Seal ® to help prevent stretching. Leather eventually stretches and rots with use.
  A binding that stretches means problems for the snowshoer. The heel and toe strap hold the wearer's boot in place; when these straps stretch, the boot slips out. The snowshoe must be put on again, with much time and energy wasted.
* A few types of bindings:
  H-Binding — allows the boot to go through the toe hole for climbing hills. It works satisfactorily as a snowshoe binding.
  A-Binding — a slip-in type with heel strap. When made out of leather, it is not always satisfactory.
  The Howe-Binding — a good touring binding; the front toe cover prevents toe slippage and movement. Also a very excellent binding for snowshoeing.
* Things to be aware of:
  Heel lift — the binding should not hinder heel lift. Since the snowshoe binding acts as a balance hinge, it would be very difficult to walk on a pair of snowshoes with no heel lift.
  Lateral movement — the more lateral movement there is to a binding, the less edging control the wearer has.
  Foot movement — the tighter the foot stays in the binding by means of the toe and heel strap, the truer the snowshoe will run. Less

movement also means less chance of the foot coming out of the binding.

* Putting on bindings

A pair of boots with a stiff toe counter and heel counter such as hiking or snowmobile boots should be worn.

Position the toe of the boot midway across the toe hole. Apply the toe strap and tighten. Tighten the heel strap by moving your boot from side to side. (This will take the slack out of the strap on the opposite side of the tightening point.) The final tightening should be done with your boot being at a 90° angle from the snowshoe.

Tighten the lateral strap.

Re-tighten the toe strap. (When traveling, examine this part periodically.)

Make sure all binding buckles are to the outside.

* Other factors:

Traction — When added traction is needed, wrap twine around the rails (or frame) of your snowshoe. Keep the wraps around the foot area, since this is where the greatest load bearing is being placed and consequently where traction can be obtained most easily.

Sliding — Can be the greatest enjoyment when snowshoeing. Sliding depends on terrain, snow conditions, and wearer's nerves.

Poles — One for balance and getting back up after falling. Two can be used when climbing, but generally tend to get in the way of most people. The poles should be at least armpit height and have a large basket.

* Snowshoeing can be fun. The greatest advantage that snowshoeing has is that almost everyone can enjoy it. It doesn't require much coordination and the initial cost is around $100.00 for boots, snowshoes, bindings, and a pole. Some effort is involved and one must be in shape to appreciate snowshoe touring. But that is just about what it takes for any aspect of backpacking.

AVALANCHES

One thing to beware of in winter travel is avalanches because they definitely ruin your whole day.

Types

Soft Slab or Dry Snow Avalanche — This type develops after a major snow storm when an extreme amount of snow has fallen (around one inch per hour). This cold powder is very unstable, and occurs more frequently on northern exposures (see below). This type is light, moves fast, and contains much air. If you are going to get caught in an avalanche, hope that it is this one.

Hard Slab or Wet Snow Avalanche — This type usually develops from remelted (metamorphosized) snowflake crystals. As the layers remelt and refreeze, through the season, they become water-saturated. This instability creates shifting of the layers causing an avalanche. This type of avalanche occurs in both northern and southern exposures. They are usually more prevalent in the months that follow mid-winter. Their mass is heavy, and refreezing takes place after their occurence. Practically all major accidents are caused by slab avalanches.

Cornice Avalanche — The cornice develops on the leeward side of ridges. Wind currents and metamorphosizing of snowflake crystals (remelting and freezing) help build the cornice from early winter to late spring. When its crown becomes overweighted with ice, it falls apart in large chunks, starting a movement of snow and ice from its base. This type has a crushing effect on anyone who happens to be in its path.

Dangerous Areas

Northern exposure (area that faces the North) — is most dangerous in mid-winter due to heavier snow pack.

Southern exposure (area that faces the South) — is most dangerous in spring and warm days due to melting of cornice areas and slabs.

Leeward side of ridge — is where the greatest amount of snow is built up.

Windward side of ridge — less snow due to wind.

Exposed areas — are more dangerous due to heat of the sun, and less stability from trees and large rocks.

Forested areas — adds more stability to the slope.

OCCURRENCE

Eighty percent of all avalanches occur after storms of one inch per hour rate of snowfall. Avalanches also favor convex areas where the angle of the hill is between 30 (60%) to 45 degrees (100%).

Winter Cold Temperatures — tend to make snow unstable because

147

snow crystals are not melted or reformed. (When the crystals reform and melt, they usually bond with one another, making them more stable). Example: Soft slab type.

Winter Warm Temperatures — make snow more stable because of the breakdown and reformation of snowflake crystals. This assumes that refreezing will take place. As refreezing occurs, the snow becomes heavier and shifting takes place as in a hard slab type and breaking in a cornice type.

Spring Cold Temperatures — usually occuring at night time tend to make the snow more stable because refreezing takes place.

Spring Warm Temperatures — tend to make the snow less stable. As the spring season progresses, temperatures start warming up. With these temperatures comes less bonding of ice crystals and a greater water content in the snow. The higher the water content (with the combination of warmer temperatures), the less bonding occurs. The rocks in which these hard slabs and cornice types attach themselves to also begin to warm up. When this happens, a greater difference between snow temperature and rock temperature takes place. At a certain differential of temperature, an avalanche occurs. Examples: hard slab, cornice types.

DEALING WITH AVALANCHE POSSIBILITIES

Travel in windward side of canyons if possible.
Stay in canyons.
Commit one person at a time when crossing exposed areas.
Travel high on ridges.
If ever caught in an avalanche, the following very simple rules may save your life!
Swim the backstroke to bring you toward the surface.
Detach any snowshoes or skis from your feet.
Form an air pocket around your face, if you can. You have between 48 minutes and 48 hours to survive with snow on top of you, depending on snow conditions and natural air pockets.
The next thing you do is spit. Gravity will pull it down; then you know which way is up. Many people have died of exhaustion digging the wrong way.
Try to keep unnecessary movements to a minimum for conservation of air.

SHELTERS

Perhaps you now have more information than you will ever want about snowshoes, but once you get properly outfitted, you may be surprised how much you enjoy winter camping. I have known some backpackers who find the summer trails so congested that they have become winter campers, enjoying the unoccupied shelters, unbroken trails, and expanses of pristine white everywhere. Miriam Underhill writes affectionately of climbing in winter all of New Hampshire's mountains over 4,000 feet high. She and her husband seem to enjoy every moment — even the frozen sandwiches which had to be thawed out. They felt, on the side of Mt. Passaconaway in mid-January, in harmony with the cold, white environment around them. Although winter climbing allows little margin for error, it is an exhilarating experience.

While many summer backpackers are content to make camp in a glade with no tent or tarp, most winter backpackers like a more substantial camp. Consequently, tents (but not waterproof ones that ice up too much) are ordinarily carried in winter camping. There is some protection from the wind, and a certain amount of heat may be generated by cooking stoves or even a candle. Expensive mountain tents, unlike inexpensive backyard hobby tents, are likely to be made of inflammable fabric, but still stoves and candles inside a tent must be used with care. A gasoline stove venting its fury through the safety valve will still give forth a two-foot flame! I had a friend who once made the mistake of priming his Svea 123 stove in his mountaineering tent. After a flash of flame, he was astonished to find the tent's framework to be the only recognizable part of the nylon structure which had surrounded him moments before.

Other winter backpackers feel more joyful, more in "synch" with nature if they improvise. Ski poles and tarps can be used for makeshift shelters. Areas around tree trunks, with a roof of frozen snow covering pine branches, can also be used. Some people dig trenches that look like graves and cover them with tarps for protection from wind and drifting snow.

Ironically, it is snow itself which makes one of the best insulators.

SNOW CAVES

A good snow cave or hole can provide better protection than a thin tent fabric. The inexperienced winter hiker tends to think of snow as the enemy, but the experienced winter hiker realizes how useful snow can be. Innumerable examples exist of where snow caves saved the lives of climbers and backpackers. Tunnelling into a fairly steep snow bank (sloping upward into the bank so the entrance is lower than the scooped-out corridor), an adequate shelter may be made. Body warmth will heat up the interior; a stove or candle will also heat such a cave up to temperatures where gloves or mittens may be abandoned.

Yet there are risks with snow caves, and I should like to mention these right away before advising anyone to construct a snow cave. Unless there is adequate ventilation (many winter hikers prefer a ventilation hole punched up through the roof from inside), including tunnel circulation, there can be an air shortage. If a stove is used, there can be a carbon monoxide problem.

There is always the danger that changing temperatures or an inadequately-built snow cave can collapse, suffocating its occupants. Some hikers have failed to carry into the snowcave their lightweight portable snow shovels and slept through a drifting snowstorm and found it difficult to dig out using a throw-a-way pie plate or a spiral notebook as a shovel.

Often a snow cave is humid, with problems of condensation more severe perhaps than a waterproof tent dripping wet from the inside. Ventilating the cave can lessen the condensation. A snow cave should come to a point, rather than a rounded circle. The water or condensation tends to run off faster on a pointed surface.

A small snow shelter can be surprisingly warm, fairly easy to build, and on occasions, a lifesaver. Perhaps that last benefit — the fact that knowing how to build a snow shelter can save one's life — is worth the effort to explain here the technique of creating snow shelters. It is much easier to learn **anything** by doing, and if I were to take you into the High Sierra some winter day and let you construct a snow cave or trench along with me, I know you would have the technique down pat in one four-hour session, along with an overnight living experience in the shelter. The best I can do here is outline the general principles of snow shelters and hope you can find someone who has built one to help you construct your first. As I shall repeat for the last time: a snow shelter can provide an emergency station which may mean the difference between life and death, so I have no apologies for including it here.

TRENCHES

The trench is the simplest of the snow shelters, and the builder is not as likely to get clothing as wet as when a snow cave is being built. The trench's cold air space, warm air sleeping benches, and air vents and wall structures are the main features of a snow trench, and once learned, the task of building other snow shelters becomes much easier.

DIRECTIONS FOR BUILDING A SNOW TRENCH

MATERIALS NEEDED

* One pair of ski poles, however, one will do.

* One pair of snowshoes or skis.

* One 5' x 7' tarp (waterproof nylon preferred).
  This tarp is your ground cover.

* One 7' x 10' tarp or 5' x 10' tube tent.

* Six snow stakes. Two sticks can be crossed and tied
    tied togethr in the middle, then attached to the
    tarp. All a snow stake is is a flat or larger surface
    area that can be used in the snow. Examples will be
    given in the directions.

1. Stamp down area with snowshoes or skis.
2. Determine doorway and wind direction, making sure
    the doorway will be cross wind. (Diagram I)
3. Lay out ski poles equal to the height of builder plus
    two feet. (Diagram 2)
4. Dig cold air trench two feet by three feet wide.
    (Diagram 2)
5. Trench
    a. Depth — keep sleeping area 3 to 4 feet deep and
        cold air space one to one and one-half feet
        deeper.
        (Diagram I)
    b. Width — keep width to three feet; make sure
        width does not exceed length of snowshoes or
        skis. (Diagram 2)
    c. Length — dig to end of ski poles, pile snow
        around edges for height. Make one side higher
        to slope tarp for moisture run-off (Diagram 2)
    d. Space — for more shoulder room, dig out sides
        one foot above sleeping platform. (Diagram 2)
6. Ribbing
    a. Lay snowshoes or skis across the trench about
        THREE FEET APART.
    B. Lay one ski pole lengthwise of trench on snow-
        shoes, the other over the cold air space.
        (Diagram 3)
7. Secure tarp — use 7' x 10' tarp or 5' x 10' tube tent
    a. Secure tarp at rear of trench with snow stakes.
    b. Secure middle of tarp with snow stakes or snow
        anchors.
    c. Pull tarp over cold air space and secure corners
        with snow stakes or dead men.
    d. Pack snow on tarp around edges to keep warm air
        in and to prevent wind from lifting tarp.
8. Make entrance
    a. Finish doorway to make it fit yourself.
    b. Cut snow blocks or use your pack to close
        entrance. (Make sure to leave a square foot
        open space for air ventilation.)

9. Construct sleeping area

    a. Lay out 5' x 7' tarp on the floor of the sleeping area.

    b. Lay Ensolite ® flat (may be difficult because of cold; if so, lay pack on top of it to flatten out).

    c. Leave sleeping bag in stuff bag until bedtime, unless you eat supper in the sleeping bag.

    d. Use cold air space for pack and equipment storage.

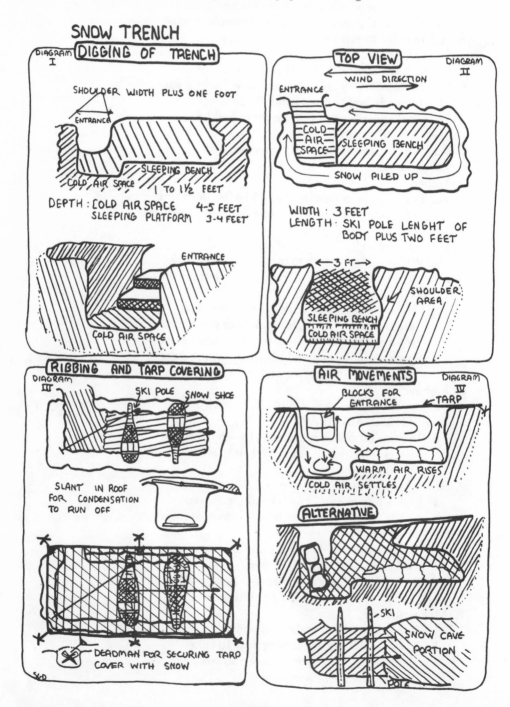

SNOW TRENCH

DIAGRAM I — DIGGING OF TRENCH
SHOULDER WIDTH PLUS ONE FOOT
ENTRANCE
SLEEPING BENCH
COLD AIR SPACE · 1 TO 1½ FEET
DEPTH: COLD AIR SPACE 4-5 FEET
SLEEPING PLATFORM 3-4 FEET
ENTRANCE
COLD AIR SPACE

DIAGRAM II — TOP VIEW
WIND DIRECTION
ENTRANCE
COLD AIR SPACE
SLEEPING BENCH
SNOW PILED UP
WIDTH: 3 FEET
LENGTH: SKI POLE LENGHT OF BODY PLUS TWO FEET
3 FT
SHOULDER AREA
SLEEPING BENCH
COLD AIR SPACE

DIAGRAM III — RIBBING AND TARP COVERING
SKI POLE   SNOW SHOE
SLANT IN ROOF FOR CONDENSATION TO RUN OFF
DEADMAN FOR SECURING TARP COVER WITH SNOW

DIAGRAM IV — AIR MOVEMENTS
BLOCKS FOR ENTRANCE
TARP
WARM AIR RISES
COLD AIR SETTLES
ALTERNATIVE
SKI
SNOW CAVE PORTION
POLE

WINTER CAMPING ODDS AND ENDS

* A great danger to a snow camper is saturated wet clothing. It can happen all to easily by falling into a stream while searching for water or crossing a brook on slippery logs. An emergency method: rolling in newly fallen snow; the flakes act like sponges that soak up water from clothing — if you brush off your clothes as you roll.

MORE TIPS

* **Easy digging** (you hope!) — As a trench is dug, the snow you take out becomes part of the walls above the snow's surface. Just hope that your digging in is not extremely hard.
* **The danger of it all** — Yes, there is a possibility of collapse and suffocation. This is where a qualified instructor and beginner must work closely. The better the structure of a snow trench, the lower the percentage of collapse. This goes for most snow homes.
* **An overall compromise** — The snow trench and cave are similar in so many ways. Then trench just happens to be a little easier and faster for the beginner to attempt. I am not trying to discourage building the snow cave. It is just that it requires more time, more knowledge, and a waterproof rain suit to build one. When one is ready, a snow cave (like the trench) can be a rewarding experience; like building your first sand castle, either at the beach or at your sandbox at home, way back when!
* Snow shovel. You can use large flat bladed shovel, such as a folding snow shovel, an Air Force snow survival shovel, a plywood shovel made at home with two hand holds on the top, or a cookie sheet with end cut out. A plain snow saw or machete will work.
* By the way, when digging a trench, you may find it easier to cut blocks out at first, then finish up the digging after the blocks have been taken out and piled along the side. This method makes digging the trench much faster and easier.

COMMENTS ON DIRECTIONS

* Secure tarp at rear of trench with snow stakes or a snow anchor. One example would be, take two sticks about 8" long, cross the, tie them together and bury in the snow.
* After the tarp has been layed out, secure it to the walls of the trench by means of small sticks, thru grommet holes, or plastic and secure them in the snow.

153

A SNOW TRENCH FOR TWO OR THREE

Follow the same directions. Of course, they will slightly change, along with the materials needed. (See diagrams below).

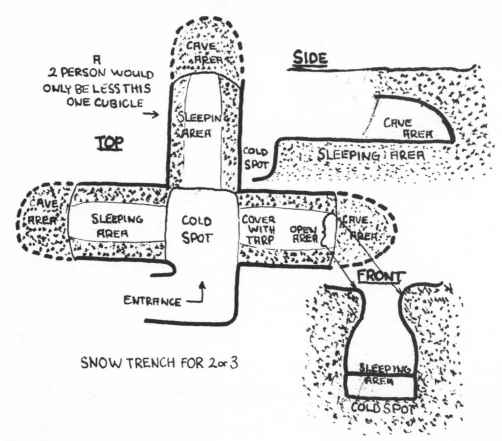

SNOW TRENCH FOR 2 or 3

HINTS ON ALL THREE

Try and start your digging in an area where the entrance will be lower than the sleeping area. When tearing them down, collapse the walls and fill in the trench. By filling up this hole, the chances of some unaware skier falling into it will be slighter.

AN EMERGENCY SNOWHOUSE

A snow house that can be made quickly (once your skill is perfected) in a snow storm is a fine accomplishment. Materials needed here are a snow saw or machete.

* **Cutting blocks** — Snow conditions may not always be perfect (wind packed snow), but usually some type of block can be cut and used. Pack down this area, preferably on a slight mound. Then stand with

your feet lower than the first block layer. Make two parallel cuts, then two vertical cuts with the last cut being underneath the entire block. Once all the cut edges join, a crunching noise may be heard. Lift the block out with your hands and arms underneath to support it. Transfer the block to the building site and continue cutting.

THE SNOW CAVE

Even though the snow cave has not been thoroughly discussed in this chapter I do want to pass along one diagram. The snow cave has many advantages as far as insulation and protection from the elements are concerned. Cave construction does take longer and is harder for the beginner. Expect to get your clothes soaked when you build a snow cave.

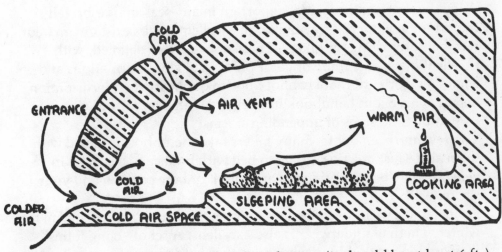

Make sure of the snow's depth before digging (it should be at least 6 ft.). Mark the snow surface above the cave, so that people do not walk on your roof. And lastly, when cooking inside, make sure you have plenty of air ventilation.

* Stamp down the snow in the general vicinity of the campsite. (Normal traffic ought to do this anyway.)
* Sometimes you may need to sleep with a stove in bed with you to keep it warm. (You think I am kidding, right? Then try to light a Svea 123 at minus 20 degrees F. some morning.)
* Store gasoline outside the shelter.
* A small piece of plywood brought from home can serve as a base or platform for a portable stove, preventing it from sinking into the snow as they warm up the snow.
* Wool — that great insulating fabric — should be used next to the body with clothes made of artificial fibres like polyester for outer

155

garments. Wool is — despite all the virtues of artificial quick-drying fabrics — a dependable insulating material. (Try crossing a stream in a pair of nylon trousers; if the water is only knee deep, the nylon trousers will "wick" the water practically up to belt level, but a wool pair of pants will show the knee-high water level mark, and no higher.)

* Most backpacking books say, "Do not wear the same clothing to bed as you have worn all day." This may be excellent advice, especially if the day clothing is saturated with sweat.

* Inner soles, perhaps felt innersoles, may be added to ordinary boots for extra warmth. Rubber boots may tend to "sweat" but they also may be practical under certain circumstances. Some hikers add a layer to their socks by inserting a plastic bag (a vapor barrier) next to the bare foot and then adding this inner and outer wool or Ragg sock respectively.

* A lookout for weather signs, important in any season, is especially important in winter. Any number of excellent books exist on amateur weather forecasting for hikers. These books are so detailed, with excellent black and white or color pictures of cloud formations and what they portend, that I cannot hope to duplicate their information here. Even a Scout handbook has pages devoted to various cloud formations and signs of impending storms.

* To prevent frozen boots, many hikers take their boots into bed with them also. (Just imagine, going to bed with boots and a stove!) In general, store boots upside down at night, inbetween you and your shelter wall.

* Fishnet underwear, a luxury in the summer, is more appreciated in the winter. Thermal underwear is also excellent. A set of "Long Johns" may not look sexy, but in winter weather outdoors, who cares?

* Crampons — whether smaller instep crampons or full-sized 10 or 12 point boot crampons — are often essential in uphill winter hiking. Crampons must fit securely to the boot. Good crampons are sharp and thus present a danger to the novice. It is best to learn how to use crampons from an experienced winter climber.

* A thermometer might be an item to carry in the winter. Mountain supply stores carry excellent portable thermometers which are lightweight. Some ordinary thermometers do not show gradation below -10 degrees. A good, light weight thermometer should register to -30° F at least.

There is a special beauty in winter. It is a black and white photographer's paradise, with sharp contrasts. The air is bracing. There is a real challenge in hiking and in staying alive, in sleeping out overnight with cold air and wind. It is interesting to see how animals hibernate, how deer get through the winter, what birds stay around in the snow. As I said at the outset, winter backpacking is not for the inexperienced unless he/she is in the hands of an experienced winter backpacker to learn the ropes. But once you are on to winter backpacking, it can be a source of great fun and joy.

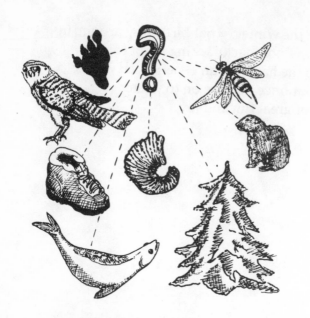

Grab-Bag

*A medley of
backpacking tips.*

Chapter Ten

In our throw-away society, we discard much that is valuable and even more that could be recycled. Discarding is such a habit, I find myself doing it in writing this book. Perhaps the fact that my chapters have been structured and devoted to a single subject forced me to cast aside a little tidbit which didn't **quite** fit in. Then, too, — and I am not hesitant to admit this — my ideas altered slightly as I came to terms with the material, so that a little tip for backpackers which might have seemed too trivial for me to mention back in Chapter 2 kept gnawing at my consciousness: perhaps I should have included it after all. Instead I stored these cast-offs the way I put uneaten food in the refrigerator **perhaps** to see another day.

All right, call this chapter what you will: a cornucopia of cast-offs, a backpacker's grab-bag, even Hikers' Left-Over Stew. I have decided to include here, in no particular order (because **order** is too confining), all those odds and ends which, to shift metaphors from the kitchen to the garage, might make up a Garage Tag Sale. Poke around, browse here and there, reject what you want — maybe you'll find a nugget here worth the whole chapter. To your astonishment, you may even find a statement that disagrees somewhat with something I said early on. (Reviewers can have a field day pointing out these discrepancies.)

James Rutter wrote after hiking the Appalachian Trail, "Hiking and backpacking are sports that have become preoccupied with equipment. This is where I split with the manner in which the sport is practiced today . . . I can never understand the endless discussions about such things as whether the Optimus of the Primus stove is better. I do not see enough difference in these stoves to warrant the discussion, and *I would not more presume to list the items a hiker should carry than I would tell him what he would have in his house."*

The italics, as you probably guessed, are mine, but the quote is James Rutter's and from a fascinating, two-volume (2009 pages) set of books which I have mentioned before: **Hiking the Appalachian Trail**, edited by James R. Hare (Rodale Press, Emmaus, Pennsylvania, 1975). Sometimes I refer to this book as HTAT.

This book deals with a subject only hinted at before: long-distance hike; an "essential item" (perhaps even a lightweight Mallory flashlight) chapters and deserves a little space.

LONG-DISTANCE HIKING

A long-contour packframe which seems perfectly adequate on a day hike in the mountains beyond Seattle may develop breaks on a long-distance hike; an "Essential item" (perhaps even a lightweight Mallory flashlight) may be discarded after three weeks on the trail to lighten the load. One's idea of food or food-preparation may also undergo changes on an extended hike through rain, cold, sweltering heat, and bug-filled woods.

Hikers who go from one end of a trail to the other are appropriately called end-to-enders. You will see them on the Bruce Trail in Ontario, on the Centennial Trail in British Columbia, on a 2,500 mile Pacific Crest Trail, the Continental Divide Trail, and on the Appalachian Trail, that venerable trail from Georgia to Maine. Less ambitious end-to-enders will be seen on John Muir Trail, part of which coincides with the Pacific Crest Trail.

Some of these long distance hikers are young, but many are middle-agers who are either taking a hiatus from the rat-race or have dropped out of their fluorescent-lit offices to rediscover themselves or maybe even (for the first time) to discover themselves.

One hiker who completed the trail three times was nicknamed Walking Grandma; Ms. Emma Gatewood hiked it in tennis shoes (the ultimate little old lady in tennis shoes) and a light homemade little bag, eschewing such things as knapsacks, ponchos, tents, and sleeping bags. Like old-time wilderness walkers, she dismissed what she called "all that heavy gear" (and which most backpackers would call "lightweight gear"). Sometimes she used a blanket and an old shower curtain. Mostly she used her large shawl — in rain and cold, in blackfly country and in unexpected sleet. Incredibly she hiked in a long maxi-skirt. To some fully-equipped end-to-enders who had spent six months planning the trip, weighing each item and figuring out mail drops for post offices en route, she must have seemed like a blueberry, ginseng, or mushroom picker out for the day. In fact, she plodded on daily, a three-time end-to-ender, a candidate for a Ripley "Believe It or Not."

Such a hiker must give the Centennial Backpacker pause: what is the **true** meaning of the contoured packframe, the Sierra cup, the lightweight, Swiss-made aluminum nestling cook-kit, the alkaline battery-powered flashlight, the $125 one-person tent with lightweight poles? How much back-to-nature is **really** involved when we let the metallurgists design a magnesium alloy frame? How much of the throw-away society are we divorcing ourselves from when we finish off a canister of canned butane for the Bleuet stove, even if we tote the empty cartridge back out of the woods to end up in the town dump?

Although I have so far shied away from recommending pieces of equipment, I do suggest that a reading of Hare's two-volume account of end-to-enders may prove more profitable for the ordinary backpacker than all the how-to backpacking books, full of little lists of what to take along, their seemingly endless discussions of trail boots. (Several end-to-enders discarded their expensive, heavy trail boots with Vibram ® soles and stopped at a K-Mart to buy an inexpensive, crepe-soled construction workers' boot — and were happier, lighter of foot, blisterless, and more comfortable!)

To hint at the flavor of this lengthy book, I am passing along a few hints — and a quote or two. First I have listed the hiker's name, then liberally borrowed with the hope you may be enticed to the original source.

Bump Smith — abandoned his 2½ pound down sleeping bag for (of all things!) a blanket.

Ned Smith: Commenting on his non-breathable tent: "Condensation did accumulate on the inside whenever it rained, but it was a minor problem. The saving in weight over a double wall tent offset the inconvenience."

James Leitzell: "The lightweight freeze-dried backpacking foods are very expensive for the amount of nutrition they furnish . . . and unappetizing." Leitzell discovered that hard-boiled eggs kept three days. On the trail Leitzell met a hiker whose eating equipment consisted of an empty soft-drink can, a throwaway pie plate, and a spoon. His initial impression was 'how ridiculous' but after spending a night with him, Leitzell's contempt turned to admiration. Leitzell then felt he was an unusually plucky young man making the best of his limitations of mind, body, and finances.

Charles Konopa: Konopa, the best writer of all the end-to-enders, wrote: "A meeting with a rattlesnake is one of the few original experiences left in the American outdoors." His detailed description of snakes and how to cope with a bite is worth reading. He advises applying an antiseptic, cutting gently (through skin and fat but not into muscle or bone) and pressing out the venom — for an hour if necessary. He feels this is better than a snake-bite kit with a suction devise. Konopa reminds us how the Indian handled a bite from a poisonous snake: the Indian wrapped him/herself in a blanket and lay immoble for two or three suns.

Andrew Giger: Found the scratchiness and friction of new bluejeans to be a bother. Later he abandoned his Levi's ® (weight 20.5 oz.) and got cotton and dacron pants; however, he wore shorts "99.99% of the time." For his tarp he carried not only 150-pound test nylon but 60-pound dacron fishline which is even lighter.

Albert Field: Often hiked nude with dry clothing in the pack. What happened if he met people? (1) Not many people were on the trail. (2) Most people make enough noise to be heard or seen ahead of time. (3) He just didn't care. When dressed, he preferred gym shorts or track shorts cut up the sides. Field is a low-shoe man, liked crepe soles. He met woodchucks, opossums, turtles, loons; he enjoyed hearing the sounds of the ruffled grouse drumming; he even patted a beaver. Of 164 days on the trail, he met hikers on only 109 days.

Bill O'Brien: Preferred the color red for his Kelty BB-5 packframe because of its visibility. Often carried a 3 ½ oz. Sony transistor radio. He found that unlined boots dried much faster than lined boots.

Elmer L. Onstott: Felt that a rectangular bag is best, with a cotton flannel liner. (Mummy shape too confining.) Liked 8 or 9-inch high boots as protection against possible snake-bites, and for streams and bogs when mud would otherwise ooze into the top of lower boots. He estimates that light boots have the following advantage: one pound lighter boots will save a wearer lifting 1½ **tons** per hour! Like many a hiker, Onstott became acquainted with the aerodynamics of a poncho. "As a rain garment, in strong winds out in the open, I found a poncho to be useless."

Jim Shattuck: Carried honey and small quantity of apple cider vinegar. Sometimes slept in abandoned cars, buses, woodsheds, Discovered extra socks performed fine as mittens. Like many a hiker, found dogs (not snakes or bears) the greatest threat to life and limb. Weight-conscious Jim (who learned a lesson from a hiker who drilled holes in his toothbrush to save weight) lightened his load after several days on the trail. Items discarded: a Boy Scout cook kit with frying pan, kettle, fork and spoon; flashlight; stove and fuel; mosquito netting; extra shoes. For his "new" mess kit he used a chile-con-carne can with a wire bail. NOTE: Food may be trapped in the bottom corners of this can, causing diarrhea if the can is reused more than a few times.

Emma Gatewood: "Walking Grandma" carried a total of seventeen pounds, including her shower curtain tarp/poncho.

Art Harris: "As much as I disapprove of the disposable society, there is an item of incredibly light weight which may interest the backpacker — the new Gillette Disposable Twin Blade Razor, retailing for 25¢. It lasts a week or two and weighs almost nothing compared with a conventional razor. Not everyone likes to grow a beard in the wilderness."

J. D. Adams: "Ever want a hiking companion and not know how to acquire one? Well, Lance Feild up in Maine has solved that. His quarterly, **The Trail Voice** has a regular section, "Hiking Partners Wanted" in which hikers explain their ability, geographic preference and time available for backpacking. Write to The International Backpackers Association, P.O. Box 85, Lincoln Center, Maine 04458."

Ron Calkins: Ron, who innovated the Calkins Method of putting on a pack, is a tall, husky chap who has always had problems with regular hiking shorts. The shorts chafe his upper leg. He now uses a pair of ski pants cut off just above the pockets. Not terribly stylish, but certainly comfortable. He has also been seen on the trail with cut-off Levi's ® which he claims he buys in a size five times larger than normal. This Calkins costume most closely resembles the "Culottes" adapted from the French for women.

Rolling Stone: This magazine, which ventures far beyond the rock and roll format, carried a full treatment of backpacking in its June 3, 1976 issue. Under the title, **The Outside Story Zen & the Art of Backpacking, Cicycling, Polar Bear Swimming, Bird Watching, Rafting, Knifing and . . . Golfing in Yosemite?**, equipment and forest behavior get an arch and often hilarious treatment. We especially enjoyed Michael Rogers's description of a mass encampment of hikers (such as scouts). Rogers said these encampments, "are usually, for nearby hikers, the aesthetic equivalent of the Monghol hordes."

Charles Ebersole: Like many an end-to-ender, learned to eat off the land. Liked the ramp (wild onion or leek) with branch lettuce and watercress, leaves from peppermit and spearmint plants. He picked a plant, hung it on his pack to wilt and dry, then put it into plastic bags for the crumbly stage.

"Identification is the secret to overcoming a fear of snakes," as there are far more harmless snakes than dangerous ones.

Max Bender: "One might question the idea of carrying canned goods, considering the weight of the can and the moisture. Bender feels the protein and other nutritive value makes these foods worth the weight. Bender singles out sardines, canned salmon, tuna fish. The water content of canned fruit, soup, spaghetti, etc., was just too high in relation to nutritive values. Bender especially liked figs. At one time Bender carried an L.L. Bean axe. Fire-making, however, consumed so much time and made his pots black and sooty (which then required still more time to clean) so he switched to a Primus kerosene stove which was lighter than the axe and not a fire hazard.

Owen Allen and **Lochlen Gregory:** Their packs seldom exceeded 25 pounds with a full week's food. Used regular gas with an Enders Benzene Baby stove. Developed a liking for hot Jello! Allen wrote: "I don't mind sleeping with bears, snakes, deer, mice, or bugs around, but I don't care for skunks."

Murray Chism and **Edward Little:** Incredibly they carried a Mirro 2½ quart pressure cooker! It cut down on cooking time and fuel.

Incidentally, many of the male hikers ran into appearance discrimination when they came onto civilization en route. Unshaven, long-haired, sometimes moist if not downright wet, these solitary walkers were sometimes regarded as "dirty Hippies" or "no-good Commies" or "eccentrics" for leaving home or spouse to hike over two-thousand miles. Police were not always kind, regarding a lone highway walker with suspicion. Yet there were also compensating incidents when ordinary folk went out of their way to be hospitable, sharing food, drinks, and tall tales with these long-distance hikers, some of whom hiked less to test equipment or their body's endurance than "to get their head together."

FINDING ONE'S SPACE

The literature of mountaineering, from stories of oxygen-assisted high altitude climbing to wilderness rambles, is often devoted **ultimately** to a new perspective toward life, a heightened awareness, an expanded consciousness. Personally, I find it difficult to go into the woods for even a day without experiencing something of this mind expansion. Increasingly, backpacking books are getting away from an obsession with equipment to focus finally on what we go for and what we gain from the experience. "You went in fat and you came out lean," writes Albert Saijo in a slender but fine book (**The Backpacker**, 101 Productions, 1972). "You saw your head through some changes. You started out nervous and excited — like a virgin. Then the hard work of backpacking got to you, and you went into a more serious mood. That broke as you acclimatized, and the trip became pure delight. Each trip has a high point. A point where you feel absolutely with it."

Nearly all **long-distance hikers have such points** — and not always on the final summit **at trail's end.** Ordinary one or two day backpackers can have such moments. It may be the sight of a deer in the dusk or evening making way through the brush toward a stream; it may be a sweaty moment when the pack is taken off for a rest and the cool of the woods seems welcome after uphill exertion. As Saijo writes, the moment can not be planned, anticipated — it just comes. It comes to a hiker with the most rudimentary, homemade equipment and to an elitist hiker, outfitted with

163

Kelty Pack, a Gerry tent, a Black's sleeping bag, Peter Limmer boots, a Holubar down jacket, an L.L. Bean chamois shirt, and a full line of Richmoor dehydrated foods. I don't say the moment is any sweeter to the hiker with the discount store work shoes and the garbage-bag poncho, but it may, in fact, be purer.

DIGESTIBILITY OF FREEZE-DRIED FOODS

Speaking of dehydrated and freeze-dried foods, Albert Saijo writes that while the lightness and compactness of these foods would seem to make them ideal foods for outdoors, there is this lingering question: "Can you submit food to such harsh treatment without devitalizing it?" Saijo writes that these foods are notorious for not digesting well. "The energy of the food is held in the chemical bonds of its molecular structure. When you process a food you break down its structure and de-energize it. It would seem that highly processed food lack the structure for proper digestion. A lot of freeze-dried food passes through undigested." He finds it depressing the outdoor stores which promote earthconsciousness offer what is essentially junk food.

Ideally, I should submit this concept of freeze-dried foods not only to the manufacturers for their comments, but to the National Space Agency which has spent time developing food, not so much for outdoor eating, as out-in-space eating where even strawberry shortcake has been reconstituted. If you have any comments on these "Hikers' foods" — or any other aspects of this book — write me in care of Jalmar Press, 391 Munroe Street, Sacramento, California 95825. In the next edition, perhaps I can add reader comments and suggestions, thus making it even more of a "People's Guide to the Wilderness."

THE RECYCLED CAN

A Planter's Cocktail Peanut can (with a plastic push-on top) makes a fine water-boiler for the top of a small stove. The 12 oz. size also can be used to repackage peanut butter if it is purchased in a glass jar. (Best way to buy peanut butter: in your own container from a "health food store" where the peanut butter is genuine, with no added oils. Neither is it homogenized. Extra bonus: it tastes better!)

SCHOOL FOR BACKPACKERS

With over ten million (estimated) people backpacking annually (I think the estimate is **high**), schools of backpacking are springing up, just as computer schools sprang up when the computer came of age. On the East

Coast, one of the best is run by Lance Feild who offers a free school of outdoor skills (SOS) twice each summer near Lincoln, Maine. Write for details to: International Backpackers Association, P.O. Box 85, Lincoln Center, Maine 04458. On the West Coast contact Yosemite Mountaineering School, Yosemite National Park, Yosemite, California 95389 (One of many). The school is open to anyone, nationwide, who want to learn more of basic skills before venturing into trail country. Fifteen is the minimum age. In addition to trail foods, camp stoves, packing packs, and trip planning, the school takes up a subject dealt with sketchily in this book — use of map and compass (best learned in the field, anyway.)

Incidentally, Lance discourages blue denim claiming that blue **definitely** does attract mosquitoes, especially damp, sweaty clothing. He says khakis or colored denim other than blue are best . . . and pants should be loose fitting.

On the trail, Lance advises the smallest, lightweight pen flashlight (with alkaline batteries preferably); a sewing kit and safety pins; a candle and waterproof match holder. He suggests a small magnifying glass, presumably a help in starting fires when the sun is out and the matches are wet. He suggests a **group** first-aid kit which can be swapped around among hikers' packs. One of the sessions, incidentally, includes a discussion of wild edible plants.

FOURTEEN ESSENTIALS

As James Rutter said (HTAT), he would not presume to list the items a hiker should carry, yet one is forever running up against lists of "must-carry" items. Examine several of these lists for ideas; discard items which you would be uncomfortable with; perhaps you can pick up an idea or two.

Mary Sturtevant of the Appalachian Mountain Club First Aid Committee lists what she calls "The 14 Essentials." She feels these items should be carried on a day trip as well as an extended trip. (The list would be amplified for winter hiking.)

1. Matches (in waterproof container).
2. Candle, to start fires (saves on matches, can be used to seal ends of synthetic rope to prevent fray and for emergency lighting.)
3. Poncho, protection from the elements, emergency shelter, ground cloth. (A rain parka may be preferable for protection from the elements.)
4. Rope or strong twine (15' or 25' minimum), for securing loose gear on packs, for emergency repair of packs or other gear, securing and supporting emergency shelters, for tree-bagging of food, securing splints.
5. Emergency rations, for unexpected overnight stays due to accident,

disorientation, or weather conditions.

6. Extra clothes, for changes in elevation, terrain, or weather; spare socks, gloves or mittens, wool hat, wool shirt or jacket.

7. Jackknife.

8. Grab rag (bandanna), an indispensible item which has at least 100 uses, some of which are: potholder, bandage, sling, sweat band, handkerchief, patch for clothing repair, emergency face mask, ear protection.

9. Whistle, communication signal for groups traveling in heavy brush or fog, SOS signal in emergency situations.

10. Water.

11. Map

12. Compass. Know how to use it!

13. Flashlight. Carry it on day trips, too. Consider the shortness of the days in late Fall or early Spring and the possiblity of underestimating hiking time or having to deal with illness or accident.

14. First Aid kit.

It may seem, after perusing this list of essentials, that a ponderous volume of gear will be added to your pack. However, if one considers carefully the size and weight of each item and the possible consolidation of some of the smaller items in a container, the inclusion of these items in one's pack seems a fair trade for prevention of a possible accident or emergency situation in the wilderness.

THE EIGHT VARIABLES

Equipment which is really not needed, but is carried, is a burden. Eight points to take into consideration when making a list are:

1. What time of year are you going? The equipment you carry varies greatly with the season.

2. In what type of terrain and altitudes are you backpacking — rock, mountains, glaciers, desert?

3. The breakdown of your equipment varies with the number of people who go. Food will be the biggest variation.

4. Number of people cooking together.

5. Equipment can vary greatly with the length of time that you are gone, plus the mileage that you cover. If you are going to be gone for from one to four days, you can get away with taking some frills. If you're going for five days or longer some of this "essential" equipment should be reexamined to make room for food space.

6. What is the purpose of your trip: to take pictures, rock climb, mountain club, collect rocks, fish?

7. Group's ability as woodspeople.
8. Personal tolerance to inconvenience.

PACKING LIST

The "fourteen essentials" are the framework of the working pack list. The eight variables are the situations that can change this list.

The beginner often finds he/she has taken too much equipment. As he/she continues backpacking, less items are essentials and those get laid aside into the non-essential bracket. The working pack list can help you:

1. Start with a basic list of your equipment.
2. Pack your pack, checking off each item as you put it in. Consider if it has one essential use or if it can be used for two or three purposes.
3. When you return — lay each item out and consider usage during trip. If it was not used, either it was an emergency item (and hopefully you'll never have to use it), or it is a non-essential item.
4. By repeating this process several times, your packbag should be filled with essential items and very few luxury items. List page 169.

BAREFOOT HIKING

Jill tells me her new boots were developing a blister when she'd traveled only two of the seven miles up Mount Carrigan in the East. So she left her boots at the side of the trail and picked them up five hours later on her return from the summit. Yes, she climbed Carrigan, an isolated mountain 4,647 feet high, barefoot!

ACCOUTERMENTS

I watch people arrive at the beach for the day. Many bring aluminum and plastic folding chairs, jugs, large beach towels, a portable radio. Others arrive with only a towel and sunglasses, lie on the sand, and listen to the waves or watch the marshy grasses move in the on-shore winds. So it is with backpackers: some have learned to travel lightly in the woods, to leave much of civilization behind. "You don't want to become an equipment freak. The wilderness trip is more than just having the latest equipment," Albert Saijo writes. He reminds us how Himalayan Yogis who got their possessions down to almost nothing seemed able to exist on the elixir of it all, of Jesus who went into the wilderness for forty days and ate nothing, of John Muir's "beautifully austere backcountry style" carrying no equipment to speak of.

167

A PACKING LIST FOR THOSE
WHO INSIST ON ONE

On Person —
- underwear
- tee shirt or fishnet underwear
- shirt; cotton or wool
- hiking pants or shorts
- (1) pair inner socks
- (1) pair outer socks
- hiking boots
- hat or cap
- sunglasses
- pocket knife
- bandana
- 35mm survival kit

MAIN BAG:
Trail Items —
- poncho; plastic or nylon
- food; trail snack and trip's food supply
- small shovel; Sierra scoop
- windbreaker
- wool cap
- water container (8 oz. baby bottle)

Camp Items —
- wool sweater
- down or polyester jacket
- socks (2 pair - 1 pr inner/1 pr outer)
- underwear (1 set)
- shorts or wind pants
- shelter - tube tent/tarp tent
- ground cloth
- gloves or mittens
- utensils (pot gripper, nylon scrub pad,
   bio-de-gradable soap, washing brush, salt/pepper)
- pots
- toilet kit (wash basin, hand soap-liquid,
   not bar, toothbrush, mirror, foot powder)
   (optional)

First Aide Side Pocket —
- individual first aid kit
- dime - for emergency phone call
- chapstick
- sunburn cream
- moleskin (blisters)
- flashlight bulbs & batteries
- insect repellent
- water purification tabs
- repair tape
- bandana

Miscellaneous Items
Side Pocket —
- map & compass
- whistle
- matches in waterproof container
- notebook & pencil
- extra boot laces
- 25 ft. of nylon cord
- flashlight
- candle
-space blanket
-pemmican bar

Top Portion of
Packframe —
- shelter - tent
- ensolite pad - insulation

Lower Portion of
Packframe -
- shelter - tent
- ensolite pad - insulation

Lower Portion of
Packframe —
- sleeping bag -
   depending on size of stuff bag, other
   items may be stuffed in sleeping bag

For Trip Home —
Leave in Car —
- dry clothing
- extra food

Special Items You May Want.
- camera
- camp shoes
- dry clothing (for return trip)
- extra food for the car
- nylon cord 30' x 1/8"
- safety pins
- sewing kit
- insect repellent
- water purifying tablets
- fishing pole/reel equipment
- pencil and notebook
- watch
-pocket thermometer
- toothbrush, toiletries

LEARNING TO LIVE WITH THE RAIN

I know an Appalachian Trail hiker who, after almost completing the length of the 2040 mile trail who said, "You learn to live with the rain." In Virginia and Maryland, he said, it had rained for two weeks. Even after the rain stopped, the deep woods were still wet. When he was not going to cross any roads, he claims he hiked naked, saving dry clothing in his pack. He did not always try to keep dry, letting the warm rain wash over his body and mix in with the sweat. At night, he expected that even with his large poncho rigged as a rain tarp, he would get lightly wet. His attitude was, "So what? What is so bad in summer with a little moisture?" You can spend too much energy, he explained, trying to keep dry when dryness is often just a state of mind.

None of these remarks take away from what I have said earlier about the damage of cold rain to the nervous system and the danger of hypothermia. However, an experienced hiker senses when there is a balance between the body heat he/she is generating, moving along a trail at a good clip, and the relative warmth or coldness of the rain coming down. Under such conditions, too long a rest might upset the balance and cause one to feel chilled.

NOCTURNAL HIKING

In addition to hiking in the rain without a care, experienced backpackers often enjoy nocturnal hiking, but hiking at night is not for the inexperienced. Most people assume nocturnal hiking is done with a flashlight, but for the **experienced** night hiker, a flashlight is seldom necessary.Most of us are so accustomed to turning on artificial light as soon as night comes, whether at home or in a car, that we have had little practice seeing at night. Actually, you can see quite well at night if you allow yourself at least a half an hour to get used to the dark. Hiking is possible even when there is no moon (with a good-sized moon, night hiking is a cinch) provided the stars are out. After awhile, you develop a sixth sense about the trail; you hike in a somewhat looser style than in the daytime when you can be precise about a foot plant.

Often getting accustomed to the dark can be done on a Friday night hike into a prospective campsite. Say you leave San Francisco on a Friday afternoon, managing, perhaps, to skip out an hour or two earlier than the usual five o'clock quitting time. You stop briefly in Sacramento for a quick meal, then on up the climbing highways to the High Sierra. Some daylight still remains when you park the car and start in on the trail, but dusk comes so gradually that before you realize it, you are hiking in the dark! Instead of reaching for the Mallory flashlight, try continuing on (if the stars are out) and letting your eyes become used to the dark; let your sixth radar-sense tell you where the trail is; develop your instincts — the instincts a blind person naturally develops. You may be surprised how far you can go without artificial light. Of course, it does help to know the trail.

It is also possible to hike with a protected candle, or a flashlight, or a Justrite carbide lamp, although these lamps can be temperamental. If attached to the forehead like a coal miner's lamp, they can leave the hands free. For a good summary of hiking by night, see Chapter 14 "Night Walkin' "in Harry Roberts **Movin' Out** (Stone Wall Press, 1975). See also: John Disley's **Orienteering** (Stackpole, 1973), an excellent book on the use of map and compass.

ALTIMETERS, PEDOMETERS, THERMOMETERS, BAROMETERS

If you are into meteorology, fine — take instruments along. Actually on serious high-mountain expeditions, instruments are carried to a fairly high elevation, but not generally to the top. An altimeter is almost useless in mapped areas except to correlate with a map whose marked altitudes are likely to be within a few feet of your altimeter reading. (Recently several mountains in New England believed to be below 4,000 feet in height were resurveyed and classified as 4,000 footers or above.) Personally, I have never carried any of these instruments, but I have seen amateur astronomers carrying telescopes into the woods and I have seen home-made wind-measuring gauges being backpacked to mountain summits. Take along whatever turns you on. mindful of the weight, of course.

Alpine magazines often contain advertisements of articles found in the woods. Sometimes I think the found articles were items a backpacker deemed unnecessary and hid, hoping to retrieve on the way back down the trail and just couldn't find again. Not too many years ago you could leave your full pack with camera and portable stove in a lean-to for days at a time while you went off to town for a movie or supplies; when you returned it would be untouched, just where you left it. Unfortunately — at least in the United States — this is not always true today.

MAP AND COMPASS

In many backpacking books "maps and compass" are given the full treatment. I've never been fully satisfied with these treatments, nor would I be satisfied with my own discussion. Fortunately there is a book that is far superior to anything that has been written on "map and compass." This is **Be An Expert with Map and Compass** by Bjorn Kjellstrom, Scribners,

1955. This book demonstrates the use of map and compass in remarkably simple terms. You'll find it most easy to understand and apply.

ON SCOUTS

Now and then backpacking magazines (like **Wilderness Camping**, 1597 Union Street, Schenectady, New York 12309 or **Backpacking Journal**, 229 Park Avenue South, New York, N.Y. 10003) will contain letters about Scouts in the wilderness. Some letter-writers think Scouts have been detrimental to the wilderness environment, hiking in large numbers, over-crowding lean-to facilities, carving initials in logs, building huge campfires, and so on. Others feel the problem lies in the Scout leadership, for many Scout leaders (volunteers all) have had little experience in the woods and yet are forced to take the Scouts hiking — the blind leading the blind. To help with this situation, experienced backpackers are volunteering their time to assist Scout leaders in troop meetings and accompanying Scouts on their hikes. Training programs for Scout leaders are available in many communities, and Scouting leaders are encouraged to take courses in backpacking. I have been a Scout and worked as an adult Scouter and found it very rewarding. My main contribution today is teaching backpacking training programs. Just one Scout leader teaching others to leave the wilderness intact without stripping birch bark off trees, building huge campfires, or defacing log structures can do much toward preserving the wilderness, especially in overused trail areas.

Stung by criticisms that backpacking, like skiing, is an elitist sport, mountaineering clubs lately have been organizing youth opportunity programs designed to allow children from poor and minority groups to enjoy backpacking. The Appalachian Mountain Club program now in its eighth year helps develop youth leaders who can take youngsters into the woods as well as develop an awareness of the outdoors in their own backyards. A youth worker for the **Colcilio Hispano de Cambridge** was asked to attend a Leadership Training Course. He anticipated a week of boring talks but found himself instead climbing and sleeping out. But when the week was over, Raymond Rodriquez said what remained as most memorable "was sensitivity to a totally new environment, where one learned to savor a breath of clean air and realize it could not be taken back to the city."

It may seem ironic that just at a time when the wilderness trails are becoming crowded, recruiting is underway for still more backpackers, but the effort is necessary if backpacking is to become a democratic sport and not one attracting (as tennis once did) mostly those with money for the best equipment and transportation from city to trail. Already mountain clubs are collecting communal knapsacks and trail equipment which can be used by disadvantaged (a euphemism, to be sure, but in some ways a proper word) people who should not be denied the pleasure of hiking because of its cost. Personally, I am in favor of any moves which will democratize backpacking, even if it means more traffic on the trails.

SLEEPING BAGS-ARTIFICAL FILLERS

My experience with dacron bags has been favorable. In the backpacking store where I worked we started carrying dacron fiber fills in 1970. The lower cost, ruggedness, and warmth have worked exceedingly well. In the Sierra (where I do most of my traveling), the weather is warm but damp. Dacron bags perform very well there. I have experimented with a Polarguard ® filled winter bag in the Sierra, and found that it dries out quickly.

C.W.D.

In backpacking, you hear a lot of talk about c.w.d. It means nothing more than **controlled weight distribution.** As good as a three-pocket rucksack is, it has no interior compartments, so although it may be packed with light items on the bottom and heavier items on top, out on the trail things may get moved around; heavier items will find a way toward the bottom of the back. Consequently a sectioned pack, especially one with horizontal pockets which can be loaded individually, is a solution to the problem of **keeping** heavy objects not only near the top of the pack, but close to the back. The packframe, of course, is designed to transmit a certain amount of thrust upward, where it is carried easier.

Since I have mentioned children throughout the book, I do not feel the need for a special section. However, I have not mentioned the Gerry Kiddie Pack (Gerry, 5450 North Valley Highway, Boulder, Colorado 80216) which you see nowadays not only on the trail but in grocery stores, where mothers can take their children along and do the shopping with both hands free. This pack carries a small child in a comfortable piggyback position. Man and woman can take turns carrying the infant, while they swap back and forth a heavier **combined** pack with their own possessions. A Kiddie Pack enables backpackers with exceedingly small children to hit the trail and make their child portable at an early age.

Harvey Manning (**Backpacking: One Step at a Time**) devotes a chapter called "Suffer the Little Children" to small fry. He makes the point — and it is a good one — that almost invariably our worries about children are groundless, that they are amazingly tough little beasts and sometimes better able than pampered adults to withstand trail vigors. "Why is it a child can dash full tilt around a playground for hours, yet collapse on the trail in minutes, whimpering and complaining?" Manning's answer? Children are natural malingerers — their only defense against adult tyranny. I recommend this chapter to anyone concerned about taking an infant, toddler, or youngster along on a trip.

I began my wilderness experience at the age of three. I was given a paper bag to help carry part of the family's backpacking load. My father, mother, sister, of course, carried a much larger proportion. Even so, I felt that I was contributing a great deal (which I was for my size and weight). This practice made me feel like part of the group. We were there for fun, but there was also work to be done, and my paper bag was part of it! So, when prospective backpacking parents ask me for advice, I tell them my experiences as a three-year old backpacker.

When I emerged from the paper bag stage (age 4½), I was given my first knapsack. What a thrill! Later, I received the hand-me-down packs of my older sister (which I really did not mind) because it meant a new old pack at least every two or three years.

There is also an excellent pack for children between the ages of three and seven called the Antelope Backpack (Child's Frame). (Antelope Camping Equipment, 21740 Granada Avenue, Cupertino, California 95014). They also manufacture an expandable backpack that can be carried by youngsters seven years old to 6'6" in height. This backpack grows as the child grows, which helps cut the cost of buying a new frame every few years.

SHORT PANTS, LONG PANTS — ONE PANT!

Have you ever faced this dilemma: your hiking shorts are too cold at night and long pants are too hot for hiking? Yet you don't really want to carry both items at the same time because of added bulk and weight. Mary Jo, an avid hiker from Colorado has one solution. She has used Navy wool dress pants for her "Short pant, long pant — one pant." She cut her pants off at the desired length for shorts and kept both legs of the pant. She then sewed Velcro ® (a two sided hook and wooly tape) to both legs of the pant with the wooly tape on the top (shorts) and the hooks on the bottom (legs). When Mary Jo wants shorts, the legs disconnect. When long pants are required the legs can be reattached. By the way, Velcro ® holds quite well. In fact when I ran into this idea. Mary Jo was wearing the long pants of her short pants one pant combination on a cold January day in the Rockies.

PHOTOGRAPHY ON THE TRAIL

It would be easy for me to gear up and go on for pages about wilderness photography. A writer of a backpacking book has actually done this — see Chapter 12 "Can Your Backpacking Trip" in C. R. Learn and Anne Tallman's **Backpacker's Digest** (Follett Publishing Company, 1973). One pleasant surprise: Learn has a good word to say about those folding cameras with bellows which one sees in second-hand stores and pawn shops. He even mentions a camera which Art Harris often takes hiking, Zeiss Super Ikonta A, which takes 16 pictures on a standard 120 roll of film. Such cameras have the disadvantages of bellows which can develop pin-hole leaks and which takes a little time to open up when the camera is folded — thus making it hard to catch that deer up ahead. But these cameras have advantages for the backpackers — they are exceedingly compact since they are folding cameras. Also, lens, shutter, and other delicate mechanical operations are well protected in the fold-up position. The works are thus protected against rain and hard knocks.

Naturally, the compact, full-frame 35 mm. cameras with automatic exposure are also ideal wilderness cameras — especially in capturing a fleeting moment when wild turkey hens cross your path or a rattler, sensing danger, is coiled on the trail just ahead.

I have found that for those who have extra cash to burn, a Minolta, Pentax, Nikormat, or Nikon camera can open another realm of nature's wonders. Lenses can be a bit of a weight problem when one starts bringing 50 MM to 200 MM lenses for different effects. But, who is to say? Bringing this many lenses is not important. After going through the multiple lense syndrome myself, I am now satisfied with a Nikormat Body with a 43MM to 86 MM zoom lense. This combination seems to meet most of my picture taking requirements.

For those who do not want to hassle with any type of camera, another solution comes to mind.

Two of my friends who have hiked in Europe, the United States, and Canada never take photographs, preferring full color "mind images" which cost nothing, can be retained through the years, are moving (rather than static), and can be easily stored and transported! "No slide," say Bob and Joe, "can possibly capture the beauty of the Austria's Inner Otzal," so they prefer to remember the August day when they hiked through the Timmelsjoch Pass rather than store it on a 35 MM cardboard slide. So be it.

WILDERNESS SKIING

For some people, wilderness skiing is more fun than summertime backpacking. The Sierra Club, a mountain club which is to the West Coast what the Appalachian Mountain Club is to the East Coast, publishes a comprehensive and inexpensive Totebook: **Wilderness Skiing** by Lito

Tejada-Flores and Allen Steck. This book is especially good when describing terrain suited to Alpine skiing (the Rockies and the West) and terrain suited to Nordic skiing (the East and Midwest). An over-simplification, of course, but their analysis of how Alpine (or downhill skiing) has gotten away from the true origins of skiing in Scandinavia and how Nordic skiing is now enjoying a real surge of interest is worth reading.

The Sierra Club, founded in 1892 by John Muir (whose books still are excellent reading) has almost fifty local chapters in the West and in Alaska and Hawaii. It publishes many helpful books, including various takealong "Totebooks."

Its three addresses are as follows: The Sierra Club, 530 Bush Street, 1050 Mills Tower, San Francisco, California 94108; The Sierra Club, 597 Fifth Avenue, New York, New York 10017; The Sierra Club, 324 "C" Street S.E., Washington, D.C. 20003.

DOWN-FILLED JAC SHIRT

George Harris is very high on his new down-filled Jac Shirt. It is neither a jacket nor a vest, but resembles a western-style workshirt, yet it is made of down and may be helpful down to about 30 degrees. (Available from Gerry in Boulder). I have yet to try one, but it does sound interesting.

Speaking of western-style clothing, I have found very suitable "western wear" that works great in a backpacking situation. I purchased a polyester vest years ago that I still carry on every wilderness excursion.

CARRY IT OUT

Conscientious backpackers — and their number is growing daily — carry plastic bags not only for their own trash, but trash picked up enroute. Yes, it is all carried out of the woods — cans, aluminum foil, plastic. Of course, uneaten food can be placed away from camp in the woods; it will either compost or soon be eaten by an animal.

ODDS AND ENDS

Here are some odds and ends items sometimes carried by backpackers: tweezers, rubber bands (many uses), toothpicks (do not weigh much, right?), dental floss (doubles as strong thread), nail file, baking soda (besides as toothpaste it has **many** other uses — makes a salve for bites, good for upset stomach, and so on), lip salve, lightweight metal mirror (for shaving, for sun signaling in an emergency and whatever). And, last but not least, a "dime" for the phone.

FREEZE DRY AND DEHYDRATED

The process by which these foods are prepared differs. Freeze-dried foods are a result of a newer process and do not require as much soaking as dehydrated foods.

A friend of mine claims that those cereals designed for quick cooking (like Wheatena ® — to be cooked 4 to 5 minutes) can be soaked in water overnight and eaten quite easily in the morning without any cooking. My friend knows one "homesteader, sometimes backpacker" who buys his grains at a feed store and finds them inexpensive indeed.

FOOD ON EVEREST EXPEDITION

Here are some food items carried on the American ascent of Mount Everest in 1963:

Hot cereal
Powdered milk
Sugar
Sweetened condensed milk
Sliced, canned peaches
Ovaltine ®
Jello ®
Canned tuna fish
Metrecal ® cookies
Fruit cake
Pepper and salt
Malt crunch
Vacuum-packed peanut brittle
Tea
Jam

Noodle soup mix
Potato soup mix
Onion soup mix
White bread
Frying potatoes
Chocolate Sustagen ®
Lemonade
Instant vanilla pudding
Meat bars
Breakfast cereal (dry cereal, coconuts, freeze-dried bananas)
Consomme
Mixed nuts
Pemmican
Assorted hard candies

YOUR GOVERNMENT AT WORK

The governments of The United States and Canada publish many pamphlets, leaflets, and maps available at nominal cost. Here are some titles available from the Superintendent of Documents, U.S. Government Printing Office, Washington, D.C. 20402: **Search for Solitude, Camping in National Parks, Backpacking in National Forests.**

Here is where to order topographic maps:

For maps East of the Mississippi; U.S. Geological Survey Distribution C Section, 1200 South Eads Street, Arlington, Virginia 22202.

For West of the Mississippi: U.S. Geological Survey, Distribution Section, Federal Center, Denver, Colorado 80225.

For Alaska: U.S. Geological Survey, 520 Illinois Street, Fairbanks, Alaska 99701.

For Canada: Department of mines and Surveys, Map Distribution Office, 615 Booth Street, Ottawa, Ontario, Canada.

A SORT OF SUMMING UP

At the risk of ending on a negative note rather than a strong upbeat, I would like to list some of the major errors made by beginning backpackers. Much of the time these errors (and I am not certain **errors** is the best word) amount to nothing — no harm is done, the backpacking trip is a success. But now and then, just **one** of these mistakes can be costly. So for the prudent (as a kind of simple review) here are the most common misjudgments made by beginning hikers:

1. **All set to go with brand new hiking boots.** So new, in fact, that they have not been broken in yet — straight from the store to the trail, so to speak. A stiff, properly-constructed hiking boot with plenty of support for ankle and foot obviously requires breaking in. On the other hand, a soft leather waffle stomper or crepe-soled, orange-colored construction worker's boot may "break in" right away. (Obviously, though, with this type of footwear, especially the waffle stomper, a certain amount of foot support and protection is sacrificed in favor of an easy "break in." Which choice of footwear you make in part depends on your **personal** tolerance to pain.

2. **Forgetting to let others when and where you're going.** Somebody — park ranger, mother-in-law, or baby-sitter — should know roughly what your plans are and when you intend to leave the woods. Sometimes a hiking party will turn up missing and the folks back home (who helped load the car) have not the foggiest notion on what trails they planned to hike or where they planned to camp. Makes it tough on search parties. Even a note left under the windshield wipers of a parked car has saved many a hiker from excessive exposure in the woods. A simple note: "I plan to head up the trail to Loch Levens Lakes tonight (the 16th) and go over to the summit of Devil's Peak tomorrow, spending the night at Cascade Lake. The following day I hope to retrace my steps and return to the car by dusk, the evening of the 18th."

3. **The overweight pack.** Can you imagine a man carrying a can of aerosol shaving cream in his backpack on a four-day hike? It has been done. Sometimes, coming across a group of hikers at a campsite, I will stop for a brief rest and chat. Often I am incredulous — there is no other

177

word — at what spills out of their packs. Would you believe — and this is four miles from the nearest highway — one of those AM/FM radios with a cassette player **and** a supply of casette tapes? If **all** the comforts of home can't be carried along, then many people feel a compulsion to carry a good percentage along. Ultimately, every excess pound begins to feel like two or even ten on sharper pitches of trail.

4. **Failing to take a compass along.** Some people think they have an inherent sense of direction, but even good climbers have been mystified in a snowstorm and wandered around in circles. Mountaineering literature is filled with poignant stories of climbers who died of exposure within a hundred yards of a shelter. A compass will not solve all problems of disorientation, but it will prevent one from wandering, using up energy, getting colder and colder and ending up hours later exactly where one started. A compass need not be fancy or expensive. Often it is never used, hike after hike, but then comes that one time when it is invaluable.

5. **Carrying too much [or not enough!] water:** Sometimes one comes across a group hiking on a trail which parallels a rushing mountain stream, crossing it here and there en route. Each of them has a belt or shoulder canteen full of home tap water, now with the added taste of aluminum. "Why, or why?" I ask myself. Is it because of a false belief that city tap water is so pure? (Recent studies on the drinking water of cities, most especially New Orleans, should put the lie to **that** belief.) Is it because these Scouts believe that a rushing mountain stream, cascading over rocks and eddying into swift pools as the water tumbles down the mountain, is not fit to drink? I am not saying **all** outdoor water is safe, but I will take my chances on a rushing mountain stream. Too often water is backpacked through areas with perfectly adequate springs or stream water for drinking. (At 2 ½ lbs. per quart, that is a heavy price to pay).

Conversely there are dry areas — and even dry periods when lively streams have turned to dry stream beds — when it is essential to carry water. Above timberline in the dazzling sun one often needs more water than usual. A little common sense is called for.

6. **Hiking without adequate footwear.** We have all seen groups of hikers with sneakers or, if you prefer, tennis shoes. Sometimes a basketball sneaker which goes higher up the ankle is seen. It is easy to be patronizing about such footgear and dismiss it as totally inadequate for backpacking without considering the economics of things: these hikers may be inner-city children from the Bedford-Stuyvesant section of Brooklyn who are on a four-week "summer camp" away from the city — so-called "fresh air children." Possibly some of them have never been outside the boundaries of New York City before. They are fortunate to have new sneakers. Not everyone can afford to order a pair of $75 Molitor Wanderhorn boots specially made by Karl Molitor in Switzerland. Is it

178

better for them to be out here climbing the rocky summit of a small mountain in trail-wet sneakers or not here at all? The answer is obvious.

We Americans often have equipment hang-ups. In Viet Nam, members of the National Liberation Front Army moved about the jungle in sandals made from discarded rubber tires. They marched incredible distances carrying great weights or pushing bicycles and outmaneuvered infantry "foot soldiers" with much better footgear. I mention this only to soften my basic thrust: sneakers or sandals are all right for hiking now and then but are not really adequate for serious or sustained wilderness backpacking. If you are strapped, hike in sneakers, waffle stompers, or contruction worker's shoes, but if you have the money, try breaking in a pair of good hiking boots. If your feet have stopped growing, the boots may last a lifetime.

7. **Carrying an axe or hatchet.** Earlier I mentioned the old-time "woodsman" approach to wilderness camping in which no hiker was properly outfitted without a hatchet and a sharp knife to strip boughs, knock down trees, and the like. In highly impacted wilderness areas today, there is no need to build a lean-to — except, of course, in a survival situation when many of our rules must be tossed aside. Nor is there any reason to hack away at trees for firewood. Fires are prohibited in many forests today. In some places, they are allowed only by permit. Leave the axe at home.

8. **Carrying canned goods.** Today, with an abundance of portable foods, there is little reason to backpack canned goods into the woods. Oh, there might be an exception here and there. Sardines and tuna fish are often carried. I know a very sensible hiker who carries a pound can of peanut butter along and I cannot second-guess her, for she knows more about nutrition than I shall ever know and feels she is properly **fueled** by all that protein. (She puts the peanut butter in a coffee can.)

Most (but not all) canned goods contain a great quantity of moisture, so you end up carrying water. Also, cans are impossible to dispose of properly and a drag to lug back out. Now with freeze-dried and dehydrated foods common in supermarkets (once they were only available in mountaineering supply stores), it is easy to avoid canned goods altogether.

9. **Inconsiderateness:** This is a ten-dollar word for forgetting where one is. Do hikers have to have in-the-woods beer blasts accompanied by loud music from a transistor radio? It does no good to preach about such things in a book like this; first of all, few people appreciate being on the receiving end of a preachment; secondly, such beer-blast backpackers are probably not readers of this book anyway.

179

PUTTING ON A PACK

1. Face the shoulder strap side of the pack.
2. Grab the frame by the side members (the pack should never be picked up by the shoulder strap) with your hands just above the shoulder strap cross member.
3. Place your right leg out in front of your body, and pick the pack up resting it on the foreleg.
4. Slip your right arm through the farthest shoulder strap away from you (the right shoulder strap).
5. Lift the pack up, swing it up on your shoulders, grab the left shoulder strap with your left arm, and put it through the shoulder strap area.
6. Hunch both shoulders to settle the pack. Put waist strap on the normal way.

TAKING THE PACK OFF

1. Spread your legs for balance, take the waist strap off your body, slip your left arm and hand from underneath the shoulder strap.
2. Grab the top of the right side member with your left hand.
3. Extend your right leg and swing the pack around. Rest it on the top of the foreleg.
4. Draw your right arm through the shoulder strap and grab the side members with both hands. Then lower the pack to the ground. NOTE: This may seem like a lot of trouble, but I've found that to protect one's pack and back this method works perfectly well, and after a little practice, seems easier than many methods. Never just drop a pack on the ground.

THE CALKINS METHOD

If you want to impress your friends and fellow hikers, then the "Calkins Method" is for you:

1. Face your pack so that the pack bag is leaning against your body.
2. Put your arms through their prospective shoulder strap sides and grab the side members on the longer half of the frame.
3. Lift the pack up, gracefully swing it over your head with arms extended skyward. Suddenly you will find your pack resting on your shoulders, with you ready to go tramping through the wilds.
WARNING: Make sure everything on your pack is tied down and secure before attempting the "Calkins Method." (Unsecured articles only tend to bang you on the head in the middle of your swing).

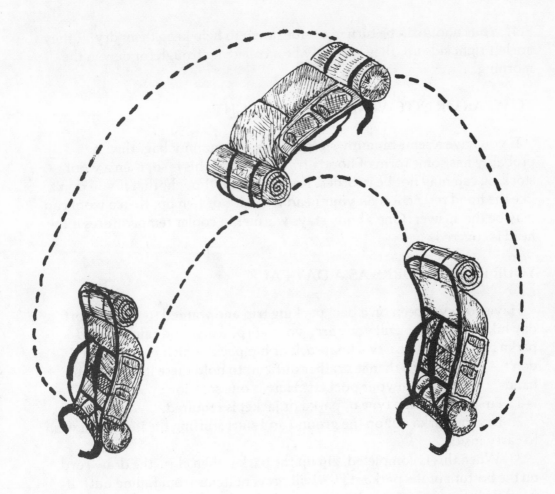

YOUR CLOTHES AND NIGHT TIME

I have been asked occasionally what I do with clothes and boots at night. And, is there anything such as a backpacking pillow? These two questions can be answered as one. Any clothing that you take off your body at night (you should never sleep in the clothing that you've worn all day) should be put into one of the following places:

1. In your sleeping bag stuff bag. Clothes that fall into this category should be somewhat dry. (Example: A down jacket). This, of course, would double as your pillow. Make sure you give the stuff bag a "whack" in the middle before going to sleep. This will prevent it from moving around at night.

2. Any damp clothing should go into your sleeping bag to dry out during the night. (Example: All inner garments, underwear, socks, T-shirt, or long underwear.)

3. Pants, shorts, or outer shirts can be laid underneath the sleeper (in the leg area) for insulation.

4. Your boots can be turned upside down to help keep them dry. If they are left right side up, they will only be a collecting trough for dew in the morning.

TO WEAR OR NOT WEAR A CAP AT NIGHT

If you have a semi-mummy sleeping bag, or mummy bag, then it probably has some form of hood arrangement. If this is so, then a wool stocking cap may not be in order. Keep in mind, though, that if you don't like the hood restriction on your head when it's drawn up, then a wool cap may be the answer. One's body stays warmer in cooler temperatures if the head is covered.

YOUR PARKA WORKS AS A DAY PACK

Have you ever been on a backpacking trip and wanted to take a short day hike? But where will you carry your gorp, water and rain or wind parka? If you didn't carry a knapsack or hip pack (which most people don't — too heavy), then it's rather difficult to hold these items in your hands, or put them in your pockets. Here is one solution:
1. First of all, some type of parka or jacket is required.
2. Lay the parka out on the ground and start stuffing the items you wish to carry inside.
3. When this is completed, zip up the parka, then close the draw cord on the bottom of the parka. (This will prevent items from falling out). If your parka has a draw cord on the hood, then do the same.
4. Roll the bottom of the parka over the items which you have placed inside. Make this roll as tight as possible and bind it with the draw cord from the bottom of the parka.
5. Take the sleeves and wrap them around your waist then tie them with a square knot. (Right sleeve over left sleeve; left sleeve over right sleeve). If the parka is made out of nylon, this knot will prevent it from slipping.
6. Now you have a hip or fanny pack for your day trip.
7. One question, what do you do if you have to put the parka on? (Stuff the items in the parka's pockets)

BANDANA FOR A HEADBAND

Many people find it difficult to wear a sun hat and use a bandana as a sweat band. (By the way, if you have a felt hat, it will absorb moisture — sweat — much better than a straw hat will). This sweat band can also be soaked in a stream (as a felt hat can) to keep more water next to your skin. You usually don't have to take as many drinks by using this method. But, what about wearing a bandana and a hat together? Not unless you have a hat that's several sizes larger than your head. One answer is:

1. When rolling the bandana, make it wider, thus this will make it thinner.

2. Make a hat out of the bandana. This can be done by folding the bandana where the tip of one of the corners is in the middle. Then place it over your head, tieing the other two ends in a knot and stuffing the last corner underneath. Voila — you have a sweat cap. This wide bandana or sweat cap makes it possible to have not only sweat absorption, but sun protection.

THE FILM CAN SURVIVAL KIT

Having carried one of these for years, I've found it to be somewhat of a security in bad times. The contents listed may be of some help (it's better than nothing), and they all fit into a 35 mm film can. It's small and compact (it should be carried on the person and not in the pack), and the film can helps keep it waterproof.

1. **Waterproof matches** — Regular kitchen matches strike anywhere. (By the way, your zipper fly has an excellent surface for striking matches). The matches should be waterproofed with fingernail polish and not wax or paraffin. (The paraffin only melts in hot weather). You should carry around eight, and the match will probably have to be shortened to fit into the can.

2. **Compass** — Small crackerjack type or toy kind. It won't find your camp for you, but it will keep you going in a straight line.

3. **Fish hooks and fly** — The smaller the hook, the better. You're fishing for food, not a prize fish.

4. **Fish line and sinkers** — Rolled on a small piece of cardboard keeps it from getting tangled.

5. **Razor blade** — A double-edged razor, cut in half (it's not meant to replace your knife, but it can be useful).

6. **Adhesive tape** — Eighteen to twenty inches, rolled tightly on a matchstick.

7. **Bandaids** — Plastic type, rolled or folded tightly and bonded with scotch tape.

8. **Gauze pad** — 2" x 2", folded tightly, but don't break the wrapper. Keep it sterile.

9. **Snare wire** — If one wants this, No. 32 copper wire can be used.

10. **A small metal mirror.**

FRUIT PEMMICAN FOR EMERGENCIES

This item, again, should be carried on the person and not in the pack. Fruit pemmican is an excellent source of carbohydrates for quick energy. It will also last without refrigeration for an indefinite time period. Here are the directions:

INGREDIENTS:

Graham Crackers
Honey
Peanuts
Moist pack apricots
Lemon juice
Raisins
Moist pack peaches
Moist pack apples
Pitted prunes

Equipment Needed:

Crank Grinder
Large Sauce Pan
Tin Foil
Large Handled Spoon
Mounting Block for Grinder

Directions:

Step 1 — Mount grinder on the top of a table; put sauce pan below it.

Step 2 — Start grinding up the fruit; alternate fruit with graham crackers and peanuts until everything is completely ground.

Step 3 — Mix all ingredients thoroughly; add lemon juice (this will take some of the sweetness out of the taste); add more graham crackers if the mix is too gooey (the crackers will help absorb the fruit juices).

Step 4 — Add honey to mixture and stir well; The honey is your preservative; the pemmican will last indefinitely.

Step 5 — Cut sheets of tin foil in half and make them 8" to 9" long. Take a handful and roll it like a rope, seal in foil and store until needed.

SEARCHING FOR A LOST FRIEND

When someone is lost, it can be as confusing for the searcher as it is for one who is lost, especially if there are no leads to work on. The first item that should be taken care of is:

1. Contact the local authorities (Sheriff, Forest Service or National Park Service personnel). Make sure you send two people out (if possible) to contact these authorities. They should also be well equipped for their journey (including flashlight and money for making phone calls).

2. If there is a time element involved, or a storm moving in or possible injury to the lost friend, then a search party may be in order. (Of course, it depends on the number of people in your group). When forming this search party, keep these thoughts in mind.

Set a time when you will call the search off for that day (before sunset, for example).

Fan the search party out enough to be effective, but don't lose sight or verbal communication with either member of the party. You don't want searchers getting lost looking for the searchee.

3. Where do you start? The last place where the "lost victim" was seen. If the victim is a youth, he/she will generally travel uphill, because more energy, and to see what's on the other side of the hill. If it's an older adult, he/she will generally travel downhill (the less energy expended, the better).

4. If the victim has a whistle, listen for it. (Three blasts — S.O.S.) Too many times, the searchers are making so much noise, they cannot possibly hear the victim.

These hints may give you some idea of where to start and, hopefully, find that friend that you're looking for.

THEFT IN THE WILDERNESS

Unfortunately, it's true, and theft happens all the time. I have a woman friend who is a wilderness ranger in the Trinity Alps. She left her camp to view a sunset on **Yonder Hill**, and when she returned, all of her equipment was gone. Not even a toothbrush was left. It's disheartening to hear about and even more sickening to experience.

To be ripped off in the wilderness is certainly one of the lowest blows that one human can deal to another. It's bad enough to have to replace equipment, and some items just can't be replaced. If someone has stolen all your survival tools, how are you going to protect yourself in the wilderness? As you can see, theft in the wilderness is a despicable act.

So, be aware of it at all times. No matter how secluded the area seems to you, stash your equipment whenever you leave it. Stashing entails gathering it up, repacking it, and covering it with a tarp either behind a tree, under large rock, or in the brush. It may seem to be a waste of energy, but, unfortunately, it's necessary.

KNOWING YOUR HIKING COMPANIONS' SHOE SIZE AND TREAD PATTERN

How could this even be important? Well, being **observant** has been mentioned throughout this book. This little item is just another feather in your cap. If one of your companions becomes disoriented (not lost) for awhile, your memory of his or her trail boot can aid you in tracking and recovering. You may, as I do, often separate from the hiking group to look at a view. By knowing shoe sizes and treads one can rejoin the group with ease. Even the freshness of the track can indicate how far ahead the group is. In the winter one can keep track of people by noticing what type of snowshoe they're wearing.

THE SNOWSHOE CHAIR

One is forever looking for a place to sit down when camping in the snow. Imagine! Not being able to sit down for 12 hour or even 2 days. It can be frustrating. Here's one solution:

1. Stamp down the snow in a six foot area with your snowshoes.
2. Stamp down the snow with your boots (or dig) creating a hole 2 feet by 2 feet and a foot deep.
3. Lay one of your snowshoes over the hole with the main part of the body lacing centered in the middle. Place the shoe in a fashion that the curved toe is facing down. (This prevents the shoe from shifting).
4. Place your other shoe vertically in back of the hole and butted up to the other which is laying down. Make sure the curved toe is out and then push the heel of the shoe into the snow until it's secure.
5. The snowshoe laying horizontally is your seat, and the standing vertically shoe is your back rest. I've cooked dinners and had long conversations in this type of chair. It's amazingly comfortable, and just think, you didn't have to carry one extra ounce for this luxury.
6. A chair such as this can also be made from cross country skis. Just avoid sitting or leaning on the running side (that wax gets awfully sticky). The weight bearing capacity of the ski might be considered.

CANDLE ON THE HEELS OF YOUR SOCKS

For years, hikers have been plagued with having their socks wear out in the heel area first. Darning, of course, can help. But, let's think of a way to prevent the hole-in-the-heel problem first. An old woodsperson friend of mine offers this simple solution. Rub the heels of your socks with a candle. This helps cut down friction, which is generally higher in the heel area. If the toe area of the sock starts looking thin, examine your toenails. They may need cutting.

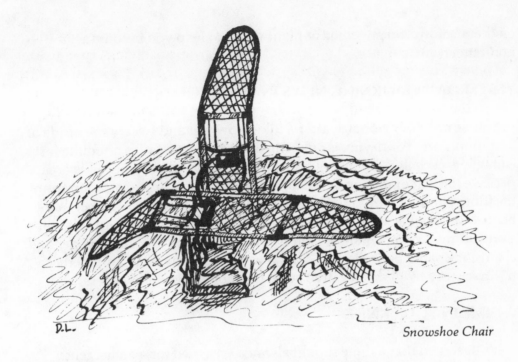

Snowshoe Chair

DO YOUR SOCKS RUB YOU THE WRONG WAY

Another problem which has irritated some hikers for years is blisters on the bottoms and sides of their feet. One cause can be the terrycloth lining of the sock. This liner is intended to cushion and absorb moisture from the foot. For some, it does, for other, it gives nothing but feet-aches.

One solution is to turn the inner wrong side out with the terrycloth liner to the outside, away from the foot. You still retain the cushioning effect, but you get rid of the abrasion which sometimes plagues those with tender feet. By having this surface to the outside, the terrycloth, which absorbs moisture, is away from your foot. You lessen the possibility of blisters which are formed by abrasion (heat) and excessive sweat. During the winter, when sweat can be a detriment, I like turning my socks inside out. This steps up the process of passing sweat from the inner sock to the outer, and up to the top portion of the boot, where it's passed to the outside air. Speaking of sweaty feet, baby powder or foot powder helps cut down friction and absorb sweat from you feet.

TOUGH ON THOSE FEET

So you won't be a tenderfoot (literally) in the wilds, you can start toughening your feet up weeks before your hike even starts. Try walking around with no shoes on (even in your house) to let your feet breathe. This, of course, also develops tougher skin and callouses. Rubbing alcohol

187

on them before you go to bed at night will also help you become a non-tenderfoot.

YESTERDAY'S MORNING NEWS IN YOUR BOOTS

You've probably noticed, after a hike, how wet and sweaty the inside of your boots are. Air drying is one remedy but sometimes it's not quite fast enough, especially with hiking boots which are padded in the ankle area. Because this padding is open celled, it absorbs water or perspiration from the foot. This moisture is trapped between the two layers of leather in the boot. If the boot leather is not thoroughly dry before the next trip, it will start rotting. To prevent this, simply stuff your boots with newspaper and change the paper periodically. After a week or so, take it out altogether. (A positive story to all the negative notes that come with newspapers).

A DIME IN YOUR KNIFE

It's been said that a dime should always be carried for an emergency phone call. There are several places this piece of copper and silver can be carried. One is in your first aid kit. Some friends of mine sew a dime into the lapel of their shirt. I carry one in my first aid kit and another in my pocket knife (sandwiched in between my screw driver and main blades).

LETTING YOUR SLEEPING BAG HANG OUT

I have mentioned in the sleeping bag section about airing your bag in storage. If you don't have room in your closet (hanging it over the dowel), then hang it from the wall. Place a nail in the corner of the ceiling and the wall. Then take a wooden or plastic hanger and place it on the inside of the hood of your sleeping bag. Draw the hood up around it, and place the hanger on the nail that's in the wall.

STUFF BAGS AND LEAKY SEAMS

I have long watched the evolution of the stuff bag. One problem that occurs with stuff bags is leaky bottom seams. Since most manufacturers use two separate pieces of waterproof material to put their stuff bags together, seams always become a water hazard especially because the stuff bag sticks out on the back of the frame. Here are two solutions:
1. Use a seam sealer (Kenyon ® is one type. Beware: Inhaling seam sealer solutions damages brain cells as do many other things, of course). This sealer waterproofs the seam. Check periodically for water leaks.
2. For those who can afford two stuff bags, place the second stuff bag

over the first, except insert going the opposite direction (Top over the bottom, and bottom over the top). A garbage bag or an oversized plastic bag will work just as well. This double layer also ensures better foul weather protection for your sleeping bag.

KEEPING THE DOWN IN YOUR BAG

Have you ever sprung a hole in your sleeping bag? Perhaps you loaned it to someone (which I don't recommend) and their cigarette got away from them. If you have a hole in your sleeping bag, here's a solution:

* Push as much of the down or polyester back into the bag.
* Patching can be done with the following:
Adhesive tape — for those on the trail catastrophes
Ripstop tape — for a more permanent patch job. Ripstop tape may be purchased from any backpacking store for 15 to 30 cents a foot. What's ripstop tape? Ripstop tape is only strips of ripstop nylon material cut into two inch strips. A sticky backing is put on one side to adhere to the sleeping bag.
* Patching the hole — cut a section off the ripstop tape (make the length generous). Round off the corners on the rectangular strip to prevent raveling. Then peel off the paper backing and apply to the nylon material of the sleeping bag. (If the sleeping bag is soiled, the ripstop may not adhere, so contact cement will help.) When applying the patch, press hard and rub from the middle out. Make sure that all the edges of the patch are in contact with the shell of the sleeping bag. Now you're all ready to go on that upcoming backpacking excursion this weekend.

THAT GOOD OLD USEFUL GARBAGE BAG

There is one item used in the home that is ideal for the wilderness. That is the familiar plastic garbage bag (Around 8 to 10 cents, 30 gal. size). A head hole can be cut in the bottom of the bag and arm holes cut in the sides (a custom fit). The garbage bag can also be used for a pack cover, as long as one side of the bag is cut away to facilitate the shoulder straps and waist band parts of the pack.

THE FIVE STEP, ONE STEP SHUFFLE

When traveling cross-country, wasted energy should be kept to a minimum. One energy drainer is traveling on the slope of mountain or hill and trying to maintain a straight and level course. With an objective in mind and in sight (on the other side of the slope), one starts off. After reaching the area of the objective, this hiker finds that uphill travel is necessary to compensate for elevation lost in travel. One way of eliminating this drain of energy, at the last minute, is the five, stop, one step shuffle." What this entails is for every five steps taken forward, one step can be taken uphill. When reaching your objective on the other side of the slope, one finds that they are fairly level with that objective.

A PACK FOR PEOPLE'S BEST FRIEND

The subject of dogs in the wilds has been discussed, but not much was said about a pack for this creature. Many people object to carrying their dog's food, and why not? They should carry their own. But, when you start looking for manufactured dog packs, you will be startled by the price ($18 to $30.00). I suggest buying a dog harness and attaching two small bags on either side (Army ammo pouches work fine. Or make your own).

WHAT'S A WILDERNESS AREA?

The Wilderness Preservation Act of 1964 has set aside areas that can be used by the walking public. Foot travel is the only way one can travel through a wilderness area. (Motorized vehicles and equipment are prohibited). Wilderness areas exist within National Park boundaries, and on U.S. Forest Service lands. Both proposed wilderness areas (N.P.S.) and primitive areas (U.S.F.S.) fall under the same rules and regulations, plus wilderness permit usage.

WILDERNESS PERMITS — A HASSLE OR A HELP?

Many people feel that wilderness permits are only an extension of Government harassment gone to the hills. Some feel that local people around wilderness areas should be exempt, or these permits are just too damn much trouble. But, the permits are part of a fairly new program (1971), and they should be tried. I agree that it does take you out of your way. You can either pick one up on the way to a wilderness area, or if it's late at night, some forest service and park stations will leave a permit taped to their door for you (please call ahead for this type of arrangement). Another way to get a permit is to fill out a **Wilderness Permit Application** and send it by mail to the prospective wilderness area station where you'll be traveling. (Allow for a week for this method.)

Another benefit is that the wilderness permit makes people aware of fire regulations and general wilderness practices. Did you know that a shovel with a 5″ x 7″ blade and twelve inch handle is required? (No more garden trowels). That some form of a bucket is required, and that no more than 25 people can travel in one group, and for some wilderness areas, the number is even lower? That all camps must be at least 100 feet away from any waterway? I could go on and on. But, as you can see, a wilderness permit helps educate the backpacking public. The wilderness permit also keeps tabs on the numbers of people who are traveling in different areas. For example, if Five Lakes Basin draws 500 permits in a year, compared to 5 at Frog Lake, just over the hill, which area do you think would have greater impact? Which area would need to be maintained more? Since Five Lakes Basin is traveled into more (popular), it needs a helping hand from both the backpacker and park and forest service personnel. I hope the idea of wilderness permits becomes a little more palatable to you. Then, maybe, the wilderness permit will seem more of a help than a hassle.

WHAT'S A FIRE PERMIT?

A fire permit is required for private land, forest service land, and national park boundaries. To get one, go to any forest service or park service headquarters, fill out the card, take a short test (this test entails knowing the regulations of building a fire), and sign the card. By the way, if you carry a stove, a fire permit is still required. If you obtain a wilderness permit, that acts as a fire permit, but fire permits are not wilderness permits.

WHAT'S THE DIFFERENCE?

I have asked many times about the difference between National Park Service and U.S. Forest Service wilderness permit requirements. Since I have never seen any answers to these questions in backpacking books, I thought I would try to give you a little insight. **Both National Park Service and U.S. Forest Service wilderness permits are required** for all day-hiking and overnight camping in all wilderness and primitive areas.

1. Wilderness permits are issued at ranger stations and field office near point of entry.
2. Wilderness permits are free.
3. Wilderness permits act as fire permits.
4. Each wilderness, primitive, and national park wilderness areas has to own specific rules and regulations (see below).
5. Good for a single trip.
6. Wilderness permits can be obtained by:
   Mail — at least 15 days prior to trip departure.
   In person — During office hours listed in each wilderness section.
   By telephone — During office hours. In some areas you can arrange a permit by phone. At others, you can secure information only.
7. Reservations are available for some wilderness areas which have capacity or trailhead entry. Reservations usually pertain to N.P.S. wilderness areas, but sometimes U.S.F.S. areas also.

Some differences between the N.P.S. (National Park Service) and U.S.F.S. (U.S. Forest Service), as far as regulations are concerned, are:

1. A wilderness permit issued by a national park for a trip starting in a national forest wilderness is valid in both the park and forest. The reverse is also true.
2. National parks do not allow dogs in the back country. Fines up to $50.00. No firearms may be carried.
3. U.S. Forest Service allows dogs in the back country. No regulation on firearms.
4. In the back country without a wilderness permit, fines and citations are levied on anyone who is within a national park boundary or national wilderness area boundary.

NOTE: Each organization and specific area does have slightly different regulations.

COMMENT: Now that you've seen the reasoning behind all this, please take out a wilderness permit. It is important to all of us as wilderness users — Thanks.

SHOWBIZ IN THE HILLS

The danger of backpacking becoming ensnared in the high price, high hype, elitist marketplace (like downhill skiing) is already with us. But as we have constantly pointed out you don't have to be trapped — you can improvise with very little money in your pocket.

Already in some Western mountains you'll meet some modern day villains on the trail. Villains, armed with point-of-purchase promotions, sales and exclusives, will confront you with the latest and expensive merchandise lines from over-enterprising backpacking and mountaineering stores. Their tee-shirts are emblazoned with store names and inevitably they are costumed in what they hope will become the new hiking costume — from multi-colored terry cloth headbands to fancy mint-condition boots (usually much too heavy for comfortable tramping). Your option is embarrassingly simple — walk away.

BEING THE CARETAKER

Inevitably, as you backpack in the wilderness, you begin to be a **caretaker**. The sight of garbage, devastated trees, floating toilet paper in the forest regions will repulse you. You wonder how you can help prevent this littering. You wonder how you can create an awareness among the occasional hikers, so accustomed to the disorder of the cities, to recognize and to be in tune with an undefiled nature.

Oftentimes when you find a hiker or hikers abusing the wilderness it is not owing to their carelessness as much as their lack of knowledge about the ecosystem. Bio-degradable soap used in a natural waterway is superior to regular soap in terms of polluting but it is still mixing a foreign material in a natural setting.

No book dealing with the outdoors is worth its salt unless it imparts the latest knowledge on wilderness conservation. So, while I join the lists of backpacking writers, I am also aware that I am promoting the sport and perhaps increasing the use of the forests, even endangering it if the new backpacker is unmindful of protecting the wilderness. Yet it is a risk that backpacking writers must take.

Backpacking as a sport is well on its way to resembling the downhill ski market with all the new offerings in lightweight and stylized equipment. This should put us all on guard. I would deem it a tragedy if children and people of all ages are discouraged from backpacking because they don't have this very poshy equipment. I would rather have caretaker-like people enjoying the wilderness experience with the most modest and makeshift equipment than to be superbly outfitted but lacking in feeling for conservation of the wilderness.

Dear Readers,

Now that I've had my say, I would welcome your comments. As backpackers we like to think of ourselves as individuals committed to one of the most individualistic of all activities. Besides the demands backpacking makes upon our physical well-being, it can claim as its very special domain — the potential to raise our levels of consciousness — and this is what makes real and whole people.

With gratitude,
Dennis Look
Sacramento, California
July 1976

Bibliography

At the request of several colleges, schools and training classes, here is a listing of books and authors noted in the text.

American on Everest, by James Ramsey Ullman (J.B. Lippincott, 1964), Philadelphia, Pa.

Appalachia Magazine, December, 1974.

Backpacking: One Step at a Time, by Harvey Manning (The R.E.I. Press, 1972), Seattle, Wash.

Backpacking Made Easy, by Michael Abel (Naturgraph, 1972), Healdsburg, Ca.

Be an Expert With Map and Compass, by Bjorn Kjellstrom (Scribners, 1955), New York, NY.

Diet for a Small Planet, by Frances Moore Lappe' (Balantine Books, 1972), New York, NY.

Give Me The Hills, by Mariam Underhills (Chatham Press, 1956), Riverside, Conn.

Hiking the Appalachian Trail, Edited by James R. Hare (Rodale Press, 1975), Emmaus, Pa.

How to Stay Alive in the Woods, by Bradford Angier (Collier Books, 1962), New York, NY.

Hypothermia, Killer of the Unprepared, by Dr. Theodore G. Lathrop (Mazamas, 1973), Portland, Or.

Movin' Out, by Harry Roberts (Stonewall Press, 1975), Lexington, Mass.

Outdoorsman's Medical Guide, by Alan E. Nourse, M.D. (Harper and Row, 1974), New York, NY.

Outdoor Survival Skills, by Larry Olsen (Brigham Young University Press, 1974), Provo, Utah.

Orienteering, by John Disley (Stackpole, 1973), Harrisburg, Pa.

Recipes for a Small Planet, by Ellen Buchman Ewald (Ballantine Books, 1973), New York, NY.

Sand County Almanac, by Aldo Leopold (Oxford University, Ballantine Books, 1949), New York, NY.

Snow Camper's Guide, by Raymond Bridge (Scribner's, 1973), New York, NY.

Stalking the Wild Asparagus, by Ewell Gibbons (David McKay, 1962), New York, NY.

Superintendent of Documents, U.S. Government Printing Office, Washington, D.C. 20402, **Search for Solitude, Camping in National Parks, Backpacking in National Forests.**

Sweet and Sour: The Sugar Menace, John Pekkanen and Mathea Falco (Atlantic Monthly, July, 1975).

The Backpacker, by Albert Saijo (101 Productions, 1972), San Francisco, CA.

The Survival Book, by Nesbitt, Pond and Allen (Van Nostrand, 1959), New York, NY.

The Ultimate Journey, by Eric and Tim Ryback (Chronicle Books, 1971), San Francisco Ca.

Three Years of Arctic Service, by General Adolphus Greely (Charles Scribners, 1885), New York, NY.

Wilderness Digest, The High Adventure Team, Western Region, 1974, Los Angeles, CA., Don M. Deck, Editor.

Wilderness Skiing, by Lito Tejada — Flores and Allen Steck, (Sierra Club Books, 1972), San Francisco, CA.

Suggested Readings

There is an overwhelming selection of books dealing with backpacking and related subjects available. The following list names books and authors with which I am most familiar. Happily, libraries, book stores and backpacking outlets are doing an increasingly good job of stocking wilderness literature.

HIKING BOOKS, EQUIPMENT, TECHNIQUES, ADVENTURE

Mountaineering, Freedom of the Hills, by the Climbing Committee of the Mountaineers (The Mountaineers, Seattle, 1960)

Basic Mountaineering, San Diego Chapter, (Sierra Club, third Edition 1970)

The New Complete Walker, Colin Fletcher (Knopf, New York 1974)

Backpacking One Step At A Time, by Harvey Manning (REI Press Seattle 1972)

Pleasure Packing, by Robert S. Wood (Condor Books, Berkeley, 1972)

The Man Who Walked Through Time, by Colin Fletcher (Vintage Books, New York, 1968)

Backpacking, by R. C. Rethmel (Burgess Publishing Co., 1964)

Backpacking Techniques, by Ruth Mendenhall (La Siesta Press, Glendale, 1967)

Lightweight Camping Equipment and How to Make It, by Gerry Cunningham and Margaret Hanson, (Charles Scribner's & Sons, New York, 1976)

America's Backpacking Book, by Raymond Bridge (Charles Scribners & Sons, New York, 1973)

Backpacking For Fun, by Thomas Winnett (Wilderness Press, Berkeley 1972)

The Backpacker, by Albert Saijo, (101 Press, San Francisco, 1972)

Woman in the Woods, by Kathleen Farmer, (Stackpolis Books, Harrisburg, 1976)

Going Light with Backpack and Burro, edited by David Brower (Sierra Club, San Francisco, 1951)

FOOD FOR THOUGHT, FOOD FOR ENERGY

Back to Nature, by Frank Ford (Harvest Press, Inc., Fort Worth, 1974)

Roughing it Easy, by Dian Thomas (Brigham Young University Press, Provo, 1974)

Edible and Poisonous Plants of this Western United States, by Calvin P. Burt and Frank G. Heyl, 1970

Stalking the Wild Asparagus, by Euell Gibbons (David McKay Inc., New York, 1970)

Stalking the Healthful Herbs, by Euell Gibbons (David McKay Inc., New York, 1970)

Backpack Cookery, by Ruth Mendenhall (La Siesta Press, Glendale 1968)

Food for Knapsackers and other Trail Travelers, by Winnie Thomas and Hasse Bunnelle (Sierra Club, San Francisco, 1971)

COMMON SENSE TOOLS

Surviving the Unexpected Wilderness, by Gene Fear (Survival Education Assn.) other pamphlets write: 9035 Golden Given Road, Tacoma, WA. 98445

Outdoor Living: Problems, Solutions, Guidelines, edited by Eugene Fear, Assisted by John Simac and Everett Lasher (Tacoma Unit of Mountain Rescue Council, Tacoma.)

Teaching for Survival, by Mark Terry (Balantine, Friends of the Earth, New York, 1971)

Mountaineering Medicine, by Fred T. Darvill, Jr. M.D. (Skagit Mountain Rescue Unit Inc., 1975)

Mountaineering First Aid, by Dick Mitchell (The Mountaineers, Seattle, 1972)

Medicine for Mountaineering, by James A. Wilkerson and others (The Mountaineers, Seattle, 1967)

American Red Cross First Aid Textbook, Standard and Advanced (The American Red Cross, Distributed by Doubleday Inc., 1973)

Hypothermia, Killer of the Unprepared, by Dr. Theodore G. Lathrop (Mazamas, Portland, 1973)

THE OTHER SEASON (WINTER)

The Cross-Country Ski, Cook, Look and Pleasure Book and Welcome to the Alice in Snow Peopleland, by Hal Painter (Wilderness Press, Berkeley, 1973)

Snowshoeing, by Gene Prater (The Mountaineers, Seattle, 1974)

Snow Campers Guide, by Raymond Bridge (Charles Scribners, New York, 1973)

ABC of Avalanches, by Ed Lachapelle (Colorado Outdoor Sports, Denver Revision Edition 1969)

The Snowshoe Book, by William Osgood and Leslie Hurley (The Stephen Greene Press, Battleboro, Vermont, 1971)

A Field Guide to Animal Tracks, by Olaus J. Murie (Houghton Mifflin Co., Boston, 1975)

BRINGING UPON A NEW ETHIC

Sand County Almanac, by Aldo Leopold (Oxford University, Ballantine Books, New York, 1949)

On the Loose, by Jerry and Renny Russell, (Sierra Club Books, San Francisco)

In Wilderness is the Preservation of the World, by Elliott Porter, (Sierra Club Books, San Francisco)

FILMS

By Nature's Rules, 28 Min., 1970, Color. Distributed by Jim Lawless, Motion Pictures Consultant, 1545 N.E. 130th St. Seattle, WA. 98125 (Excellent presentation showing the effects of Hypothermia upon outdoor people)

Backpacking, 16 Min., 1975. Distributed by Westwind Productions, P.O. Box 3532, Boulder, CO. 80803
(Since there are still very few basic backpacking films, this film has at least made an attempt; not too bad.)

MAGAZINES

Backpacker, 65 Adams Street, Bedford Hills, N.Y. 10507
Wilderness Camping, P.O. Bo 1186, Scotia, N.Y. 12302
Off-Belay, 12416 169th Ave. S.E., Renton, WA. 98055
Mountain Gazette, 2025 York Street, Denver, CO. 80205
Mariah, 3401 W. Division Street, Chicago, Ill. 60651

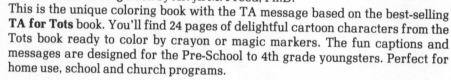

AVAILABLE FROM JALMAR PRESS

The Book That Tells Teenagers They're OK. Dr. Freed does it again!*

TA for Teens (and other Important people) by Alvyn M. Freed, Ph.D. #5 in Transactional Analysis for Everybody Series. This vital new book is aimed at telling Teens and their PIC's (People in Charge) that they are OK. **Teens** is designed to bring teens, parents, relatives, teachers and friends into closer and more satisfying relationships. Dr. Freed offers new choices and options to teenagers in dealing with the dilemmas of growing up in a positive way.
* Author of TA for Kids, TA for Tots.

Perfect Bound $7.95

How to Use TA to Solve People Problems in Business and Industry

TA for Management: Making Life Work by Theodore B. Novey, Ph.D. #3 in Transactional Analysis for Everybody Series. If you are a manager, boss, supervisor or leader of a company or organization, Dr. Novey's book can help you deal with people and people-problems. **TA for Management** applies TA principles to organizational dilemmas. Dr. Novey's description of crisis handling, middle secence and busting out of group games is easily the best treatment ever given the subject.

Perfect Bound $7.95

At Last . . . a Usable Guide for Teacher of Modern Dance

A Time to Teach, A Time to Dance by Margaret DeHaan Freed, M.A. Especially recommended for secondary school teachers and teacher-training institutions. **A Time to Teach, A Time to Dance** is a unique approach to teaching modern dance. The author, a master teacher, encapsulates her years of successful dance experience in this lucid, easily read book. Marge Freed's belief that dance fulfills young people's need for emotional and affective experience is further expressed through the striking photography of Alex Ortiz.

Hardbound $14.95

The First Backpacking Book To "Clean up the act."

Joy of Backpacking: People's Guide to the Wilderness by Dennis Look.
A very special book for either the novice or seasoned backpacker. You'll find Look's book non-sexist, non-elitist and non-ageist. The author writes from his own woods' training and his extensive experience in the classroom. With the aid of world-traveler and author Art Harris you learn the essentials of backpacking as they apply to United States and world mountains. Author Look still in his twenties, brings a candid approach to equipping yourself for the sport so you'll be comfortable while having fun. Look has fashioned an outdoor classic.

Perfect Bound $5.95

ORDER HERE
Check, money order or purchase order must accompany order.

TA for MANAGEMENT: $7.95 each plus $.75 postage and handling.
Quantity _____

THE JOY of BACKPACKING $5.95 each plus $.75 postage and handling.
Quantity _____

TA for TEENS: $7.95 each plus $.75 postage and handling.
Quantity _____

A TIME TO TEACH, A TIME TO DANCE: $14.95 each plus $.90 postage and handling.
Quantity _____

Enclosed is my check for $ _____ California residents add 6% sales tax. Discounts to Trade available upon request.

Send to
JALMAR PRESS, INC.
391 Munroe St., Sacramento, CA 95825
(916) 481-1134

Name _____

Address _____

School or District _____

City/State/Zip _____